PRAISE FOR *EXTRAORDINARY LEARNING FOR ALL*

"In my experience as an educator and leader, I've seen bold visions for educational change fall short when the community is not part of the solution. That is what makes this book so important: it shares lessons about how communities come together to make lasting, meaningful change so every student has the ability to succeed."

—**Kaya Henderson**, Former Chancellor of the District of Columbia Public Schools

"The future of public education depends upon communities coming together to learn, envision, and develop approaches that truly put learners at the center. As a leader with decades of experience in public schools, I have witnessed firsthand the powerful impact of Transcend's work. Transcend is my 'go-to' organization for innovative thought leadership, and I am thrilled that their approach is now captured in this book. It's essential reading for leaders at every level of the system who care about ensuring that *all* young people thrive in the 21st century."

—**Susana Córdova**, Colorado Education Commissioner

"As a system leader driving innovation and transformation across multiple districts, I saw the profound power of community-based design. This book offers you inspiring stories of real districts doing this work combined with practical tools and insights that you and your community can implement immediately. This is required reading for any system looking to move beyond the industrial model toward one that truly unlocks the potential of each and every learner."

—**Christine Fowler Mack**, Former Superintendent of Akron Public Schools

"At a moment in American history when the clarion call to help 'all children' has morphed into a rhetorical placeholder for polite conversations between legislators, researchers, and philanthropists, this book breaks through fashionable clichés and decades-old misconceptions about what it takes to a create a meaningful learning environment for urban and rural communities. By utilizing a school design framework, the authors provide a smart mix of science- and professional-based practices we must consider to truly place a premium on supporting principals, teachers, students, and families."

—**Gerard Robinson**, Former Secretary of Education in Virginia and Florida Education Commissioner

T0244110

"If our transformation journey in Lindsay Unified has taught us one thing, it would be that engaging the community in a design process with learners at the center matters deeply. Transcend has played a pivotal role for years as a key partner in our journey, and I'm thrilled that this book will enable far more communities to benefit from Transcend's insights and actionable tools. If you are a leader looking to put your learners first, this book is for you."
—**Tom Rooney**, Superintendent, Lindsay Unified School District

"Systems produce the outcomes they're designed to produce. That's a truism when it comes to our schools, but fortunately Jeff, Aylon, and Jenee offer us a roadmap to reinvention so that all students can thrive through a robust and practical design process with inspiring real-life examples of educators doing the work. It's time to design our way to success for all!"
—**Michael Horn**, Author of *From Reopen to Reinvent: (Re)creating School for Every Child*

"Too often, our field looks for silver bullets that do not exist. This book doesn't fall into that trap. Rather, it shares practical methods and powerful examples of communities coming together to imagine and build a promising future for public education. The book expresses wisdom that Transcend has accumulated by working with hundreds of school systems across the country. I hope it spreads far and wide, so innovators know they are not alone!"
—**LaVerne Srinivasan**, Vice President, National Program, and Program Director, Education, Carnegie Corporation

Extraordinary Learning for All

Extraordinary Learning for All

How Communities Design Schools Where Everyone Thrives

AYLON SAMOUHA

JEFF WETZLER

JENEE HENRY WOOD

JB JOSSEY-BASS™

A Wiley Brand

Copyright © 2025 by John Wiley & Sons, Inc. All rights, including for text and data mining, AI training, and similar technologies, are reserved.

Published by John Wiley & Sons, Inc., Hoboken, New Jersey.
Published simultaneously in Canada.

ISBNs: 9781394230549 (Paperback), 9781394230556 (ePDF), 9781394230563 (ePub)

No part of this publication may be reproduced, stored in a retrieval system, or transmitted in any form or by any means, electronic, mechanical, photocopying, recording, scanning, or otherwise, except as permitted under Section 107 or 108 of the 1976 United States Copyright Act, without either the prior written permission of the Publisher, or authorization through payment of the appropriate per-copy fee to the Copyright Clearance Center, Inc., 222 Rosewood Drive, Danvers, MA 01923, (978) 750-8400, fax (978) 750-4470, or on the web at www.copyright .com. Requests to the Publisher for permission should be addressed to the Permissions Department, John Wiley & Sons, Inc., 111 River Street, Hoboken, NJ 07030, (201) 748-6011, fax (201) 748-6008, or online at http://www.wiley.com/go/permission.

Trademarks: Wiley and the Wiley logo are trademarks or registered trademarks of John Wiley & Sons, Inc. and/or its affiliates in the United States and other countries and may not be used without written permission. All other trademarks are the property of their respective owners. John Wiley & Sons, Inc. is not associated with any product or vendor mentioned in this book.

Limit of Liability/Disclaimer of Warranty: While the publisher and author have used their best efforts in preparing this book, they make no representations or warranties with respect to the accuracy or completeness of the contents of this book and specifically disclaim any implied warranties of merchantability or fitness for a particular purpose. No warranty may be created or extended by sales representatives or written sales materials. The advice and strategies contained herein may not be suitable for your situation. You should consult with a professional where appropriate. Further, readers should be aware that websites listed in this work may have changed or disappeared between when this work was written and when it is read. Neither the publisher nor authors shall be liable for any loss of profit or any other commercial damages, including but not limited to special, incidental, consequential, or other damages.

For general information on our other products and services or for technical support, please contact our Customer Care Department within the United States at (800) 762-2974, outside the United States at (317) 572-3993 or fax (317) 572-4002.

Wiley also publishes its books in a variety of electronic formats. Some content that appears in print may not be available in electronic formats. For more information about Wiley products, visit our web site at www.wiley.com.

Library of Congress Control Number: **2024027746 (print) | 2024027747 (ebook)**

Cover Design: Wiley

SKY10086724_100424

To our heroes: all the courageous and hard-working educators, administrators, young people, their families and caregivers, and those who support their challenging but important work to create extraordinary, equitable learning for all.

"And how are the children?"

—Daily Maasai greeting

Contents

About the Authors

Aylon Samouha is a cofounder and the chief executive officer of Transcend. He has dedicated his career to driving transformative change in American schooling. Before cofounding Transcend, Aylon served as the chief schools officer at Rocketship Education, where he led the design of a community-centered breakthrough model of school. Additionally, Aylon spent several years as a senior vice president at Teach For America, focused on pre-service training and in-service support of teachers. Aylon earned a bachelor's degree in English from Columbia University and is a Pahara-Aspen Fellow. He delights in his roles as husband and father and is a professional jazz guitarist.

Jeff Wetzler is a cofounder of Transcend, where he currently focuses on exploring new strategic horizons for the organization. Prior to Transcend, he was the chief learning officer at Teach For America. He earned a doctorate in adult learning and leadership at Columbia University Teachers College and a bachelor's degree in psychology from Brown University. While at Brown, Jeff studied under Ted Sizer, whose beliefs about school design shaped his worldview. Jeff is a Pahara-Aspen Fellow and an Edmund Hillary Fellow. He is also the author of *Ask: Tap Into the Hidden Wisdom of People Around You for Unexpected Breakthroughs in Leadership and Life.*

Jenee Henry Wood is the chief learning officer at Transcend, where she oversees learning and development. She plays a key role in shaping and communicating Transcend's mission, insights, and impact. Prior to that, she was the vice president of knowledge at Teach For America. She started her career as an educator in Atlanta, Georgia, and has been nationally recognized for outstanding teaching. Jenee studied economics and Russian at Sarah Lawrence and Wadham College, Oxford. She was a cellist in the Oxford University Orchestra. She lives in New Haven, Connecticut, with her husband and a beagle they call Esteban.

Acknowledgments

This book would not have been possible without the contributions, commitment, and care from the school partners we've been privileged to partner with, from the members of the Transcend team and board, from our supporters, and from the broader Transcend community.

We share our deepest appreciation for the school communities and their leaders, teachers, community members, and young people who contributed directly to this work, especially the following:

- The team at Van Ness Elementary led by Cynthia Robinson-Rivers, Maquita Alexander, and Aly Roberts
- The team at Northern Cass School District led by Cory Steiner and Tom Klapp
- The team at Brooklyn STEAM Center led by Kayon Pryce and Damiano Mastrandrea
- The team at Intrinsic Public Schools led by Melissa Zaikos and Ami Gandhi

We are grateful for the unwavering support and leadership of our board members, past and present, and our Advisory Council:

- *Current board members:* Trevor Brown, Stacey Childress, Greg Gunn, Angel Morales, Vanessa Rodriguez, Deb Sawch, Bror Saxberg, Gisele Shorter, Diane Tavenner, and Adeola Whitney
- *Past board members:* Jean-Claude Brizard, Jemina Bernard, Christy Chin, Michael McAfee, and Gerard Robinson
- *Advisory Council:* Norman Atkins, Stephen D. Arnold, Greg Bybee, Andy Calkins, Matt Candler, Ulrik Juul Christensen, Aimee Eubanks Davis, Rich Eldh, Michael Goldstein, Alex Hernandez, Paula Hidalgo, Michael Horn, Todd Kern, John B. King Jr., Vanessa Kirsch, Wendy Kopp, Jal Mehta, Adam Pisoni, Deborah Quazzo, Art and Lindsay Reimers, Tom Rooney, Irene Rosenfeld, Chris Rush, LaVerne Srinivasan, Elisa Villaueva Beard, and Giselle Wagner

This book represents the collective contributions of every individual who has and continues to shape Transcend as an organization. We commend and celebrate each of them: Sarah Akhtar, Diego Arambula, Kimberly Austin, Alejandra Arrue, Kaitlyn Baldwin, Courtney Bell, Lavada Berger, Sujata Bhatt, Anirban Bhattacharyya, Ellen Bhattacharyya, Katie Bowen, Willie Brewster, Myra Brooks, Jane Bryson, Emily Bush, Trevor Bynoe, Abby Callard, Rachel Carlson, Mary Carlton, Pedro Carreño, Briana Castano, Catherin Casado, Dariana Castro, Benita Cervantes, Jenn Charlot, Leslie Colwell, Mark Conrad, Susana Cordova, Amber Cross, Nikki Darden, Kirsten Dargis, Jarad Davis, Jami Dean, Kendal Dooley, Jamie Downs, Nicole Dray, Lillian Dunn, Kyndal Easter, Josh Edelman, Indi Ekanayake, Brittany Erickson, Kaytlin Ernske, Arisha Farquharson, Paula Fernandez Baca, Sarah Field, Jackie Fisher, Lyric Flood, Noelani Gabriel, Kat Gaubert, Chastity George, Thaly Germain, Deborah Gist, Zachary Goldman, Freddy Gonzalez, Sofi Gonzalez, Ashley Gordon, Mitra Grant, Sarah Hakes, Helen Hailemariam, Anna Hall, Ryan Hall, Melissa Harris, Adam Haywood, Celestina Hidalgo, Elaine Hou, Eveleen Hsu, Celeste Huizar, Kelly Hung, Nikhil Iyer, Frank Jemison, Christina Jenkins, D'yahna Jones, Phil Jones, Nikhil Kawlra, Juetzinia Kazmer-Murillo, Alison Guglielmo Kerr, Caitlin Keryc, Jeeyoon Kim, Arielle Kinder, Samina Kingsley, Shamaa Lakshmanan, Leanna Lantz, Shari Lawrence, Cynthia Leck, Alison Lee, Monica Lee, Ross Lipstein, Estefany Lopez, Lindsey Lorehn, Josh Lotstein, Jamila MacArthur, Divya Mani, Christian Martinez-Canchola, Justin May, Vanessa Mendoza, Ashley McHam, Manuela Monsalve, Kaci Morgan, Archie Moss, Sarah Nager, Nik Namba, Lizeth Navarro Mancillas, Alisha Neptune, Hanah Nguyen, David Nitkin, Sultana Noormuhammad, Okie Nwakanma, Jenny O'Meara, Morolake Odeleye, Saskia Op den Bosch, Carmina Osuna, Penelope Pak, Jenn Perniciaro, Ali Picucci, Melissa Ponce, Amore Porter, Mika Rao-Kalapatapu, Tess Reed, Radhika Rengarajan, Meaghan Roberts, Rivers Cynthia Robinson, Emily Rummo, Keptah Saint Julien, Leah Samaha, Lizzy Sanders, Andy Schaefer, JT Schiltz, Youssef Shoukry, Andrew Smith, Dottie Smith, Joanna Smith, Sarah Spadaccini, Rob Strain, Saya Taniguchi Reed, Aileen Tejeda, Tyler Thigpen, Candace Thompson, Denise Thorne, Marthaa Torres, Taina Torres, Catherine Townes, Sarah Tucker, Margaret Van Cleve, Ana Vargas, Sara Vaz, Michael Vea, Danielle Veal, Shanika Verette, Stacey Wang, Crystal Ward, Sara Weaner, Becca Weinhold, Oliver Wells, Jeremy Williams, Renise Williams, Andrea Wistuba, Sung-Ae Yang, and Jimmy Zuniga.

Our thanks to Transcend's leading individual and institutional supporters (current and past): Ballmer Group, Barr Foundation, Bezos Family Foundation, Bill and Melinda Gates Foundation, Carnegie Corporation of New York, Chan Zuckerberg Initiative, Charles and Helen Schwab Foundation, Draper Richards Kaplan Foundation, Einhorn Collaborative, KLE Foundation, Catherine Lego, Steve and Sue Mandel, Margulf Foundation, Dr. David Milch,

Myerson-Wagner Family, New Profit Inc., NewSchools Venture Fund, Oak Foundation, Overdeck Family Foundation, Adam Pisoni, Prosper Road Foundation, Raikes Foundation, Art and Lindsay Reimers, Robertson Foundation, Arthur and Toni Rembe Rock, Dr. Irene Rosenfeld, MacKenzie Scott, Siegel Family Endowment, Margie Thorne, the Whitman Harsh family, William and Flora Hewlett Foundation, and Rick Witmer. We are grateful to *all* of our donors for their insights, belief, and investment over the years.

We thank the individuals who helped bring this book from concept to the page:

- Tess Reed for her instrumental leadership throughout the development of this book.
- Marni Seneker for her expertise and dedication that helped bring this book to life.
- Ross Lescano Lipstein for his insights, guidance, and help in telling the story of how community design journeys launch, deepen, and sustain.
- Kendall Dooley and Cynthia Leck for their leadership on graphics and the entire Usable Knowledge team at Transcend for the resources and products incorporated throughout the book.
- Kaytlin Ernske for research support throughout the book.
- Leslie Colwell for her expertise and support on policy-related content.
- Geoffrey Canada for writing such an inspirational foreword.
- Each person who reviewed content of our book and offered comments, including Jenny West Anderson, Monique Darrisaw-Akil, Susana Córdova, Margaret Crespo, Ivan Durab, Ami Gandhi, Greg Gunn, Damiano Mastrandrea, Lyn Moody, Tom Klapp, Eugene Pikard, Kayon Pryce, Joel Rose, Christoper Rush, Deb Sawch, Bror Saxberg, Max Silverman, Anibal Soler, Cory Steiner, Chris Timmis, Michael Thomas, Adeola Whitney, Tamara Willis, and Melissa Zaikos.
- Tom Rooney and all the Learner-Centered Leadership Lab participants who taught us about learner-centered leadership.
- And the members of the Transcend team who reviewed and commented, including Lavada Berger, Katie Bowen, Mark Conrad, Jarad Davis, Josh Edleman, Lyric Flood, Deborah Gist, Mitra Grant, Ryan Hall, Melissa Harris, Alison Guglielmo Kerr, Cynthia Leck, Ross Lescano Lipstein, Estefany Lopez, Vanessa Mendoza, Nik Namba, Cynthia Robinson-Rivers, JT Schiltz, and Sarah Spadaccini.

Lastly, we thank our publishing team at Wiley for believing in and supporting this book.

Authors' Note

The stories within these pages are drawn primarily from the communities Transcend has been privileged to support and partner with throughout the years. In some chapters, we also highlight examples from innovative communities we haven't partnered with directly. Names and details vary in whether they are real or altered to protect privacy or are part of composites to best illustrate key concepts. First and last names are used in places where we have permission or we are referencing something already in the public domain. Student names have been replaced with pseudonyms to protect their identities.

Schools and models are worthy of learning from for many different reasons. When we cite examples of school communities, our intention is to highlight particular aspects of their design, parts of their learning experiences, or dimensions of their journeys that illustrate concepts and points we share throughout these chapters. We do not aim to imply any example we share is a model of excellence on *every* dimension—this would be an unrealistic bar for any school. When we bring in relevant student data, we only share information that honors student privacy regulations.

As we are writing this book, artificial intelligence (AI) capabilities are rapidly evolving. We avoid making specific claims about how AI will impact the future of K–12 education innovation because it is too early to know for sure how AI will influence school communities and young people. It is also too early to know for sure the benefits and risks AI will raise. What we do know is that the world is changing very fast. We firmly believe that any technology, including AI, needs to be thoughtfully designed into school, never as a replacement for talented and committed human beings. We will continue to offer our thoughts on the possibilities of AI for education. You can stay up to date by using the following QR code:

Foreword

I believe in the brilliance and infinite potential within *all* young people. When we invest wholeheartedly in our young people, we place them, their families, and their communities on a path to a more prosperous future. And a quality education is the foundation of that path. Our young people deserve an education that unleashes their potential, allows them to thrive personally, and equips them to make a difference in the lives of others. Every child is capable of rising to high expectations when they have the right educational experiences and opportunities for growth.

Every child deserves schools outfitted with the people, culture, and services that ensure their academic success *and* healthy physical and emotional development. Every child deserves enriching experiences to foster learning within and beyond the four walls of the classroom. We need every single young person's potential realized to tackle the most important issues of our time—from the local and community level to national and even global challenges. We all must commit to this effort, in service to our kids and our nation's future.

We live in a country with immense wealth, but to make it possible for *all* kids to succeed—especially those who are furthest from opportunity—we need to think differently than we have before. The way that mainstream schooling is designed—which hasn't fundamentally changed in more than one hundred years, by the way—is particularly ill-suited for what many of our young people need today. In a rapidly ever-changing world, the education provided for young people needs to reflect the realities they face as lifelong learners and contributors. Our young people also deserve experiences of schooling that fit who they are and what they care about. They deserve schools that can foster a sense of deep connection and community with those closest to them. All of this can happen both within and outside the four walls of schools.

I know firsthand that transformational change *is* possible. I've seen this kind of change happen through my work at Harlem Children's Zone (HCZ). For more than twenty-seven years, HCZ has worked to advance student success in our schools and transform the neighborhood environment in Central Harlem to disrupt cycles of intergenerational poverty. We have closed the

Black-White academic achievement gap and sent more than one thousand young people to and through college by saturating our ninety-seven-block neighborhood with a comprehensive pipeline of wraparound supports that meet the needs of young people from birth through early adulthood.

We will never realize our educational aspirations for young people with answers that are imposed on communities in top-down ways. We've seen time and again that this doesn't work. The most important, relevant, and lasting solutions come from *within* communities—those who are most impacted by issues of poverty and inequity. Communities have deep reservoirs of assets— starting with the love they possess for all young people—as well as insights, ideas, and resources. Collaborations between schools, nonprofits, local businesses, and community organizations can offer students real-world learning opportunities, mentorship, and access to resources like internships and job shadowing that enrich the curriculum. This kind of coalition can also come together to design schools that better serve *their own* young people. But we can't leave all the burden of redesigning schools on communities alone. They deserve deep reinvestments of resources and support, and they deserve to benefit and learn from the evidence and expertise of those doing this work elsewhere.

Transcend is an organization created to support communities in just these ways. In its earliest days, Transcend's founders visited with me at Harlem Children's Zone, and I had the opportunity to share my advice as they built this promising organization. We discussed the importance of *both* rigorous academics *and* broader learning outcomes. We discussed the importance of *both* community leadership *and* support from expert partners. We discussed the importance of serving *every* young person, regardless of their starting point or needs. We discussed how important it is to understand the unique challenges *and* assets in every community, engage deeply with the communities to understand these dynamics, and support the design of schools that are responsive to local contexts. In short, we discussed what became many of Transcend's deeply held tenets.

Nearly a decade later, I could not be more thrilled to see how far they have come. Their work with communities from New York to North Dakota and everywhere in between has shown what's possible when leaders come together to design schools where all children can thrive. In my own New York City backyard, Transcend is partnering with amazing schools, from the Bronx to Brooklyn, from charter to traditional district to independent. For example, in the Bronx, their work to co-create the Rev-X model with the Concourse Village Elementary School community has shown how project-based learning can be relevant, rigorous, and community-based—all while addressing real needs. Their work with the Brooklyn STEAM Center gives young people the opportunity to take charge of their learning, get on-the-job training, access relevant paid internships on-site, and pursue careers that create wealth. In both cases, not only do academic outcomes improve, but young people get the kinds of experiences they deserve, they work on things that matter to them and their communities, they develop professional skills in real-world settings, and much more.

The community design journeys that Transcend supports are not another top-down solution. But neither do they leave under-resourced educators to figure it all out by themselves. Transcend has found a third way: an approach to help communities harness their inherent strengths while also offering proven models and expertise to support them. Transcend's expertise in learning science, design thinking, and change management are all in service of each community's unique vision for its young people—one that reflects the community's hopes, dreams, assets, and realities. What they're sharing in this book is not a hypothetical theory. It's based on their work in hundreds of different places—rural, urban, big, small. It's an actionable, manageable, and achievable approach for transcending the outdated factory model of school and reimagining what's possible—to build learning environments where *every* young person thrives.

In this book, you'll not only find real stories of diverse communities doing this work, but you'll also find practical ideas and methods for your community to start innovating. And if you're already down the path of redesign, what you'll find will enable you to accelerate and deepen your work, and perhaps share it with others beyond your realm. It takes a village, but every village is made of individuals with the ability to work in service of our young people, and we must all take accountability. Let this book be your guide— whether you are a superintendent, central office administrator, school principal, educator, concerned parent, funder, policymaker, employer, or, yes, a student. We *all* have important roles in leading and supporting the work of making opportunities for kids great.

The work of transforming our schools has never been more possible. We have methods, tools, and examples—even new technologies—that put the wind at the backs of communities committed to doing whatever it takes on behalf of young people. The time for doing this work is now! I am inspired by the real-life stories in this book about young people whose opportunities are forever changed and whose potential for greatness is possible because of the courage and persistence of the changemakers dedicated to doing whatever it takes. Join me in learning about this important, innovative approach to help all children thrive.

—Geoffrey Canada
Founder and President of Harlem Children's Zone, and
Founder of William Julius Wilson Institute

Introduction

You've come to this book because you believe that all children have infinite potential. But to realize this potential, we must redefine "schooling" as we know it. Perhaps you have already witnessed the power of extraordinary learning in your school or an out-of-school experience and it has ignited a spark within you. While the current educational system may seem intractable, you refuse to be discouraged. You recognize that our young people deserve nothing less than the very best, and you are ready to be a catalyst for this transformation.

TWO SCHOOLS, TWO DISTRICTS, TWO POSSIBLE FUTURES

Joanna is a ninth grader at General High School. All her life she has been artistic, creative, and curious. Her family moved to this community because all the common wisdom said that it was a "good school district." Test scores were high, as were graduation rates. By all measures, this was an enviable place to be. But over time, Joanna's family notices that their artistic and adventurous child appears stressed and withdrawn. Her creative spirit has dimmed. She is buried underneath homework, grades, and test prep.

Joanna's school day is typical of many American students. She arrives around 8:30 a.m., sits in fifty-five-minute content subjects with students her same age, takes notes from a teacher at the front of the room, hurries through lunch, and completes mountains of work that she finds disconnected from the issues she cares about most. Joanna likes her teachers, who are thoughtful and hardworking, but school is tedious.

Across town, Ali is having a very different experience at Discovery High School. Like Joanna, he is highly creative and has long shown interest in filmmaking. When he was in middle school, he participated in a yearlong learning experience that helped him to understand his passions and sense of purpose. He discovered that he loved interviewing people and telling stories. He created a thirty-minute documentary about the experiences of small business owners in his downtown. The experience was transformative. Now, Ali's high school experience looks very different from Joanna's.

When Ali arrives, he's already completed a math and science class, focused on the fundamentals. His school offers online courses for students who want to expedite their learning and have shown they can master competencies. In person, Ali attends a math and science hybrid seminar—his working group is attempting to create efficient solar ovens. They are applying concepts from geometry, optics, and energy. They are varying the designs, angles, and thickness of materials to test hypotheses. Ali's team is solving a challenge he and his classmates care about: life on a warming planet.

Ali's next experience is a small-group Advisory Circle, where he reflects on his weekly goals with peers. He then attends a writing workshop where he tests ideas for a documentary series he's creating. His friends from Advisory encouraged him to expand his horizons, so he is taking a hands-on construction class where he and a small group are exploring how to prevent flooding in a greenhouse they are building.

Ali is motivated to be at school. His learning environment allows him to practice new skills, learning from his triumphs and failures. Ali has a sense of control over his learning, being able to pick how fast or slow he progresses through content. Every day, he has opportunities to increase his self-understanding and feels that he belongs here.

Joanna and Ali are not radically different young people with wildly divergent dreams for their futures. However, they are immersed in fundamentally different learning environments that are creating different outcomes and experiences. Joanna attends a high school that many of us recognize. It is what we call "industrial-era education"—schooling that reflects the needs and structures of a bygone age when jobs in factories or fields were the expectation. Her learning is characterized by a set of experiences that are often narrow, inflexible, and confined to the four walls of the school building.

When you think about the learning environment that you want for your own children or the children in your district, which would you choose? While Joanna and Ali still have so much more life to experience, their life trajectories could be different. Students from Ali's high school are not guaranteed a perfect future, but they are armed with myriad experiences that have cultivated growth in all kinds of transformative ways. Ali's learning environment is one nearly everyone would choose for their children *and* themselves.

What makes Discovery High School and the school system that supports it so extraordinary? It's the design.

OUR CASE FOR CHANGE

In this book, we ask and answer one big question: *How do communities create extraordinary learning for all?*

As educators, we know the reality for most young people in school today is merely fine. School is neither awful nor extraordinary. Students make their way through the education system as it was intended to unfold. But when we reflect and allow ourselves to think expansively about what matters, for all children, we see in Ali's journey something extraordinary happening that is worth learning from.

This book has three big ideas. If you read no further, take these with you:

Big Idea #1: School has a design, and it can be redesigned. A set of basic practices, structures, and assumptions has historically shaped the American public school system: students grouped by age progress through a subject-based curriculum, assessed at the same time, within a singular building structure. Scholars have called this the "grammar of schooling"[1]—practices ingrained in the education system and resistant to change, much like the grammar of a language. School as we know it was designed more than a century ago for efficiency and control over students. It incorporated ideas at the time—that emphasized managerial philosophy, such as standardization and specialization, in an economy built on factories or farms—but that are far from sufficient for developing the skills and habits that young people need today.

Big Idea #2: We must redesign school from the ground up by making big "Leaps" away from outdated approaches. We have developed the Leaps for Equitable 21st Century Learning framework to describe the key ways we believe the student experience must change so that schools can prepare all young people to thrive in and transform the world. These ten Leaps invite us to reimagine how we educate young people—centering on personal growth and equal opportunity for every child—so that all young people will not only maximize their own potential but also tackle society's greatest challenges.

Big Idea #3: Community-based design is a proven process by which communities can make these Leaps. It is a strengths-based approach to school change that draws upon our proximity to real communities making these strides as well as a century of learning and progress in the education sector. This approach combines the latest in learning and cognitive science with a community's wisdom, needs, and goals. Through community-based design, schools rethink every aspect of teaching and learning, from curriculum and culture to scheduling and facilities. The result is a 21st-century learning environment that leaves students more intellectually engaged, emotionally connected, and personally empowered.

For many of us, our conception of school change has one of two archetypes: we are pursuing either "top-down" initiatives headed by visionary leaders or "bottom-up" change emanating from classrooms, schools, or parents. Community-based design offers a third way: a local process where young people, educators, administrators, and caregivers come together—supported by expertise in learning science and design thinking, as well as evidence-backed models—to collaboratively pursue better learning experiences and outcomes. This process is grounded in the belief that young people deserve learning environments that cultivate comprehensive human development and value communities as a powerful resource for building better schools.

At this point you may be thinking, "Terrific, I've purchased another out-of-touch, fanciful education book that can be achieved only if my community is wealthy, connected, and preferably both." Suspend that skepticism! Innovation and change have never been more possible in *all* schools than now, today.

The last ten to twenty years have brought tremendous insights from the interdisciplinary field of the science of learning and development. It is teaching us how humans actually learn.[2] Technology is increasingly enabling personalized, self-paced learning that accommodates each learner's unique strengths and weaknesses. Teachers are embracing new technologies in the classroom, which have the potential to revolutionize learning.[3] Platforms that allow young people to see their progression on learning competencies and self-pace toward mastery empower students to own their learning in profound new ways. AI-powered tutoring systems can provide individualized support, answer questions, explain complexities, provide high-quality feedback, and enable practice. By the time you read this book, there could be even more significant advancements that we cannot yet foresee.

This book is about inspiration and hope, not only a critique about how no-good-and-very-bad American schools are. We aim to offer a positive vision for how communities come together to dream up and create schools that look like Ali's Discovery High School. Our goal is to inspire and equip communities everywhere to embark on community-based design, work that is done *by* communities, not to them. **At a time when so much of the country— including education—is polarized, we need approaches that bring communities together more than ever.**[4]

But first, we need to understand Big Idea #1: school has a design, and it can be redesigned.

SCHOOL AND ITS INDUSTRIAL-ERA DESIGN

When you think of the word "design," certain images spring to mind: a chair made for maximum lumbar support, the kitchen's famed triangle layout for greater cooking efficiency, or the latest Apple product. Rarely does "the school day" or "social studies class" come to mind as a designed experience intended to meet a need. We unconsciously limit "design" to the objects that we use, but more and more people are coming to terms with "experience design" as a serious endeavor.[5] At its core, this kind of design is about making choices, both explicit and implicit, about how humans engage with the world around them. These choices are shaped by the purposes that guide them, whether clearly stated or subtly understood.

Schooling as most of us know it today is the result of design choices made more than a century ago that continue to dictate how young people and adults experience learning. Joanna and Ali are experiencing wildly different learning environments that are nurturing their potential in ways that will have a lasting impact on their lives. The educators within Joanna's school district are no less committed to the development of their students than Ali's. But these educators are separated by different conceptions and choices. They are separated by design.

Learning environment design, specifically, is the subject of this book. It is the set of cumulative choices, implicit and explicit, about how learners (young people *and* adults) are supported within a given community. In our view, the schedule that dictates how learners spend their time or the content of their learning is as much a product of design as the physical school building itself. Understanding schooling as designed experiences opens new possibilities for change: if schools were designed one way, they can be designed in other ways. Looking at it this way, we no longer have to accept that schooling is a small, fixed box that we must tinker within, working to squeeze out incremental improvements. We believe that schooling requires a meaningful redesign if we are to achieve the outcomes that young people deserve to prepare them for the world ahead.

Unlike Ali's school, the prevailing design of school today rests on industrial-era assumptions. The experiences of teaching and learning mimic the precision and uniformity of the most cutting-edge technology of the late 19th and 20th centuries: the industrial factory. Students arrive at a set time, move through the day with learners of their same age, use a standardized curriculum, and focus on the same thing at the same time. Learners are batched, sorted, and sent into the world in ways that replicate and exacerbate inequity. This is the school experience that mirrors what most of us can recall for ourselves, and so can our parents, and their parents.

The story of the industrial design of school is not singular. It's not only the fire-breathing dragon bent on destroying our hero; neither is it the gleaming knight coming to the rescue. The story is a mixed one, with progress in some areas but also entrenched unfairness and disadvantages that are fundamental parts of the system. The results show themselves. On the one hand, the industrial model increased access for many, where millions of Americans became literate, were able to receive wage employment, and experienced a significant rise in living standards; this upended centuries of the status quo where education was reserved for the wealthy or was interrupted and infrequent due to the demands of agrarian life.[6] The industrial model made mass education affordable and scalable across countries and contexts, providing unparalleled pathways of opportunity. Without it, we might still live in a world where reading and writing are reserved for the very few and where social mobility is nonexistent. However, decades of research have consistently shown that the industrial-era schooling model perpetuates societal inequities, marginalizing generations of young people and failing to cultivate the full potential and talent of our nation.[7]

Our work is informed by myriad scholars, organizations, and thinkers who have extensively studied the American school system;[8] we do not attempt to provide a comprehensive review of the entirety of this literature. However, to provide a positive vision for the future, we need to understand the basics of the industrial design of school, how we inherited it, and the major efforts to reform it.

In early American education, one-room village schoolhouses served students of various ages with a curriculum that varied dramatically between communities. Governed locally, these schools had teachers with limited formal training. However, by the late 19th and early 20th centuries, the "Administrative Progressives" saw these decentralized schools as barriers to educational and industrial advancement, advocating for a standardized, efficient system with professionally trained educators using scientific methods. This era emphasized managerial principles that brought significant reforms like compulsory education laws, teacher certification, and standardized curricula, aligning with the factory model of efficiency.

However, these reforms often perpetuated and exacerbated racial inequities in education. Segregated schools, unequal funding, and discriminatory practices limited educational opportunities for students of color.[9] The standardization and sorting of students based on metrics like IQ tests and tracking systems disproportionately disadvantaged students of color, reinforcing marginalization and limiting their access to high-quality education.[10]

Innovations such as departmentalized subjects and standardized testing aimed to measure and enhance education but often led to rigid, one-size-fits-all approaches and high-stakes environments that could undermine holistic learning. While standardization ensured a baseline of quality and specialization could optimize teaching, the intense focus on metrics and sorting often perpetuated inequalities and limited personal educational growth, particularly for students from marginalized communities. These practices highlight a conflict in goals: managerial efficiency can effectively sort and rank, but it may fall short in nurturing diverse talents, addressing broader educational objectives, and promoting educational equity for all students regardless of where they are from, what they look like, or what their parents do for a living.

Industrial-era schooling has resisted change despite major reform efforts.[11] The Progressive education movement of the late 19th and early 20th centuries advocated for child-centered, hands-on learning and a curriculum fostering critical thinking and personal development, countering the rigid, factory-like model. The Civil Rights Movement of the 1950s and 1960s brought legal and legislative changes aimed at desegregation and ensuring educational equality, impacting racial integration, bilingual education, and special education. However, these structural changes did not fully overcome inequities. The 1990s and 2000s saw new reforms focused on high academic standards and accountability, like the No Child Left Behind Act and Common Core State Standards, attempting to address quality and consistency. Yet, many argue that the system remains ill-suited for today's challenges, underscoring the need for a transformation in educational paradigms to better serve all students in a modern context.[12]

HOW TO READ THIS BOOK

This book introduces a systematic yet flexible approach to school redesign supported by a body of practical tools and resources. Throughout, you will see QR codes you can use to find more robust explanations and examples of the frameworks, concepts, and methods mentioned within this book.

In Part 1, you will find an overview of what school would look like if it were extraordinary for all. In Chapter 1, you will explore a vision for redesigning the industrial model by making Leaps that define extraordinary experiences. As you move on to Chapter 2, you will be introduced to the concept of community-based design; you will discover what it is, why it matters, and how it differs from the historical approaches to school change.

In Part 2, you will explore the journeys of four school communities embarking on community-based design: Van Ness Elementary in Washington DC; Northern Cass School District in Hunter, North Dakota; Brooklyn STEAM Center in New York City; and Intrinsic Public Schools in Chicago, Illinois. As you delve into this part, you'll discover key community-based design concepts, such as learning environment design, community conditions that enable design journeys, the Design Cycle, and the visionary leadership that guides the process. You'll also find a comprehensive example of a community's journey, allowing you to understand the whole process.

Part 3 presents the framework and methods for implementing community-based design in your community. Chapters 7 and 8 outline the early activities of your design journey, while Chapter 9 shows you how to sustain it long-term.

Part 4 explores the broader context in which schools operate, focusing on the critical role of your leadership (Chapter 10) in creating the conditions for innovation and how you can navigate (or transform) common policy barriers

(Chapter 11). In the conclusion, you'll find support that you can draw upon to build capacity and move the work forward.

WHO IS THIS BOOK FOR?

This book is for anyone in a community ready to move beyond industrial-era learning to create extraordinary outcomes and experiences for all learners. Whether you aim to design a new school or reimagine an existing one, this book is a valuable resource for system leaders, administrators, parents, community leaders, and even young people.

If you are a system leader (e.g., superintendent, director of innovation, division head), you will

- Understand the community conditions that lead to innovation and what a culture of innovation looks like in a school system context
- Have a basic command of the design process necessary to move away from industrial-era learning and an idea of how to lead stakeholders in a community-based design effort
- Have a framework to think about learner-centered leadership and steps you can take to lead innovation in your system

If you are a school-based administrator (e.g., principal, department chair, dean) or educator, you will

- Gain inspiration from a framework we call the Leaps for 21st Century Learning and ideas from innovative designs that might be possible in your own schools or classrooms
- See opportunities for professional learning and ways to shift your mindset toward learner-centered learning
- Envision a role for yourself in the community-based design process
- Build a sense of agency in implementing innovations on a small, iterative scale in your own schools or classrooms

If you are a parent or caregiver reading this book, you may

- Gain a deeper understanding of the ways that school design impacts your child's experience and what may be missing (or working) about those learning experiences

- Understand what's possible for your community and what you can expect of your schools
- Develop the knowledge that as a caregiver your insight matters and you have an important role to play in designing school

If you are a community member (e.g., board member, union leader, business owner, etc.), you will

- Understand that student experiences (not only outcomes) are part of an extraordinary school design and that your collaboration is necessary to make them possible
- Realize that a learner-centered mindset means you are thinking of what best serves learners in every decision you are making
- Understand that you are a key stakeholder in design decisions and your ability to support community conditions for innovation is critical to the success of any community-based design journey

And if you are a student reading this book, you will

- Find out that school does not have to be boring; it can be designed to engage you, inspire you, and help you reach your full potential
- See that your voice matters; you are an essential stakeholder in the community-based design process
- Learn that schools become great when people work together to make it so; through a community-based design process, your very own community can come together to reimagine school

ABOUT US

The heart and soul of this book lie in the experiences of school communities blazing a path toward extraordinary learning for all, and their journeys have shaped our design frameworks and methodologies. Over the past decade, our organization, Transcend, has walked alongside these communities as they envisioned, built, tested, and implemented new learning experiences. We have celebrated their successes and stood by them during challenges, recognizing that change, even when deeply desired, is rarely straightforward.

Transcend is a diverse team of educators, innovators, and changemakers with experience as school and system leaders working to create a world where all young people learn in ways that enable them to thrive and transform society. We believe our school system—encompassing district, charter, and private schools—plays a crucial role in fostering a pluralistic, welcoming, and just society. Education is our greatest hope for ensuring that a child's future is not predicted by where they live, what they look like, how they see themselves, or what their parents do for a living.

We believe that the work to reimagine schooling must be done *with* communities, not *to* them. Our 125 dedicated staff members are on the ground in schools, learning alongside educators and students every day. For the past decade, we have had the privilege of working with hundreds of visionary, cutting-edge school communities at various stages of their design journeys. Through this proximity, we have identified patterns, understood them, and produced clear knowledge to help others embark on their own journeys. This book reflects their learning and tireless efforts.

The three authors of this book—Aylon Samouha, Jeff Wetzler, and Jenee Henry Wood—first crossed paths at Teach For America. Wood was a classroom teacher in Atlanta before joining staff, while Wetzler and Samouha led teacher training and support. Over time, we observed thousands of teachers and students in schools across diverse geographical contexts in America, consistently seeing educators and learners trapped within the confines of the industrial-era classroom, a flawed design demanding more intensity, more hours, more testing, and more endurance. We believe learning should not be this way. This book shares what we, and our entire team at Transcend, have learned so far about how we can collectively move toward extraordinary learning for all.

Extraordinary Learning for All

In this part, we introduce three concepts that comprise our vision of extraordinary learning for all: Graduate Aims, Leaps for Equitable 21st Century Learning, and the community-based design journey.

In Chapter 1, we describe three categories of Graduate Aims (intellectual prowess, wayfinding, and well-being) that we have synthesized from the vast literature on outcomes by researchers, practitioners, education-focused organizations, and schools themselves. You will discover why these outcomes matter and how they are supported by the science of learning and development.

In Chapter 2, we articulate what we call the community-based design journey. You will see how community-based design creates extraordinary outcomes and experiences for students by bringing together young people, educators, administrators, caregivers, and experts to collaboratively redesign their learning environments. At the heart of this process, you will find the Design Cycle that aids communities in refining their learning environment design. You will see how the process of these Design Cycles strengthens Community Conditions for innovation.

CHAPTER 1

Extraordinary Experiences and Outcomes

Key Points

- Students need to develop in a wide range of areas—cognitive, life skills, and physical and emotional well-being—to thrive in the 21st century.
- Experiences are the variety of activities and interactions that help learners develop. The Leaps for Equitable 21st Century Learning articulates the ten most important experiences for learners to thrive. Experiences are not solely a means to outcomes; they also matter as ends in themselves.
- To foster these outcomes and experiences, learning environments must evolve beyond industrial, one-size-fits-all approaches to schooling by applying the science of learning.

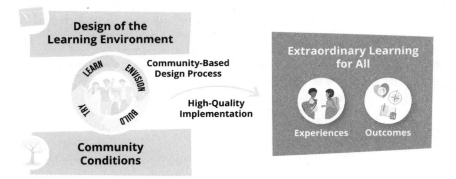

This chapter defines "extraordinary learning for all" by laying out a vision for the outcomes *and* experiences that young people most need to thrive and transform their worlds. First, we describe the outcomes that matter most for learners today. Next, we present a framework called the Leaps for Equitable 21st

Century Learning ("Leaps") that articulates these experiences—activities and interactions that allow students to acquire knowledge, behaviors, and attitudes. Experiences must change for schooling to move beyond a one-size-fits-all model toward a new paradigm for learning that can maximize every child's potential.

As we lay out this vision for outcomes and experiences, we describe insights from the science of learning and development that ground the Leaps. We also provide examples of these Leaps in action at real schools making significant progress. (These examples illustrate the Leaps but do not suggest that each school has achieved perfection).

EXTRAORDINARY OUTCOMES FOR ALL

In the education field, "student outcomes" is a widely understood concept. For many communities, the most prominent aims have typically been academic or easily quantifiable, such as grade point average (GPA) and standardized test scores. Recently, it has become more widely accepted that schools must drive toward a more expansive set of outcomes to better attend to their students' needs and prepare them for the demands of our changing world. To build this more expansive set of outcomes, communities broaden the definition of a learner's skillset. Districts and schools have many different names for the idea—"Portrait of a Graduate," "Portrait of a Learner," or "21st-Century Skills." At the core, these outcomes refer to the knowledge, skills, behaviors, and attitudes that learners develop as a result of educational experiences.

Graduate Aims are also important because in the work of school design, they determine the rest of the learning environment. Many organizations have done the exceptional work of creating frameworks to broaden our understanding of the outcomes that matter most for learners in this century.[1] We have synthesized a review of more than thirty frameworks from across the field that describe these learning outcomes and organized three areas of focus that provide a set of Graduate Aims that describes the most important outcomes: intellectual prowess, wayfinding, and well-being.

Intellectual Prowess

Schools play a foundational role in fostering cognitive development throughout a learner's life. Educators and caregivers alike have known that key skill development must be built on a foundation of reading, writing, and arithmetic—which is necessary but insufficient for the kinds of skills and knowledge that young people need today.

Intellectual prowess includes the key skills listed previously but also includes the knowledge and skills needed to understand, analyze, and apply ideas from various disciplines and cultures. It includes artistic knowledge and skills as well as an appreciation of the visual and performing arts; critical thinking, problem-solving, generating ideas or forming and expressing arguments; and content-specific learning, including math, science, and social studies. In this new century, it's also imperative that young people possess computing knowledge such as programming or artificial intelligence (AI) literacy.

At Northern Cass High School in Hunter, North Dakota, the community is undergoing a community design process to migrate from a standards-based system to a competency-based one, where learners are assessed on what they *know* and *can do*, rather than on what they've completed. One of their Graduate Aims is "Problem-Solving and Design." The community aims for students to be knowledgeable about how to define and frame problems, create an approach, and tinker toward solutions. Their Studio high school model is a self-directed, interdisciplinary, project-based learning module that spans six weeks within a semester. As part of Studio two students are working together to construct "Quiet Pods" on campus, where classmates who have attention issues or need peace and quiet can retreat during the hectic school day. The Quiet Pods are the result of this student-designed and -constructed solution. This is one of many examples of students cultivating intellectual prowess through relevant, hands-on learning.

Wayfinding

The role of school in developing young people's cognitive abilities is widely recognized. Yet, caregivers and young people themselves frequently report that school didn't do enough to give them "life skills" such as how to manage their finances and maintain good credit. Schools that aim to develop the whole child know that "wayfinding," described as the ability and assets needed to plan for, manage, and follow through on key decisions about one's life path, has become increasingly important to help young people navigate the vicissitudes of college and career.

Intrinsic Public Schools in Chicago, Illinois, has articulated their Graduate Aims in two dimensions: academic and agency outcomes. Intrinsic's agency outcomes are to develop learners who are independent and persevering—they have the ability to set goals and chart a path toward those goals. To achieve these outcomes, Intrinsic developed an experience for juniors and seniors called "Seminar," a two-year program that prepares students for the world they face after graduation. Learners complete projects where they compare the cost of attendance for various collegiate institutions. They learn financial literacy by pretending to open credit card accounts and evaluate various offers and rates. Students engage in "Networking Night," where they practice talking about their skills and interests with local business leaders and community members in Chicago. All of these experiences help cultivate skills like adaptability, self-direction, and knowledge of the post-secondary landscape to plan, manage, and follow through with their own best life path.

Well-Being

Students today report higher levels of stress and anxiety than ever before.[2]

To meet the social and emotional needs of young people, learning environments that strive to move beyond the limitations of traditional, industrial-era learning aim for well-being outcomes, including the beliefs and behaviors that support one's mental, emotional, and physical wellness.

For instance, at Van Ness Elementary School in Washington DC, compassion is a key Graduate Aim. Students build compassion by taking time to notice when they observe it and identifying ways that they can care for their class community. For example, during their morning routine, students are often invited to share and celebrate examples from the previous day when a classmate showed compassion. This builds their awareness of what compassion looks like in action and helps them identify strategies they can use to show compassion to themselves and others throughout the day.

But building extraordinary learning environments for all requires something else. Not only do these environments attend to the *outcomes* that students will achieve, but they also think about the *experiences* of learning, both inside and outside the classroom. Too often in our field, we focus singularly on outcomes, and even more singularly on outcomes that are easy to measure and quantify. Rarely are schools and systems thinking about the activities and interactions that characterize learning.

Experiences are not merely a means to better outcomes. Experiences are meaningful in their own right. In the next section, we will lay out our approach to experiences in the Leaps for Equitable 21st Century Learning framework.

EXTRAORDINARY EXPERIENCES FOR ALL

Learning experiences are the variety of activities and interactions that allow people to acquire new knowledge, skills, behaviors, and attitudes. When you think about the best learning experiences you've ever had, likely they had some features in common: perhaps they were multisensory, requiring movement or tactile objects, or maybe these experiences made you feel confident because they built on your knowledge and skills. These profound moments have likely occurred when the outcomes are meaningful and the experiences attend to our heart, mind, and body.

Experiences are often framed as a path to the outcome—you do the hands-on science activity to pass the test. **But we have seen that experiences in and of themselves are critical for learners, and we must take them seriously as we design the learning environments of the future.** The following are the ten key experiences that define traditional, industrial-era learning, as well as the ten Leaps that can help us reimagine how we educate young people.

We narrate each Leap by defining it, explaining why it matters for learning, and giving examples of how the Leap shows up in some of the most innovative and extraordinary learning environments across the country. These Leaps work together to support the holistic development of intellectual prowess, wayfinding, and well-being.

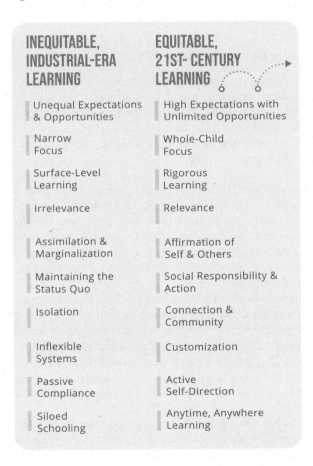

INEQUITABLE, INDUSTRIAL-ERA LEARNING	EQUITABLE, 21ST-CENTURY LEARNING
Unequal Expectations & Opportunities	High Expectations with Unlimited Opportunities
Narrow Focus	Whole-Child Focus
Surface-Level Learning	Rigorous Learning
Irrelevance	Relevance
Assimilation & Marginalization	Affirmation of Self & Others
Maintaining the Status Quo	Social Responsibility & Action
Isolation	Connection & Community
Inflexible Systems	Customization
Passive Compliance	Active Self-Direction
Siloed Schooling	Anytime, Anywhere Learning

1. High Expectations with Unlimited Opportunities

The science of learning and development suggests that experiencing high expectations can boost students' confidence in their ability to succeed.[3] It can also help mediate against identity threats young people may feel due to stereotypes and bias. In addition, having a broad range of learning opportunities helps students build a deeper understanding of themselves and their purpose and passion. When all young people are held to high expectations and have a wide variety of opportunities to learn, they are able to make more progress and succeed.[4] This in turn helps ensure that all learners are prepared for college, career, and beyond.

To achieve outcomes that are not determined by birth or class, all learners must experience a belief that they are capable, are worthy, and have unlimited potential to progress toward their aspirations.

What This Leap Can Look Like in Action

DaVinci RISE[5] does not compromise on its high expectations of youth who are navigating foster care, housing instability, probation, and/or other circumstances that have caused disruptions in their academic journeys. To uphold high expectations while also attending to the additional responsibilities students have, RISE provides various flexibilities and supports that enable students to meet those expectations:

- **Colocation Model with Nonprofit Organizations:** In-person learning occurs across three "learning sites," allowing RISE students to master RISE's curriculum in the places that work best for them. Each site is located within a well-resourced social service provider where students access counseling, case management, tutoring, job readiness training, career pathways, internships, extracurricular opportunities, leadership development, and more.
- **Independent Studies Hybrid Model:** RISE has developed a hybrid curriculum inclusive of hands-on project-based learning, career exploration, and adaptive learning technologies. Students digitally access coursework that supports the in-person instruction and project work time they receive on campus. This provides students with additional flexibility in terms of when and where they learn as well as 24/7 access to learning materials in case they need to spend more time with them or would like to accelerate their learning.
- **Flexible Schedule:** Students are able to customize their schedule to meet their unique life circumstances. It is mandatory that students attend in-person courses at least two days per week. However, students can mix

and match course schedules to meet this requirement. When extenuating circumstances prevent students from attending in-person courses, there are added layers of flexibility to complete coursework virtually.

2. Whole-Child Focus

The science of learning and development suggests that learning is a complex process influenced not only by how we cognitively process information but also by how we feel physically and emotionally, our knowledge of ourselves, and our skills and mindsets. For example, destructive emotions stemming from loneliness, anxiety, or insecurity, as well as physical discomfort stemming from hunger or illness, can make it hard to focus on, manage, and make meaning of learning. Nurturing students' social, emotional, and physical selves helps buffer against this and places students in a state conducive to deeper, more lasting learning. For more information, you can use this QR code to delve into Transcend's Designing for Learning Primer:

In addition, a whole-child focus builds knowledge, skills, and mindsets critical for successfully navigating one's professional pathways, personal relations, and health. This is especially relevant given trends like the rising prevalence of mental health challenges[6] and employers' increasing interest in skills like self-direction and collaboration.[7] We know from these examples that so much more matters for the development of human beings. We have social, emotional, and physical selves. While the cognitive and academic dimensions of learning remain foundational, for all young people to truly thrive in and transform the world, school must increasingly nurture the *whole* child. This includes the totality of cognitive, emotional, social, and physical factors that impact their learning, development, character, and overall health and well-being.[8]

What This Leap Can Look Like in Action

Van Ness Elementary School in DC Public Schools,[9] which you will read about more in Part 2 of this book, serves an intentionally diverse group of young people ranging from ages three to eleven. The community supports learners in becoming compassionate, creative, critical thinkers who are constantly working to be positive, contributing members of a cross-cultural community. Van Ness believes that, to achieve these goals, the school must take a whole-child approach, which entails a variety of practices:

- **Strong Start:** To begin each day, students engage in a set of routines that foster safety and connection and that give them practice with strategies to disengage stress. These routines include being greeted by a staff member upon arrival and then receiving a personalized greeting from their teacher at their classroom door to help kids feel connected to at least one adult. Students eat breakfast in their classroom and engage in activities aimed to foster social connection with their peers. Then, students participate in activities that build awareness of how they are feeling and learn strategies for coping with stress. Finally, they set a commitment for how they will contribute to the community that day.
- **Centering Place:** Each classroom has a "centering place" where students can go during the day to regain focus or a sense of calm. In these areas students have a menu of activities that build deeper awareness of what they are thinking and feeling and self-regulate.
- **Multi-Tiered Supports:** The previous two practices are available to all students. Students who need more support also have access to customized interventions and mental health supports that promote appropriate participation. For example, a sensory-motor room allows students to meet sensory and motor needs, facilitating their appropriate participation throughout the day.

3. Rigorous Learning

Rigorous, higher-order thinking promotes deeper, longer-lasting learning because it involves analyzing, synthesizing, and applying.[10] All this helps embed it into long-term memory. While there's a place for memorization, rigorous learning activities are often more interesting than rote activities. As a result, learners see more value and are more motivated and engaged.

Rigor also prepares learners for changing workforce demands. Employers now expect new hires to have a broader range of skills, including critical thinking and problem-solving skills.[11] As a result, expanding the use of higher-order thinking skills can improve the chances of career and college success for all children and prepare learners to solve the increasingly complex challenges our society faces. By making rigorous learning accessible to every child, we can improve the quality and impact of education for all young people.

What This Leap Can Look Like in Action

Long-View[12] is a micro school in Austin, Texas, that serves roughly eighty students from second to eighth grades. They believe learning is meaningful and transformative when young people are producers with chances to create, make, build, and do instead of being passive consumers of knowledge. They design experiences that foster critical thinking, communication, collaboration, and creativity—all of which are oriented toward the "long view" to prepare young people to be lifelong learners. Key parts of the Long-View experience include:

- **Learning Blocks:** Academic blocks are typically two hours, which enable deep exploration.
  - The Math Block follows the Number Lab's Generative Framework, which is grounded in supporting learners to construct concepts through connective ideas that fuse arithmetic and algebra. (The Number Lab and Long-View Micro School share the same founders.) Long-View learners engage in the work of deeply understanding mathematical ideas and have the opportunity to interact with each other in many of the ways that professional mathematicians do, exploring mathematical concepts, creating proofs, making critical observations of the work of their peers, and productively arguing as they make sense of the math before them.
  - In Computer Science Blocks, the curriculum is focused on computational thinking and problem-solving. According to Long-View, "Computer Science prepares kids for something we know will be required in nearly every profession they may one day choose: the ability to look at problems or systems in a way that considers how computers could be used to help solve or model the problem."
- **Build Week Challenges:** Several times a year, learners engage in weeklong experiences where they tackle a complex challenge as a team, problem-solve, and make connections across disciplines. For example, one Build Week Challenge was to design an inclusive playground to meet the needs of a specific community. In the lead-up, learners observed a local playground, learned about design principles that architects often employ, and researched playgrounds around the world. During the week, learners mocked up scale renderings on paper, modeled using computer-aided design (CAD) software and other tools, and refined a narrative explaining the story of their concept and its viability. They ultimately presented their playscape concepts to their peers and guest critics.

4. Relevance

Relevance supports learning and development by increasing student motivation; learners see more value in learning about topics connected to their interests and goals and, as a result, will be more engaged and invested.[13] In addition, relevance makes what is learned more memorable because young people can connect new ideas to prior knowledge and experiences. Relevance also helps learners feel a sense of belonging and connection, which promotes mindsets that are conducive to learning. When school is relevant to all learners and leverages a high-value, balanced curriculum, then every young person has a greater opportunity to thrive.

What This Leap Can Look Like in Action

Gibson Ek[14] is a public choice high school located in Issaquah, Washington, open to all district eighth graders. Their mission is to personalize learning for each student, guiding them as they engage in authentic project work to find and develop their passions and purpose to make a difference in the world. They adopted the Big Picture Learning Model,[15] which is designed to create student-driven, real-world learning. Students work with their teachers to create custom learning plans, pursue internships based on their unique interests, and demonstrate their learning through exhibitions.

- **Independent Projects:** Students earn academic credit through independent projects based on their interests and goals rather than teacher assignments. Their assessment approach enables interest-driven learning. Rather than earning grades and credits, students demonstrate mastery of competencies. Students are assessed through public displays of learning that track their growth and progress in their areas of interest. Assessments and evaluations are personalized to the real-world criteria of the work.
- **Internships:** Two days per week, students travel to internships at local businesses or organizations in fields like social work, video production, real estate, mechanics, and more. Students often work on Independent Projects at their internship sites in three ways: a) Authentic Projects where students create something in the business or organization, b) Parallel Projects where the student imitates the project their mentor is working on, and c) Preparatory Projects where the student researches a specific topic or field related to their internship.
- **Design Labs:** Young people can apply the skills they learn to their independent projects and internships through the Design Thinking in Design Labs (D-Labs) curriculum. D-Labs brings together small groups of students for four-and-a-half hours spread over the course of six weeks.

Students choose from an array of interdisciplinary, real-world problems to explore in areas like forest restoration, stage combat, forensic science, and more.

5. Affirmation of Self and Others

To maximize the potential of all children, schools can acknowledge, celebrate, and nurture the diverse identities of all students in meaningful ways; help each learner develop a unique, positive sense of self; and support learners to have respect for the identities and perspectives of others. When schools affirm each learner's unique identity, they promote the success of all learners.[16] Seeing one's community, values, beliefs, traditions, stories, and language reflected in the learning environment promotes a sense of belonging and self-efficacy. When young people feel confident in their ability to succeed and feel like they belong, they are more likely to see value in coming to school and are better able to learn when there. Additionally, when schools truly view students' identities as a valuable source of prior knowledge and connect learning to these identities, schools can deepen learning and make it more long-lasting. Doing this work helps all students recognize that worthiness, beauty, and brilliance come from every corner and cultural background.

What This Leap Can Look Like in Action

A growing number of middle and high schools across the country are implementing nXu's CASEL-aligned Purpose SEL and College & Career Readiness curriculum[17] through which students are experiencing measurable growth in their sense of purpose and associated social-emotional constructs. Through identity exploration, social-emotional learning (SEL), social capital development, and community building, nXu catalyzes students and educators to develop their purpose, invest in their career-related futures, and live thriving lives. According to nXu, purpose is a fundamental human motive at the root of major markers of success throughout one's life.

Their Purpose SEL and College & Career Readiness curriculum has integrated key developmental constructs so that students (and educators) can develop their purpose, foster critical SEL skills, explore a range of career pathways that align with their sense of self, and be ultimately well-positioned to live thriving lives. Highlights of nXu's curriculum include:

- Students reflect on memorable life experiences and how they impacted who they are today. They also learn about the intersections of identity and engage in discussions around how their intersecting identities shape their experiences in the world. With each exploration, students learn to own and celebrate their sense of self. They explore the need for belonging, and they delve into the topic of peer pressure, provoking dialogue on fitting in versus maintaining one's sense of self, all the while simultaneously practicing critical social skills including effective communication.

- Opportunities for relationship building and social capital development are embedded throughout the model. To build relationships, every nXu lesson begins with Connect—a ritual where students respond to a series of prompts that allow students to form and sustain relationships, establish points of connection, and practice vulnerability. nXu offers both middle and high school lessons designed to aid students in exploring the value of developing positive relationships while expanding their social networks—they explore how to make personal and professional connections and brainstorm actionable strategies to reinforce relationships.

- Through a network mapping project focused on social capital development, students take stock of their personal and professional connections and organize them into relationship groups using categories like family/ family acquaintances, peers/near peers, employment/service/internships, and more. Students create a networking map by placing themselves in the center of the map and then drawing lines of connection to community members, taking note of those with whom they have strong ties.

6. Social Responsibility and Action

Ensuring learners have opportunities to tackle adversity can foster feelings of empowerment and motivation. These opportunities are relevant to learners' lives and, as a result, bring value to learning. They also provide learners with an authentic opportunity to impact change and, in doing this, foster agency or a sense of control. For learners who have personally experienced adversity or injustice, this can be especially empowering and may bring even greater meaning to learning. In addition, at a time when our society can seem more and more polarized, it is critical for every young person to learn how to act against injustice in ways that are grounded in their own values and the values of their communities.

What This Leap Can Look Like in Action

RevX[18] encourages learners, especially those from under-resourced communities, to identify and tackle local issues—over time, helping them grow into our next generation of changemakers and leaders. At the heart is the Discover, Examine, Engineer, Do, and Share (DEEDS) Instructional Framework, a five-phase journey that equips learners with a process for engaging with the world. Through these phases, young people embark on a learning journey that integrates academic rigor with real-life application and further asks learners to explore their identities.

RevX students at Concourse Village Elementary in the South Bronx were challenged by the Office of Sustainability to help reduce reliance on fossil fuels in schools. They explored how much energy was used in the school (Discover); assessed local energy needs, causes, effects, and renewable energy solutions (Examine); created renewable energy devices for school to replace current electrical sources (Engineer); implemented these systems to power their school and collected data on the effectiveness (Do); and educated their community about sustainable practices, reflecting on their contributions to environmental preservation and community resilience (Share).

The model is influenced by several research-based approaches to learning but at its core is project-based learning (PBL), proven to boost engagement and standardized test performance while aligning closely with future work-force needs. It supports social responsibility and action in three ways:

- **Community Solutions:** Supports young people in developing solutions to their own challenges within their communities by providing resources, networks, and opportunities for problem-solving. This is reflected in the challenge-based curriculum and the requirement for young people to implement their solutions in the real world.
- **Personal Development:** Integrates personal development work one-on-one and group coaching, as well as reflections on data and feedback from others and the community.
- **Professional Skills Development:** Prioritizes equipping young individuals with professional skills essential for success in the broader world.

7. Connection and Community

School experiences that build connection and community in all directions prepare young people to thrive.[19] From these actions students can be known and respected by a variety of adults and peers, collaborate closely with one another, and form meaningful relationships across lines of difference that nurture empathy, support inclusion, and build social capital.

Developmentally supportive relationships and a sense of belonging can flourish in environments that prioritize connection and community for all learners. This helps learners explore their diverse identities, buffers against stress and trauma, and contributes to positive emotions and mindsets. It also helps young people see value in the experiences they have at school, provides a critical scaffold that makes learning more manageable, creates opportunities for discussion and higher-order meaning making, and allows learners to give and receive feedback from one another. Learning environments that prioritize connection and a sense of community also build skills and mindsets—such as collaboration, empathy, and communication—that are critical for the emotional and economic well-being of all learners. These skills and mindsets enable learners to thrive in a diverse, globally connected society where the employment landscape increasingly requires the ability to build and maintain personal relationships.

What This Leap Can Look Like in Action

St. Benedict's Prep[20] is a K–12 school located in Newark, New Jersey, and operated by the Benedictine monks of Newark Abbey to support students who have faced significant challenges related to chronic poverty and racism. Building community is at the core of St. Benedict's approach to helping its students fulfill their potential. When young people enroll at St. Benedict's, they join a lifelong community. Guided by the motto "Whatever hurts my brother or sister hurts me; whatever helps my brother or sister helps me," students and staff strive to grow in mutual respect, to work and pray together, and to take responsibility for one another. St. Benedict's focus on building community is reflected in a number of their core practices:

- **The Group System:** St. Benedict's middle and high school students are divided into multi-age groups named after a St. Benedict's alumnus or a prominent figure from the school's history. The groups become an important part of students' academic and social lives. They meet for thirty-five minutes each day, compete in events, and work together to run the school. Each group elects a group leader who is responsible for knowing about the whereabouts and well-being of all group members, oversees group activities, and represents the group in leadership meetings.
- **Convocation:** Each school day begins with "Convo," where all students, faculty, and staff gather as a community for forty-five minutes. Convo includes time for group leaders to stand up and account for any members of their group who are not in attendance that day and, if possible, provide a reason why. This is followed by time for prayer, announcements from students or faculty, and sometimes a message from the school's leader, Fr. Edwin. Convo enables students to build intentional brotherhood and accountability for every student in their group.
- **Overnight:** All incoming students attend this intense, five-day orientation during the first week of school. The purpose of the Overnight is to teach incoming students about St. Benedict's history, logistics, school songs, and aspects of what it means to be a Gray Bee, and induct them into the community. At the conclusion of the Overnight, alumni, faculty, and older students administer oral exams to individual students. Passing this test is a rite of passage.

- **Trail:** At the end of freshman year, students complete a 55-mile hike on the Appalachian Trail in groups of approximately eight students. The purpose of the trail is to foster leadership and a sense of collaboration among students, who are expected to stay together throughout the entirety of the trail. Students prepare for the hike for almost a full month through practice hikes and classes on topics like cooking, camping, leadership, and first aid. It is largely older students, not faculty, who make the hike possible. The older students work as instructors before the hike and play coordination and support roles during the hike itself.

8. Customization

Customizing young people's learning experiences in response to the ways they vary can nurture their identities, fuel motivation, and support learning.[21] In fact, for these experiences to be truly relevant to and intellectually challenging for every learner, at least some degree of personalization is essential. Technological advances can enable this like never before. By increasing customization in all learning environments, more learners can receive personalized academic and social experiences that support their developmental needs, educators can become masterful interventionists and relay just-in-time support to every child, and classrooms can promote continuous progress while also fostering a respect for differences. By personalizing learning in response to these differences and by ensuring learners who need something more or something different receive it, our education system can become more effective for all.

What This Leap Can Look Like in Action

Metropolitan Regional Career and Technical Center (the Met)[22] is a network of six schools located in Providence and Newport, Rhode Island. The Met's mission is to educate and empower youth through relentless commitment to student-centered learning and personal growth. The Met aims for all students to graduate as skilled and responsible, diverse thinkers and civically active citizens who gain fulfillment in their life and work. The school's approach is highly personalized, based on students' interests and needs:

- **Personalized Curriculum:** Students' interests are honored with a personalized curriculum designed by the student, advisor, mentors, and parents. Professionals from the community help students pursue those interests through real-world projects completed on-site with the professionals who become mentors to the students. The projects provide opportunities for the students to explore and master the content and skills outlined in their personalized curricula.

- **Learning Through Interests and Internships:** Through real-world projects, each student works with a mentor who is an expert in a field the student is interested in. The student and mentor work together to engage in project-based work that addresses authentic problems and works toward real goals. The projects are a major driver of students' academic growth but also benefit mentors and the larger community or sector.
- **Individual Learning Plans:** Each student has an individualized Learning Plan. Plans are created and updated each marking period with the student's learning team, which includes the student, a family member, the student's advisor, and, whenever possible, the student's mentor. Learning plans are built around a student's interests, talents, and needs.
- **Flexible Scheduling:** The Met encourages students to explore their interests outside of traditional school hours and awards credit for doing so. In addition, students are grouped flexibly; they engage in one-on-one and small-group work around their interests and needs, and these groupings evolve regularly.

9. Active Self-Direction

Research shows that when students direct their own learning, it drives motivation and deepens learning.[23] This is because they have a sense of control and are able to shape learning to be relevant to their interests, needs, and goals. In addition, active learning helps to more meaningfully encode knowledge, skills, and mindsets into long-term memory, which makes learning more long-lasting. Ensuring young people are active participants in the learning process also prepares them for postsecondary success, whether this means college or immediate entry into a fulfilling career. If current trends persist, like the rise of automation and the rate of scientific advancement, our learners will need a different set of skills that enable them to be self-driven, autonomous, lifelong learners who are able to make decisions that fit their unique needs and goals.

What This Leap Can Look Like in Action

One Stone is a student-led and directed nonprofit organization based in Boise, Idaho, with an independent lab high school and robust after-school and summer school programming for K–12 students throughout the Treasure Valley. One Stone's high school, Lab51, recognizes that each student brings a unique background, skillset, and passion to the learning environment. Students have many different learning opportunities, all aimed at growing durable skills such as collaboration, communication, empathy, problem-solving, and critical thinking, as well as practicing ownership and agency via real-world opportunities that give them a "toolkit for life."

- **Design Thinking Labs:** Based on experience, Lab51 offers three labs, (X), (D), and (Y), that use human-centered design thinking to solve challenging problems. Design labs partner students with local community partners to understand, empathize, ideate, and solve challenging problems collaboratively. Each lab is designed and implemented in collaboration between learners and coaches.
- **Experiences and Immersions:** Experiences and immersions are multidisciplinary project-based learning opportunities designed with students, creating opportunities for them to explore their interests and practice their skills. They range from eight-to-ten-week experiences or three-to-four-week immersions where learners can pursue personal learning goals. Students can opt into experiences and immersions or codesign one aligned to a personal interest with a coach. Themes and topics integrate mathematics, humanities, science, and technology studies in hands-on, real-world environments.
- **Living in Beta:** The Living in Beta program empowers students to explore their interests, curiosities, and passions and uncover their purpose. Using a personalized, immersive process, students discover their purpose while developing the tools to live, learn, and practice with intention. Through engagement in scaffolded wayfinding activities in groups and one-on-one work with their mentor, students use their Living in Beta insights to design experiences relevant to their learning. Students develop a greater sense of identity, belonging, and purpose as they unpack their passions, identify their values, and create a personalized and meaningful "why" statement.

10. Anytime, Anywhere Learning

"Learning" has been largely confined to schools—physical spaces with a fixed schedule. Imperfect but viable experiments in anytime, anywhere learning happened during the pandemic closures. Some communities partnered with local museums, libraries, and other schools, or even connected with working professionals volunteering their time. These kinds of learning experiences go a long way toward breaking down the barriers between school and life that are so entrenched in our thinking.

Anytime, anywhere learning can help meet the unique needs of learners.[24] It means that learners who need or want to dedicate additional time to a task are able to do so. It also means learners can choose to work at times or in places where they can be most engaged, receive additional support, or easily attend to personal responsibilities.

Anytime, anywhere learning also reflects changes taking place in the workplace, including an increase in remote work and gig work. These changes stem from a shifting economy and technological advances for which schools must prepare young people. In many ways, anytime, anywhere learning helps prepare young people for life beyond graduation by allowing them to acquire and apply a range of skills and knowledge in real-world contexts.

What This Leap Can Look Like in Action

With two campuses in the Greater Yellowstone area, Jackson, Wyoming, and Teton Valley, Idaho, Teton Science Schools (TSS)[25] leverages the power of place and connects learners to communities and the world around them. According to TSS, "Place-based education is an approach that connects learners and communities to increase student engagement, boost learning outcomes, impact communities and promote understanding of the world around us." TSS views place through the lens of a community's ecological, cultural, and economic perspective. Key practices include:

- **Community as Classroom:** Community as classroom expands the definition of the classroom beyond the four walls to include community experts, experiences, and places. Community as classroom can be carried out in three venues for learning: a) bringing the community into the classroom through guest speakers and content, b) bringing the students into the community on learning journeys, and c) simply going outside the classroom to do something you could have just done inside. These venues develop strong relationships between students and their community. Breaking down barriers between the classroom and community enhances students' appreciation for the natural world, as well as their interest in engaging in improving both community vitality and environmental quality. Emphasizing hands-on learning grounded in community increases academic achievement, develops stronger student commitment to community, and encourages the development of active, contributing citizens.
- **Community Impact:** Place-based education goes beyond surface exchanges between learners and the world around them; instead, through inquiry, design thinking, and project-based learning, students ask questions, codesign solutions to real problems, and execute projects that have an authentic audience and practical application. The connections developed in Community as Classroom evolve into community impact projects. Teachers guide learners to identify problems or needs, help students co-design solutions with their users, and facilitate locally relevant projects designed to lead to learners' mastery of outcomes, ideally from multiple domains. Learners and teachers actively contribute to their community's vitality, and the school helps the community to be more ecologically resilient, economically vibrant, and culturally inclusive.

In a new paradigm for school, outcomes focused on intellectual prowess, wayfinding, and well-being better align with the world learners navigate daily. By incorporating experiences and Leaps grounded in the science of learning and development, we can redesign schools where young people flourish.

The solution is not to create a one-size-fits-all new model to replace the outdated one. Rather, every community that desires it can go on a community design process, bringing together educators, young people themselves, experts, administrators, and community stakeholders around a common table to collaboratively design better learning experiences *and* outcomes.

This work doesn't happen overnight. In the next chapter, we define the community-based design process.

CHAPTER 2

Community-Based Design

Key Points

- Community-based design is an iterative, collaborative process that brings together diverse local voices, including students, to reimagine learning experiences and outcomes.
- The Design Cycle, consisting of Learning, Envisioning, Building, and Trying, guides communities in evolving their designs over time, while simultaneously strengthening their local conditions for innovation and change. These conditions play a huge role in determining the success and sustainability of a community's design journey. They include Conviction, Clarity, Capacity, Coalition, and Culture.
- Design journeys can be accelerated by a supportive ecosystem, which includes adoptable learning models, Design Partners, supportive policy, and leadership.

You've come to this book because you want the kinds of aims and experiences we just discussed in Chapter 1. The question is, *how* to get there. Often big systemic change is coming either from "top down" (e.g., a newly hired superintendent wanting to pursue a bold new vision) or from "bottom up" (e.g., teachers in classrooms trying new approaches or parents and stakeholders lobbying for change at school board meetings). We've seen over time that neither of these approaches works in isolation. Top-down change tends to fizzle and fray as district leaders cycle in and out of the job, and bottom-up change is typically unwieldy to manage, study, codify, and scale.

Other traditional methods to improve schools often involve discrete projects or interventions, such as introducing a new way to teach reading or providing additional tutors during different parts of the day. These approaches to school improvement assume that the current model of school is the best one available and that by working harder and implementing initiatives more effectively, we will achieve the desired outcomes.

In this chapter, we share an approach that we call the *community-based design* process, where communities engaged in this process are on a "journey." **This design journey is a local process where young people, educators, administrators, caregivers, and experts come together—supported by expertise in learning science and design, as well as models that have been proven in other contexts—to collaboratively design better learning experiences and outcomes.** The ingredients forming this approach draw from other fields such as community organizing, design thinking, and participatory change. Community-based design applies this deliberate, human-centered, design-based thinking to the institution of school. Our partnerships with education leaders and communities across the country have taught us that making schools not just better but *extraordinary* for young people means thinking differently about *how* we pursue change in school systems.

> Community-based design is a process where young people, educators, administrators, and caregivers come together—supported by expertise in learning science and design, as well as by models proven in other contexts—to collaboratively pursue better learning experiences and outcomes.

Community-based design differs from other school improvement initiatives. First, it takes a comprehensive approach, helping a community redefine the overall purpose and learning experiences of school for young people and educators. Second, the process brings together the most important participants of a school (young people) and key stakeholders (e.g., system and school leaders, caregivers, and community leaders) to collaborate on a shared vision.

> "Community design is a unique process because it involves students from ideation to implementation. They are at the table coming up with new ideas, and they are at the back end of the process giving feedback."
> —Dr. Tamara Willis, Superintendent of the Susquehanna Township School District

Community-based design is not a one-time event where feedback is collected and plans are made in a single night; it's a sustained journey and commitment. The goal of this process is not to replace a hundred-year-old model of school with another hundred-year-old model of school. It isn't a one-time act, but a new way of understanding the school as a dynamic learning organization built to change to meet the needs of new learners or effectively use new technology. This way of being is more closely aligned to other institutions like science, medicine, technology, or aeronautics. Ultimately, we have seen that this approach generates durable and long-lasting changes because it involves system leaders and other decision-makers who tap into the insights and leadership of young people, educators, and families.

Through this process, we have witnessed educators rekindling their passion for teaching, caregivers embracing their vital role in shaping their children's learning experiences, and students experiencing that their voices matter. Community-based design unleashes energy and creativity from a range of perspectives.

The design process, and all that it entails, can energize the community because leaders and all participants feel empowered to effect change. Addressing critical issues that impact student well-being and teacher satisfaction is incredibly rewarding. Community-based design improves outcomes, validates effort, and strengthens the community by doing and sustaining the work.

THE BASICS OF COMMUNITY-BASED DESIGN

A Community's Design Journey

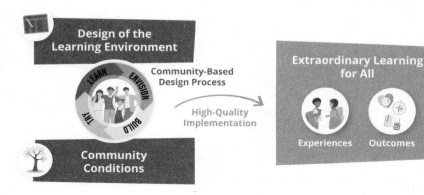

Powerful School Designs Enable Extraordinary Learning for All

In Chapter 1, we laid out a vision for extraordinary learning for all. This foundational belief holds that every child deserves to have extraordinary experiences *and* outcomes, regardless of where they live, their appearance, how they see themselves, or their family's occupation. By defining the extraordinary experiences with the Leaps for learning, as well as the outcomes with the Graduate Aims of intellectual prowess, wayfinding, and well-being, we have a direction for what a school could and should be. The community design process is how we get there—how to create powerful new school designs that prepare young people for this century's greatest challenges.

Community design doesn't hold one design of schooling to be supreme. Rather, it aims to create improved student experiences and outcomes through a sustainable process, bringing communities together in powerful ways that foster ownership and involvement beyond the influence of any single leader or top-down process.

The Design Cycle: The Engine of a Community's Design Journey

Every community has its unique design journey that is responsive to the history, conditions, and needs of the community. Because this effort is complex and often takes years to see to fruition, a design journey needs a sustained and focused process as a guide. **The Design Cycle is a four-stage iterative process that helps to refine a community's ideas over time and leads to better implementation.** Many leaders and educators do some version of this cycle every day!

There are four activities that every community continually cycles through as they bring their learning environment vision to life:

- They **learn** together: They gather knowledge by exploring research, visiting or reading about innovative learning environments, catching up on the latest social science, reflecting on past experiences, and listening to students, caregivers, and "alumni" of other community design journeys to gain insights and wisdom. Because this cycle is continuous, learning also happens after the "try" phase as teams take in new information and data from their attempts and start the process again.

- They **envision** together: Using the knowledge they've gathered, the community expresses its biggest hopes and dreams and gathers them into a Blueprint, an organizing document that holds all the key pieces of the design (more information in the following section).

- They **build** elements of school to bring the vision to life: At this stage, communities gather everything needed to turn their ideas into real experiences. The term "build" does not necessarily imply starting from scratch, as communities have the option to "build in" or adapt existing learning models developed elsewhere for their own community—more on this in the next section.

- Finally, they **try** these new learning experiences: They put their ideas into action with real students and educators, collecting data and evidence to understand what works and what needs improvement. This guides the beginning of the next cycle where "learn" activities are reignited, as teams look at the evidence of what's been tried to make responsive decisions about what to improve, what to expand, and what to throw out.

The School Design Blueprint: Design of the Learning Environment

SCHOOL DESIGN BLUEPRINT:

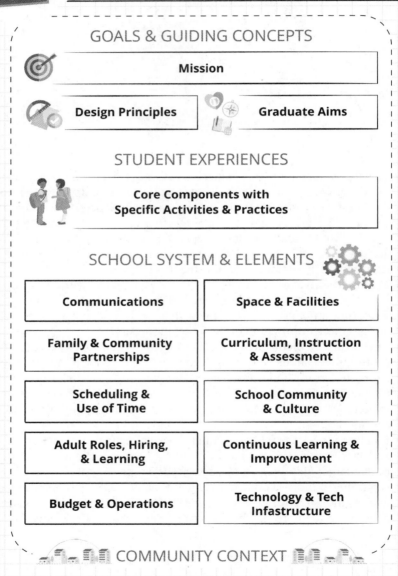

GOALS & GUIDING CONCEPTS

Mission

Design Principles   **Graduate Aims**

STUDENT EXPERIENCES

**Core Components with
Specific Activities & Practices**

SCHOOL SYSTEM & ELEMENTS

Communications	**Space & Facilities**
Family & Community Partnerships	**Curriculum, Instruction & Assessment**
Scheduling & Use of Time	**School Community & Culture**
Adult Roles, Hiring, & Learning	**Continuous Learning & Improvement**
Budget & Operations	**Technology & Tech Infastructure**

COMMUNITY CONTEXT

A blueprint is a tool typically associated with physical buildings, not learning environments. In the world of architecture, blueprints provide detailed two-dimensional visuals to guide construction based on the final design. This is a useful metaphor to apply to designing a learning environment. Schools can map out their designs for the learning environment using a "School Blueprint" ("Blueprint," hereafter), which outlines what the school ultimately aims to achieve, how students will experience learning, and which key elements, like staff roles or schedules, may need to adjust to meet the goals.

Blueprints articulate three major components of any school: its goals and guiding concepts, what the student experience will look and feel like, and school and system "elements" (such as the schedule, the curriculum, etc.) that bring everything to life. Over time, the Blueprint becomes a plan for building a new learning environment that changes important aspects of how the school operates. These changes may include curriculum, teaching methods, school layout, facilities, budget, roles for different adults, the hiring process, and ongoing professional development. The Blueprint is a detailed snapshot of the design choices for a learning environment, but it's not set in stone. It's a tool the team can continue to revisit, make changes to, and use to document new ideas. Just like a Blueprint in architecture, the designers of a school Blueprint continuously make sure all the elements work well together.

In a community-based design process, working together and including many voices means communities can dream boldly and work together toward a clear, cohesive design of the learning environment.

The School Design Blueprint is comprised of three sections:

- Goals and guiding concepts (See Figure 2.1)
- Student experiences (See Figure 2.2)
- School and system elements (See Figure 2.3)

The Blueprint: Goals and Guiding Concepts

SCHOOL DESIGN BLUEPRINT:

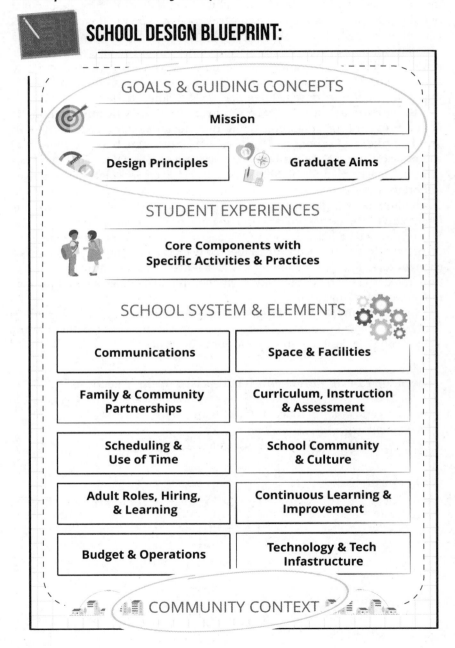

FIGURE 2.1

The Blueprint: Student Experience

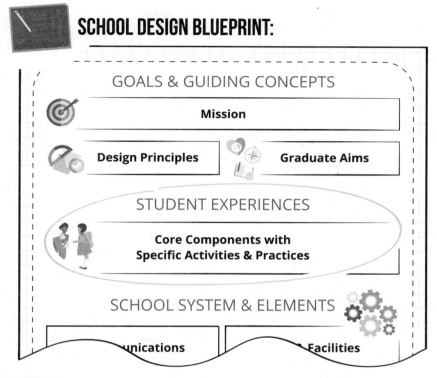

SCHOOL DESIGN BLUEPRINT:

GOALS & GUIDING CONCEPTS

Mission

Design Principles   **Graduate Aims**

STUDENT EXPERIENCES

**Core Components with
Specific Activities & Practices**

SCHOOL SYSTEM & ELEMENTS

...nications   ...Facilities

FIGURE 2.2

Community Context: This is a summary of insights about your local community that inform your design journey with knowledge and appreciation for the community's past, present, and future. As you embark on your design journey, work to capture the full complexity of your community context, focusing not only on the challenges and barriers but also on the opportunities and assets.

Mission: Your mission, typically crafted in a paragraph or less, expresses the ultimate purpose of your learning community—its North Star. It illuminates what will hold true for students in the long run as a result of being part of your learning community.

The Brooklyn STEAM Center Mission Statement

"The Brooklyn STEAM Center provides a tangible pathway to economic mobility and wealth creation for young New Yorkers from a diverse range of socioeconomic and educational backgrounds, by preparing them, through

project-based learning in a real-world environment, with the technical, professional, career and financial skills to create their own futures. With a focus on building their own identity, agency, and social capital, scholars are prepared to adapt across their careers in the 21st century economy."

Graduate Aims: Graduate Aims distill your mission into more concrete, measurable outcomes that you can work toward with your students. They anchor your design by helping you decide what to include or exclude in the student experience and can help you monitor progress. These Graduate Aims should encompass experiences that promote intellectual prowess, wayfinding, and well-being. By spanning this range, your Graduate Aims acknowledge that young people need to develop a wide range of knowledge, skills, and mindsets to thrive. Insights from your community and beyond will illuminate why each Graduate Aim is important to cultivate.

Design Principles: These are the core characteristics that describe the overall atmosphere and values of your learning environment, which are upheld across all experiences to achieve your mission. Creating Design Principles supports the development of a coherent school design by establishing a set of characteristics that should be reflected throughout your environment. These principles help you communicate the fundamental beliefs and values of your learning environment to those within and beyond it. Design Principles describe the environment your young people will engage with, whereas Graduate Aims describe the student outcomes your environment will lead to. For this reason, your Design Principles should reflect what you believe needs to be true about your school to achieve the Graduate Aims you aspire to. These Design Principles should make a clear statement about how your school environment makes the desired experiences and outcomes possible.

Core Components with Specific Activities and Practices: This is where your plans come to life as you translate your goals and guiding concepts into tangible experiences for your students. This part of the Blueprint captures your community's thinking about the activities that students directly engage in, like goal setting, and practices they encounter, like consistent teacher tone, that drive toward specific Aims and honor your Design Principles. Documenting the various Core Components of the overall experience your students will have in your learning environment supports the successful build-out, training, and implementation of these Core Components. Just as a Blueprint in architectural design ensures a smooth flow, articulating the details of activity and practice can ensure flow and alignment with your Graduate Aims and the larger learning environment.

The Blueprint: School and System Elements

SCHOOL DESIGN BLUEPRINT:

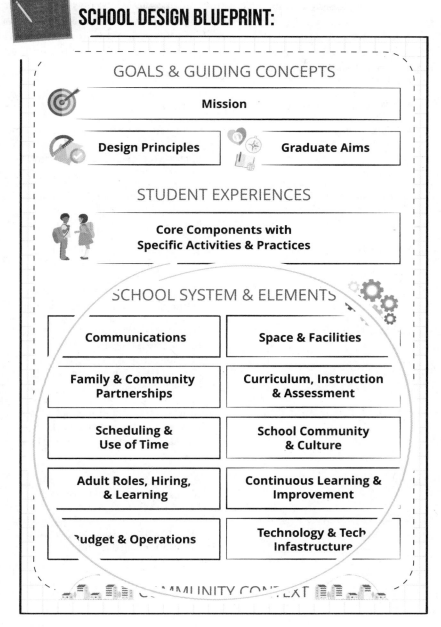

GOALS & GUIDING CONCEPTS

Mission

Design Principles

Graduate Aims

STUDENT EXPERIENCES

Core Components with
Specific Activities & Practices

SCHOOL SYSTEM & ELEMENTS

Communications

Space & Facilities

Family & Community
Partnerships

Curriculum, Instruction
& Assessment

Scheduling &
Use of Time

School Community
& Culture

Adult Roles, Hiring,
& Learning

Continuous Learning &
Improvement

Budget & Operations

Technology & Tech
Infastructure

COMMUNITY CONTEXT

FIGURE 2.3

School & System Elements: These are the various approaches, structures, and resources that make your student experience possible. The decision-making authority for each may reside at your school level, the system level, or some combination of both. You and your school system must make decisions about a number of instructional, cultural, and operational factors to support the student experience you envision. In the following table, we've identified ten key areas these decisions span:

School & System Elements	Description
Curriculum, Instruction, Assessment	The content young people learn and how they learn it, as well as how they demonstrate their learning and progress toward new goals.
School Community & Culture	The makeup, rituals, and community practices of the entire learning environment.
Adult Roles, Hiring & Learning	The roles adults play; the knowledge, skill, mindset, and experience profiles those roles demand; and resources that support how adults communicate, interact, and develop.
Schedules & Use of Time	How learners and adults move through time—when they arrive and leave, how long they spend engaged in different experiences, and how this varies by individual.
Community & Family Partnerships	How learners and staff interact with families and the broader world outside the immediate learning community.
Space & Facilities	The design and organization of the physical space where learning occurs.
Technology & Tech Infrastructure	The hardware, software, and connective infrastructure used to support communication and learning.

School & System Elements	Description
Budget & Operations	How budgets are allocated, as well as operational dimensions such as transportation, nutrition, and meal systems.
Communications	How the work of the school is shared externally with families, the local community, and the larger field of education to ensure understanding and garner support.
Continuous Learning and Improvement	How everyone in the learning community understands success and progress, learns and reflects together, and influences the evolving model.

Conditions for Community Design

In your time in education, you have likely been part of an exciting new initiative or rollout of a program, where seemingly everything was set for success—a strong mission, a clear strategic plan on paper, and dedication from the district level—only to see those initiatives fall flat or peter out. There are many reasons that initiatives can fail. But the main culprit we see is that "the soil" wasn't quite right for innovation and change. The Community Conditions are guideposts that can help you determine how healthy your community's soil is for new ideas to be planted and take root.

The design process is a transformative tool for your school community. As you engage in this journey, your designs and conditions will strengthen together, creating a momentum that becomes an essential part of your thriving learning community. By developing more robust designs and cultivating an environment that fosters innovation, you'll be better prepared for the critical task of implementation: translating designs into actionable steps. Strong implementation serves as the bridge from your well-crafted designs and favorable conditions to the extraordinary, equitable experiences and outcomes your young people deserve.

The Community Conditions describe how well-equipped a person or group is to pursue change in a specific aspect of the community's learning environment through a community-based design process.

Conditions do not mean *preconditions*. We have observed that communities build their Conditions throughout a design journey. Conditions serve as a framework for aligning on strengths and areas of improvement among various stakeholders.

There are five Community Conditions:

- **Conviction** in the importance of the journey and a deep, shared belief in the need for change.
- **Clarity** on their vision and what it will take to achieve that vision over the short and long-term.
- **Capacity** to design and implement their ideas.
- **Coalition** of broad and diverse stakeholders who share this conviction and clarity.
- **Culture** of innovation, trust, and learning.

Conditions do not mean *preconditions*, as we have observed that communities build their Conditions throughout a design journey. Conditions exist on a developmental progression that is strengthened by what we call "intentional turns of the Design Cycle," as communities work to bring their learning environment designs to life.

The following table is a framework that school communities might refer to as they reflect on their ongoing design journey:

CONVICTION
A deep and sustaining belief in the importance and potential of the work being undertaken that fuels engagement and ensures it is prioritized

Conviction to redesign this part of the learning environment: *We* believe deeply that for all students to be successful, *this part of the learning environment* must look and feel very different from how it has looked and felt for the last 50 years.

Conviction to engage in a community-based change process: *We* are invested in ensuring that the process of changing *this part of the learning environment* is done in ways that both draw on outside perspectives and also deeply involve all groups within the community and especially center students and families.

Conviction to improve equity through this change: *We* have a clear position on the role *this part of the learning environment* should play in supporting all young people to learn in ways that enable them to thrive in and transform the world.

Conviction to prioritize this change: *We* are willing to make changing *this part of the learning environment* one of our highest priorities, now and for as long as it takes to see this change through.

CLARITY
A comprehensive and crisp understanding of the work ahead that provides direction and a path forward

Clarity in community aspirations: *We* are clear on what various members of our community want for *this part of the learning environment*.

Clarity in vision: *We* are clear on the design choices we want to make for *this part of the learning environment* to meet our collective aspirations.

Clarity in journey path: *We* are clear on the approach that we're taking to improve *this part of the learning environment* toward our vision.

CAPACITY
The support of personnel, funding, and time required to successfully carry out the work

Capacity in skills and capabilities: *We* have the skills, knowledge, and mindsets we need to help shape and implement improvements to *this part of the learning environment*.

Capacity in time and bandwidth: *We* have the time, headspace, and flexibility we need to help shape and implement improvements to *this part of the learning environment*.

Capacity in resources and supports: *We* have the supporting resources—physical, financial, and human—needed to help shape and implement improvements to *this part of the learning environment*, now and into the future

Capacity through continuity: There is enough continuity in people in key roles across our community—as well as healthy turnover when needed—for *us* to effectively shape and implement improvements to *this part of the learning environment*, now and into the future.

COALITION
The investment of a committed group of stakeholders who are helping the work become a sustained success

Coalition with students and families: *We* are better able to improve *this part of the learning environment* because students and families are consistently involved and invested in making this change successful.

Coalition with educators and school administrators: *We* are better able to improve *this part of the learning environment* because educators (and any unions they're organized into) and school administrators are consistently involved and invested in making this change successful.

Coalition with district staff and administrators: *We* are better able to improve *this part of the learning environment* because district-level staff and administrators are consistently involved and invested in making this change successful.

Coalition with others within and beyond our community: *We* are better able to improve *this part of the learning environment* because others within our community (e.g., our Board, religious and political leaders who represent diverse perspectives in our community, etc.) and outside of it (e.g., support organizations, sources of funding and policy support, etc.) are consistently involved and invested in making this change successful.

CULTURE
Values, norms, and practices that support effective, sustainable, and equitable innovation and learning

Culture of trust: *We* trust each other to fulfill our commitments, execute our roles effectively, make thoughtful decisions, and do what is right for all learners above all else.

Culture of learning and innovation: *We* authentically celebrate saying "what if," digging into evidence (in multiple forms), trying out bold improvements, and openly sharing successes and failures.

Culture of inclusion and connection across lines of difference: *We* relate with all members of our diverse community in ways that cultivate authentic interactions, that honor each of our strengths and differences, and that share power in decision-making to help us contribute to change together.

In our work, we have seen that when communities grow their underlying conditions, design journeys are more likely to be successfully initiated and sustained over the long term. They serve as a framework for aligning on strengths and areas of improvement among various stakeholders. The key idea here is that when communities are on successful design journeys, they can only move at the "speed of conditions."

How the Design Cycle Nurtures Conditions

The Design Cycle supports Community Conditions and three critical dynamics within communities: power, narratives, and relationships. This is achieved by building an inclusive Coalition of stakeholders engaged in the process. Power refers to the decision-making dynamics between community members. In industrial-era systems, decision-making power usually rests with district leadership and school boards, with students, families, and educators being informed of decisions or offered a "feedback period." The Design Cycle requires the community undergoing a design journey to center critical voices, like students and families, in decision-making. Tending to narrative within a Design Cycle ensures that school designers bring together different kinds of expertise, lived experience, and wisdom to improve the design. Relationships are strengthened as people work side-by-side to solve a common problem. By building a strong Coalition of stakeholders, conditions for innovation are strengthened, and community power dynamics become more equitable.

We believe that communities often do not have all the resources to undertake this work on their own, on top of the burden of running schools. There are three key factors that speed up a community's progress: adoptable learning models (programs that fundamentally reshape the educational experience), Design Partners who can facilitate and support a community's journey, and the ecosystem that leaders cultivate around them. We will go into greater detail about these elements in Parts 3 and 4.

For now, here is a brief description of each of these critical community-based design accelerators:

■ **Adoptable learning models**

Communities will decide whether they are ready to create new learning experiences or embrace and modify proven innovations used in other communities. Our experience shows that almost all communities will benefit from adapting existing learning models and integrating them cohesively to establish a strong overall learning environment. We've developed the Innovative Models Exchange, a free platform where you can search for and share compelling innovations that fundamentally reshape the educational experience. The Exchange includes details on each model's design and the resources and supports available to help implement it.

The following QR code will take you to the Innovative Models Exchange:

The Innovative Models Exchange is a free platform where you can search for and share compelling innovations that fundamentally reshape the educational experience. The Exchange includes details on each model's design and the resources and supports available to help implement it.

■ **Design Partners**

A Design Partner is a valuable collaborator who supports a community throughout its design journey. This partner possesses the skills, knowledge, and experience necessary to guide the community through the various stages of the design process. The Design Partner ensures that the community stays on track and achieves its design goals effectively and efficiently.

One of the key responsibilities of a Design Partner is to surface design options and provide well-informed recommendations. They leverage their expertise to identify and present a range of design solutions that align with the community's needs, values, and aspirations so the community can make informed decisions and select the most appropriate path forward.

In addition to their design expertise, a Design Partner excels at making connections and bridging gaps. They have the ability to identify and tap into useful resources, both within and outside of the community, that can support and enhance the design process. This may include connecting the community with relevant experts, securing necessary funding or materials, or facilitating partnerships with other organizations that share similar goals.

Additionally, a Design Partner helps build capacity within the community. They work closely with community members, sharing their knowledge and skills and empowering them to actively participate in the design process. By fostering a collaborative and inclusive environment, the Design Partner ensures that the community's voices are heard and that the design outcomes truly reflect their collective vision.

Throughout the design journey, a Design Partner serves as a trusted advisor, advocate, and facilitator. They bring a fresh perspective, challenge assumptions when necessary, and help the community navigate complex challenges and decision-making processes. By combining their technical expertise with a deep understanding of the community's context and aspirations, a Design Partner plays an invaluable role in helping the community achieve its design goals and create meaningful, sustainable change.

You will read more about the role of Design Partners in Chapters 7 through 9, and this book's conclusion.

- **Ecosystems of support**
The third factor that speeds up community design is the local support system that leaders can enlist. The most effective leaders of community-based design processes know how to harness the power of their surrounding ecosystem. They engage with local funders, establish connections with support providers, and possess a profound understanding of how to navigate (and even influence) the policies and regulations that either facilitate or hinder innovation. System leaders play a pivotal role as enthusiastic advocates throughout the community-based design journey, securing resources and building the necessary buy-in to sustain years-long design journeys.

Every school system is part of larger networks that can greatly influence school redesign. Local philanthropists and business leaders can provide crucial resources such as funding and skilled human capital. Beloved religious or civic leaders and experts from healthcare, housing, or other sectors can act as important advisors, connectors, and advocates for the community-based design process. In some cases, it will take some advocacy to shift policies and regulations so they are more conducive to innovation, such as more funding to develop new designs or making it easier for kids to learn outside the school building.

Now more than ever, we need processes that unite communities to address difficult problems. Community-based design is a solution that creates sustained engagement and interaction between students, educators, caregivers, and system leaders all in pursuit of extraordinary and equitable outcomes and experiences for young people.

The solutions we need in education won't come from a quick fix or one perfect policy change, no matter how well-intended. Instead, real, enduring, and inventive solutions must emerge from the very communities where they are most needed.

Communities across the country want and need profound change in the design of school. In the next four chapters, we take you through four real communities that have used this community-based design framework to redesign their learning environments toward extraordinary experiences and outcomes where all young people can thrive.

II

Stories from Four Community Design Journeys

In this section, you'll meet four school communities undertaking community-based design. Their stories will illustrate various aspects of our approach and hopefully inspire you to pursue this work.

Chapter 3 highlights Van Ness Elementary, a school within DC Public Schools, where we delve into the design of their learning environment. You'll witness how the power of cohesive, intentional design has allowed this model to expand and replicate across the nation.

Chapter 4 takes you to Hunter, North Dakota, where you'll see how the Northern Cass School District has used the Design Cycle in transitioning from a standards-based system to a competency-based one.

Chapter 5 introduces you to the Brooklyn STEAM Center and their innovative workplace learning environment, which equips students with skills to earn middle-class wages upon graduation.

Chapter 6 highlights the story of Intrinsic Public Schools, in Chicago. Their visionary cofounders created a school that continuously adapts to meet the needs and aspirations of its learners. You'll witness how all the elements of community-based design come together to create a dynamic learning environment.

Regardless of whether you are in a dense, urban neighborhood or amid the stillness of the open prairie, community-based design is accessible and applicable to all communities.

CHAPTER 3

DC Public Schools' Van Ness Elementary | Washington, DC

Key Points

- DC Public Schools' Van Ness Elementary developed the "Whole Child Model" to support students emotionally and academically.
- The design Blueprint helped them create a cohesive environment that supports young people to feel safe, connected, and ready to learn.
- Van Ness's model honors the Leaps of Whole-Child Focus, Connection & Community, and Affirmation of Self & Others.

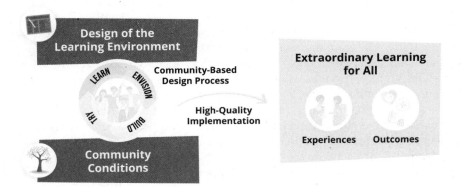

In a socially and racially diverse context, where learners are navigating adverse childhood experiences and varying levels of trauma, the young people at Van Ness can emotionally self-regulate and co-regulate better than most adults. As a consequence, the learning environments at Van Ness are collaborative and empathetic, cultivating deeper instructional time.

The Whole Child Model, developed by DC Public School's Van Ness Elementary, is a learning approach that supports students to make the neurological progression from their "survival state" to their "learning state";[1] it focuses on the beliefs, actions, habits, rituals, and systems that support academic learning and enable learners to develop critical skills such as empathy, trust, and self-regulation. "When students are regulated and feel related, they are ready to reason,"[2] goes the saying at Van Ness. The school is nearly ten years along in their community-based design journey, a process that continually renews their vision.

In this chapter, we focus on two aspects of their community-based design journey: learning environment design (supported by the Blueprint) and Community Conditions. We analyze several student experiences to illustrate what a cohesively integrated design looks like, one that skillfully marries several frameworks and insights around early childhood development. We also examine how the act of refining the design deepened Community Conditions, such as Conviction, Clarity, and Capacity.

Jalissa arrives at the front door of Van Ness Elementary School, her hair in afro puffs adorned with pink barrettes, wearing a purple and white puffer coat. She's walking slower than normal. Something seems off. Jalissa is welcomed warmly by Ms. Jones, a teacher she had in second grade. As she walks up the stairs, more greetings come her way—from another teacher, the custodian, and the security guard. Though generally in good spirits after some early school year bumps, today Jalissa is struggling. The adults take notice, aware extra support may be needed.

Jalissa hesitates going into class, but seeing Ms. Nguyen is comforting. Ms. Nguyen sits smiling widely on a short stool by the door, coffee mug in hand. She asks Jalissa how she'd like to be greeted today. Unusually, Jalissa requests a high-five instead of her normal hug. Ms. Nguyen makes a mental note to tell Senior Freddy, noting Jalissa's preference.

At the start of her day, Jalissa has had an intentional sequence of experiences with the adults at school—all designed to welcome her and make her feel safe. Her teacher greeting her at the door might seem like an arbitrary nice gesture, but it's actually the first step within the Whole Child Model, called "Strong Start," a daily routine derived from the cognitive insight of "serve and return," which tells us that when adults respond to a child's expressions with a hug or smile, this builds neural connections in the child's brain that support communication and social skills. This makes students feel seen and cared for. Ms. Nguyen is squatting down at Jalissa's eye level, not standing over her. This is especially important if a student has faced developmental trauma, since standing over a child can be a trigger. Ms. Nguyen is also registering critical information about each of her students. A lot can be achieved in a simple greeting.

Jalissa high-fives Ms. Nguyen and then enters the classroom. A eucalyptus scent hangs in the air as cozy lamps line the room. After dropping off her bags, Jalissa heads for the breakfast cart. Passing by, she sees her grandmother's face on the wall. Earlier that year, students brought in pictures of family members they admired to share their stories. Jalissa told of how her grandma is cherished for taking in youth without families due to incarceration or hardship. Seeing her grandmother's warm face, Jalissa feels a swell of emotion.

After breakfast, students head to the carpet. While walking, Lorenzo accidentally bumps Jalissa. She gets angry and yells, "Hey, can't you walk right? Don't hit me!"

Ms. Nguyen notices Jalissa's distress and approaches the two students. As she moves toward Jalissa and Lorenzo, Ms. Nguyen's energy is calm, and her expression remains composed. She checks her own emotions before beginning to speak. "It looks like something happened," she opens the conversation.

"Lorenzo bumped me while he was walking!" says Jalissa.

"Lorenzo bumped you, and you felt frustrated," says Ms. Nguyen. Her tone remains assertive and warm, consistent with how she speaks to her students throughout the day. Ms. Nguyen takes a breath and so do both students, the temperature of the situation lowering as Ms. Nguyen's own sense of calm is shared with her students.

Observing that both Jalissa and Lorenzo are ready to engage in the conversation, Ms. Nguyen reminds Jalissa of the language they have been practicing as a classroom community. Pointing to a visual on the wall that the class created together, Ms. Nguyen says, "Jalissa, we use kind words when we talk to our teammates. You might choose to say to Lorenzo, 'It bothers me when you bump me. Next time, try to leave more space.' You try it, Jalissa."

Jalissa nods, reminded of the practice she and her classmates have been doing using this sentence stem. She turns to Lorenzo and says, "I didn't like it when you bumped me. Next time, please give me more space."[3] Lorenzo nods and says, "I can do that."

In most classrooms, this situation would be unfolding differently. Ms. Nguyen might have felt compelled to "be in control" and react to Jalissa's emotions in ways that would shame or upset her further. This would have disrupted class time and affected all students' learning. As part of the model, Ms. Nguyen has received coaching and feedback from colleagues on how she responds to these kinds of situations. Van Ness has developed and codified their own language guidance for staff that is aligned with the practice of compassionate assertiveness, a research-based communication style that ensures language and tone that supports empathy, safety, and learning. Ms. Nguyen has undergone professional development that has encouraged her to reflect on her responses to strong feelings and even to reflect on her experiences of discipline in school. The Whole Child Model is designed with students at the center, but it cultivates adults as well.

As Lorenzo makes his way to the carpet, Jalissa feels a wave of emotion after this conflict. Tears filling her eyes, Jalissa feels her friend Amara take her hand. Amara invites her to the "Centering Space" in the back classroom corner—a little couch, bookshelf, and lamp.

Amara shows Jalissa a feelings chart with emoji faces. She asks how Jalissa feels right now. Jalissa points to the sad emoji. The two do the breathing exercise they learned earlier that year. Afterward, Amara asks if Jalissa is ready to rejoin class. They smile and hug before heading back.

When Jalissa and Amara return, Ms. Nguyen says, "Welcome back, Jalissa. We are so glad to have you with us." Turning to Amara, she says, "Amara, you checked on Jalissa when she was upset and helped her use the Centering Space. You showed compassion for a friend. That was kind."

In this fourth-grade class, students feel empathy and responsibility toward each other. They also have a strong sense of ownership over their learning. Communicating in these thoughtful ways is learned behavior. It requires intentional design, practice, and reflection, even for adults. As any grown-up knows, it takes work to repair relationships and reflect after disagreements, as Jalissa did. We have to learn how to generously accept apologies, as Lorenzo did. Ms. Nguyen stays calm and composed. She is able to respond to Jalissa in ways that reduce stress in the classroom. While an excellent teacher, Ms. Nguyen isn't Superwoman. In this class and others at Van Ness, teachers aren't expected to be superhuman. They are equipped with the tools of self-regulation and empathy. This is because the school design itself helps strengthen their own emotional skills and habits.

Later in the day, Ms. Nguyen texts Jalissa's Aunt Shauna. She shares a photo of a happy Jalissa after recess and describes how Jalissa overcame her "strong feelings" during carpet time. Ms. Nguyen asks how the class can support Jalissa as her grandmother copes with illness. Shauna quickly replies, relieved and thankful. She gives Ms. Nguyen more background on Jalissa's current challenges.

With this, Ms. Nguyen gains further insight into her students' lives. As their teacher, she can now approach them with even more empathy.

What's happening in this classroom happens in classrooms throughout Van Ness. The routines and systems have been thoroughly tested and codified to create classrooms that are joyful, calm, and proven by science to generate the proper conditions for learning. In many schools, traditional practices encourage students and teachers to rush this neurological process, and there is little time for young people to make the neurological transitions needed to learn effectively. Research suggests that more time isn't the differentiator but rather the quality of learning time and the conditions surrounding learners.

The Whole Child Model was built to create experiences that foster cognitive development but also self-awareness and emotional regulation. Caregivers frequently report, with amusement and amazement, how their children bring home practices for emotional regulation, coaching their families to do pretzel breathing, five-finger breathing, or other strategies in moments of frustration. The model also helps to affirm their sense of self and their interests, deepening their self-respect and respect for their peers.

Even as Van Ness was developing and refining their model, the school excelled in many measures. They performed highest in the district on the Insight survey for instructional culture and ECE CLASS assessment and consistently had Panorama student and family satisfaction rates greater than 95 percent.

COMMUNITY AND LEADERSHIP CONTEXT

DC Public Schools (DCPS) is an innovative, urban school district that has undergone tremendous transformation in the last twenty years. DCPS is showing what's possible when visionary leadership and community-based organizations come together to support students and families. The current chancellor, Dr. Lewis Ferebee, has put DCPS on a mission to become a whole-child, anti-racist district, sharing in his most recent strategic plan: "Our legacy is defined by an unwavering commitment to student success, deep investments in and from our educators, and vital partnerships with our families and community." The district has partnered with Flamboyan Foundation to work with families and Turnaround for Children (now the Center for the Whole Child) to ensure staff members have a trauma-informed approach.

The story of the Whole Child Model begins far earlier, though, with Cynthia Robinson-Rivers, Van Ness's founding principal. In 1998, Robinson-Rivers started teaching early childhood education in Oakland but felt eager for adventures. She spent a year traveling Central America. She informally volunteered in classrooms supporting students. Robinson-Rivers was, and is, deeply curious and was constantly trying to understand how brain science intersects with child development and how traumatic experiences impact students as learners. By 2005, she was ready for new challenges. She relocated to DC, taught, and worked as an assistant principal, before joining DCPS's central office working on human capital initiatives related to teacher evaluation, recognition, and retention.

Robinson-Rivers' curiosity deepened. She became a fellow at Harvard's Project Zero, exploring learning connected to the arts. There, she discovered interdisciplinary teaching. She learned from researchers like Ron Ritchhart, along with practices like Reggio Emilia, playful learning, teaching for understanding, and visible thinking. In her roles as a teacher evaluator for the school district and later as the director of teacher retention and recognition, Robinson-Rivers visited schools across DC, observing what distinguished the best teachers and classrooms. By 2015, she felt prepared for a new adventure: founding her own school.

Van Ness had been closed for years. But as the Navy Yard area was repopulated with new townhomes and apartment buildings, the new families needed a neighborhood school. The demographics of the community had changed. For decades, it had been majority Black, with most families living at or below the poverty line for generations. Now, homes for low-income families were interspersed in mixed-income buildings. The school would reflect this diversity.

As with all new ventures, the full vision doesn't emerge instantly.

In 2016, Robinson-Rivers found an opportunity: a ten-month, cohort-based program convening educators from school districts and charter networks around a shared vision. Their aim was designing innovative school models worthy of realizing students' potential. This collaboration between Transcend and New Schools Venture Fund would help participants explore user-centered design, learning science, innovative learning environments, and best practices in research and development. This matched what Robinson-Rivers needed—partners in developing her burgeoning school design, one that centered the whole-child.

Robinson-Rivers led a coalition of stakeholders (at the school and district level) on the design team that shared her passion and conviction. They partnered with other educators to build capacity for innovation. This knowledge and experience added clarity to their vision—and ultimately the implementation—of the design.

THE BLUEPRINT: OVERVIEW OF THE WHOLE CHILD MODEL LEARNING ENVIRONMENT DESIGN

In Chapter 2 we introduced the idea of a planning guide, or "Blueprint," for school design. This outlines what the school ultimately aims to achieve, how students will experience learning, and which key elements, like staff roles or schedules, may need adjusting to meet the goals.

School Blueprints articulate three major components of any school: its goals and guiding concepts (as shown in Figure 3.1), what the student experience will look and feel like, and school and system "elements" (such as the schedule) that bring everything to life.

SCHOOL DESIGN BLUEPRINT:

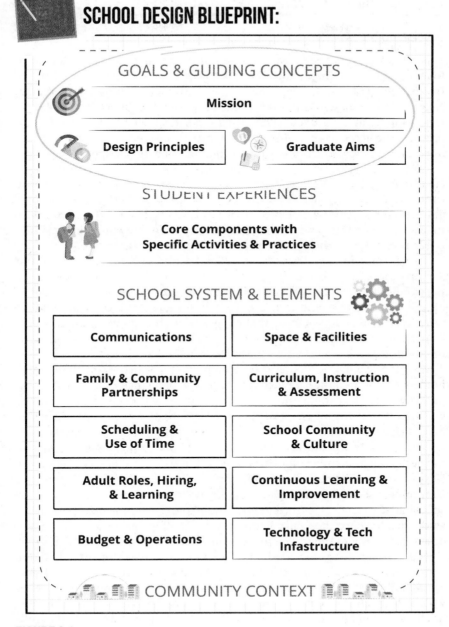

FIGURE 3.1

THE BLUEPRINT: GOALS AND GUIDING CONCEPTS

Developing the Mission

The initial Van Ness design team consisted of a handful of teachers, Robinson-Rivers, and DCPS representative Jason Kamras, then the chief of the Office of Instructional Practice. Participation from such a senior DCPS official was game-changing for the design team, as it worked to ensure the school and the district were running at the goals together. Chancellor Kaya Henderson and Kamras provided the necessary permission and spiritual guidance, illustrating just how important systems leaders are within a community-based design journey.

"We were very serious about co-designing the school with the community," Henderson reflects, **"My experience has shown me over and over again, then when you engage the community truly, you get better answers. You get 'stickier' solutions. Because, ultimately, it's not about the leader who made the decision. The community has to own the solution. . .When the leader is gone, the community will keep the dream alive."**

Robinson-Rivers reflects, "Chancellor Henderson's leadership and our deep partnership with Kamras played such an invaluable role in setting up the conditions for trust. We knew our ultimate goal was to ensure we developed a school that would enable outstanding student achievement, and we were trusted as leaders to make that happen. Even though we followed all the district guidance around instructional minutes, we never felt constrained by the status quo. This is because we had partners in the district."

In other words, DCPS was a powerful partner within the Coalition, stakeholders who shared the Conviction and Clarity for change.

The design team didn't simply document their own visions for the school's goals and animating ideas; they applied the lessons of human-centered design and engaged the "users" of school, the families and learners who would make up the Van Ness community. They conducted home visits, a method that all the design team members had experienced but were new to some other Van Ness educators. The notion of going door to door and meeting families in their own context seemed intuitive but certainly wasn't standard.

What the teachers learned proved invaluable. They gained deeper macro-level knowledge of the whole community as well as insights into each student's home environment. Some students lived in a single apartment of six within a larger three-story building. Others had the span of three floors to enjoy their toys and their childhoods. Some had nannies. Others had live-in grandmothers and stay-at-home mothers. Some were coming to Van Ness with unblemished disciplinary records. Others had previously been expelled in kindergarten for extreme behaviors. As a neighborhood school that enrolls any student within its geographic boundary, Robinson-Rivers insisted that all children would be welcome.

Home visits advanced several Conditions for Community Design at once. Design team members deepened Conviction in the power of community-based design and Capacity (skills, knowledge, and mindsets) for teaching, while caregivers and other community members became part of the school's Coalition. The design team developed this mission for Van Ness:

Children, families, and educators come together to create an inclusive community that provides authentic experiences and engages the whole child.

Our aim is to cultivate critical thinkers and develop a generation of confident, curious, and compassionate members of society.

Plenty of hard-wrestled, beautifully written mission statements adorn school walls all over the world. The design team had to keep iterating and asking new questions: *If this is our mission, what student outcomes are we driving toward to achieve this mission?*

> *"Home visits [are] fascinating and very important for me as a teacher. They really provided me with a different perspective on each child's personality and their interests; this obviously helped me when I was tailoring classroom activities. But it also helped me see the dynamics between family members. It's one thing to see a kid in your classroom; it's another thing to see them with their auntie and their siblings."*
>
> —*Raquel Sarvis, Van Ness Elementary teacher*

Articulating the Graduate Aims (Student Outcomes) Aligned to the Mission

"One aspect of teaching at Van Ness that makes this school so unique is that we are here to cultivate all their needs as human beings," one teacher describes. "It matters that my students can read and do math, especially given how important math is as a gate-keeping function in the world. It's *equally* important that they know how to apologize when they've made a mistake. I truly hold myself accountable for all dimensions and so does everyone around me."

This sentiment nicely summarizes how the Van Ness design team went about articulating the outcomes for their learning environment. They took an interdisciplinary, "both/and" approach. The learning environment at Van Ness would not strive to produce a one-dimensional learner, with strong cognitive abilities and little by way of other human skills. Children deserve to learn to read, write, do math, and be humans that can function wholly in the world. At the time, there were many forceful voices in education firmly on either side of the divide, advocating for what matters most for young people. In the end, Robinson-Rivers, the avid reader, the observer of hundreds of classrooms, would take a holistic, scientifically grounded view: this school community would drive toward holistic outcomes that nurtured cognitive, emotional, social, and physical development. Van Ness would be a school all about well-being.

The design team took in two critical inputs of information when discerning their student outcomes: community input and external knowledge. They had learned from their DC families, living in a dense urban community, that being able to work and communicate across lines of difference truly mattered to them. They didn't want children who could only empathize with and understand kids who looked like themselves. Parents wanted their children to connect and collaborate with others across lines of racial difference. But it's not just parents advocating for this need. Contemporary trends in economics, employment, and demographics indicate the value of these skills. The learners at Van Ness would be part of one of the most racially diverse generational cohorts ever in America. Additionally, they'd be navigating an increasingly connected world requiring more advanced skills and increasingly structured by independent work.

Insights from the science of learning and development informed the design team too. Long gone is the common wisdom in education that *all* you need to know is readin', ritin', and 'rithmetic. Scientists have discovered that there is so much more that goes into learning than we previously knew.[4] **Learning itself is a deeply individual and variable process. Emotions play an important role in many parts of learning.** And critically, social connections support deeper learning. This all matters, because outcomes need to reflect what we have come to learn about learning itself. Outcomes that are only aligned with the cognitive dimensions of learning are not adequate.

As the design team took in all these inputs, they identified the five big outcomes aligned with their mission, shown in the following table:

Graduate Aim (Student Outcome)	Definition	Underlying Knowledge, Skill, Mindset	Alignment to Mission
Compassionate	Van Ness graduates are kind and caring. They listen to their peers and fellow community members, seek to understand new perspectives, and contribute positively through their relationships and actions.	▪ Recognizing/ identifying emotions in self and others ▪ Perspective taking ▪ Empathy	". . . compassionate members of society."

Graduate Aim (Student Outcome)	Definition	Underlying Knowledge, Skill, Mindset	Alignment to Mission
Cross Cultural Community Members	Van Ness graduates can collaborate. They can get to know, learn from, and appreciate others who come from a different background than their own.	■ Perspective taking ■ Relationship building ■ Collaboration ■ Problem-solving	"Children, families, and educators come together to create an inclusive community."
Creative	Van Ness graduates think boldly and creatively in the face of tough problems. They apply inventive problem solving to their lives and work in school and in their communities.	■ Self-regulation ■ Self-efficacy ■ Problem-solving ■ Communication	". . . develop a generation of confident, curious, and compassionate members of society."
Critical Thinkers	Van Ness graduates think critically about the world around them. They question the status quo, evaluate multiple sources of information to understand complex and evolving topics, and form their own opinions and ideas.	■ Interpret and organize information ■ Understanding perspectives ■ Analyze information ■ Curiosity ■ Problem-solving ■ Making decisions/reflecting ■ Empathy/creativity	"Our aim is to cultivate critical thinkers. . ."
Constant Learners	Van Ness graduates are dedicated to learning in and outside the classroom. They know their own passions and interests and continuously pursue new knowledge and skills in pursuit of their passions and goals.	■ Self-awareness ■ Reflection/metacognition ■ Growth mindset ■ Analyze information	". . . develop a generation of confident, curious, and compassionate members of society."

Now, the Van Ness design team had an even sharper portrait for the kinds of young people they were aiming to cultivate. This portrait was informed by caregivers, the expertise and knowledge of the educators themselves, and the expert insights of the science of learning and development. But we've learned that even this is just not enough when articulating the goals and guiding concepts of a learning environment. You also need an important set of ideas that are often missed and are indispensable for ensuring the cohesion between your words/aspirations and the experiences that you create for learners: Design Principles.

> *"Something I am proud of about myself is showing compassion. We got a new student last January, and me and my friends have been making her feel included. We invited her to dress up like us for twin days, and we even created fake holidays together. This makes her feel included, and she knows she can come to me when someone is bullying her."*
> —*Eve, a fourth grade student at Van Ness Elementary*

Crafting Design Principles

When you think of some of the best learning environments you've experienced, the role that "Design Principles" have played in the success may not be front of mind. Design principles are core characteristics that describe the felt experience or ethos of the learning environment and are held true across all experiences to achieve the mission.

Now, the design team had a mission, they had articulated a powerful set of community-informed student outcomes, but they needed to articulate what needed to be true about how Van Ness looked and felt, which would enable these aims to come to life. Much as the science of learning and development had informed the student outcomes, they would come to deeply inform the Design Principles as well.

Two frameworks that animate the design of the Whole Child Model speak to the importance of safety: Dr. Bruce Perry's Neurosequential Model[5] and Dr. Brooke Stafford-Bizard's Building Blocks for Learning.[6] Inspired by the neurosequential model and its implications on education, the Whole Child Model assumes that learning and critical thinking happens in a child's (a person's) reasoning state. For students to be in this reasoning state, they must feel safe and connected. To connect with others and to learn, we must be physiologically regulated—having a relaxed autonomic nervous system. At school, this enables us to be related, connected, and engaged with peers and with adults. Then comes reasoning, our ability to think and determine. Only after we are regulated and related can we reason. That's when the prefrontal cortex is in charge and we are truly ready to learn.

In the Building Blocks for Learning framework, "school readiness" includes executive function, the cognitive control functions needed to concentrate and think (to reason). Executive function rests upon a foundation of healthy development, where children have attached properly, have skills of stress management, and have self-regulation.

As the design team engaged and debated these ideas, the Design Principle of "safety and connection" emerged. This principle reflects the developmental insight that children learn best when they feel physically and psychologically safe and have their needs met. Caring relationships with adults and peers contribute to students being in their executive states. Given the diversity of the children in the Van Ness community, many families face significant stress or trauma that impacts their ability to develop deep attachments and interrupts their ability to feel safe. The design team understood that they had to create a sense of safety and connectedness all throughout the learning environment.

Over time, they arrived at a total of four Design Principles, as shown in the following table:

Design Principle	Description	Why This Principle Matters
Safety & Connection	Children learn best when they feel physically and psychologically safe and have their basic needs met and when they have trusting, caring relationships with adults and peers.	Learning and critical thinking happens in the executive state. For students to be in their executive state, they must feel safe and connected. Many of our children have faced significant stress or trauma, which may impact their ability to develop deep attachments or increase the sensation that they are not safe, making it additionally important that we focus on creating such an environment.

(*continued*)

Design Principle	Description	Why This Principle Matters
Equity through personalization	Children learn best when their individual needs, strengths, and preferences are accounted for and celebrated. They learn best among a diverse group of learners.	Equity means providing every student with what we understand they need (from research) and from what they voice. No two children develop at the same pace and in the same way, and we must provide students with the support they need to help them reach the highest expectations. A groNguyeng body of schools has proven that when learning is even further personalized and tailored to the specific needs of students, not only do student achievement rates rise but children also are more deeply engaged in a positive school experience.
Every interaction matters	Students learn from every interaction. The way we behave shapes the way they behave. Children learn best when every interaction reinforces our belief that they play a meaningful role in our school community, that they have valuable ideas, and that they can learn to handle challenges, conflicts, and stressors.	Our vision for students is not limited to the skills and experience they have after they leave us; we have a vision for their daily experience with us. We know that the skills and habits they practice daily in our care will be skills and habits they can draw on forever. We aim to create a joyful learning environment in which children are trusted to shape their classroom, and in which the adult behavior models the type of skills we aim to nurture in students.

Design Principle	Description	Why This Principle Matters
Rich, rigorous, and active learning	We prioritize opportunities for children and adults to practice creativity in service of new ideas and solutions. We value smart risk-taking, inventive thinking, and multiple ways to solve tough problems in and outside the classroom.	It is clear from surveys of employers that, while graduates may have basic reading/writing skills, they often lack the ability to collaborate with peers and approach problems with creativity and critical thinking. Providing opportunities for this throughout PK–12 is critical to ensuring students are well prepared for college and career. In addition, we believe children learn best when they have a chance to grapple and make meaning of new experiences. They deepen understanding through real-world experiences.

THE BLUEPRINT: STUDENT EXPERIENCE

In reality, Van Ness's design process followed a nonlinear path with unpredictable twists and turns. New obstacles arose, which they navigated through recurring Design Cycles—more on that later in this chapter. But having established goals and guiding concepts, they could begin the tough work of transforming those ambitions into genuine student activities and experiences.

In this chapter, we will not detail how the team designed each student's experience. Instead, we'll focus on the experiences themselves—how they combine into a unified environment driving outcomes and honoring the Design Principles.

Next we explore one core component of the student experience and its related student activities (See Figure 3.2). While reading about these experiences, recall the opening story of this chapter with Jalissa, Amara, Lorenzo, and Ms. Nguyen. Where are the outcomes demonstrated in each student? And where do you see the Design Principles upheld?

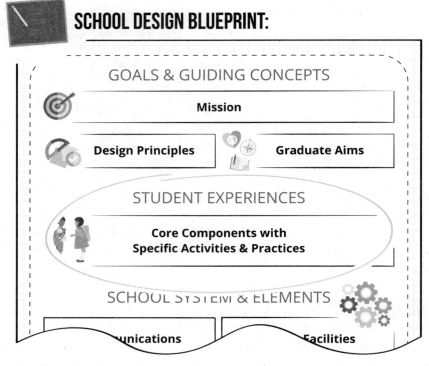

FIGURE 3.2

Student Experience: Compassion, Assertiveness, Routines, Environment

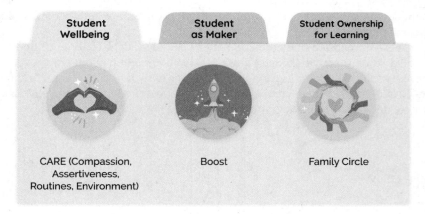

Overview Schema of The Whole Child Model

The Van Ness team uses the World Health Organization's definition of mental health and well-being: a state in which an individual realizes their own potential, can cope with the normal stresses of life, can work productively and fruitfully, and is able to make a contribution to their community. Van Ness supports student well-being through three vital components: Compassion, Assertiveness, Routines, and Environment (CARE), Boost, and Family Circle. The design team, and broader staff of teachers, developed numerous practices over time to bring these well-being elements to life, continuously refining the activities.

CARE Practices

CARE Practices

- Compassion & Assertiveness
- Routines
- Environment

CARE practices are a set of universal supports that all children receive. These practices have three components:

- Compassion and assertiveness
- Routines
- Environment

Earlier in this chapter you saw all of these practices at work. Recall how Ms. Nguyen responded to Jalissa's big emotion when Lorenzo bumped her on the way to the rug. She didn't yell "Demerit, Jalissa!" or "We don't yell in this classroom, Jalissa!" Instead she affirmed the emotion that Jalissa was experiencing—"Lorenzo bumped you, and you felt frustrated"—mirroring back in the language of empathy. But then, she offered a warm correction in the language of community and learning: "Jalissa, we use kind words when we talk to our teammates. You might choose to say to Lorenzo, 'It bothers me when you bump me. Next time, try to leave more space.' You try it, Jalissa."

These compassionate yet firm adult reactions help cultivate an environment where students become more caring toward each other. They learn to perceive peers' emotions and respond with empathy. If "every interaction matters" is a Design Principle and teacher conduct influences student actions,

Ms. Nguyen's response was highly impactful. Students closely observe each interaction, continually learning.

"There's a tremendous amount of learning to do as a teacher," reflects Aneesah Blount, a kindergarten teacher, "but no one tells you how much *unlearning* is required too."

Van Ness has been particularly intentional in how it approaches adult learning and development. As you've seen in this chapter, the Whole Child Model is not a one-off lesson on self-regulation or empathy. It is a complex, codified, coherent, and well-defined innovative school model that requires rigorous, continuous, and world-class learning experiences for adults.

CARE practices also include routines. *Routines* are very important for reinforcing a sense of physical and emotional safety. Van Ness's most lauded routine, "Strong Start," does significant work in helping young people transition from a stress state to their learning state.[7]

Strong Start is a morning routine where a child receives a personalized greeting, sets an intentional goal for the day, has breakfast in the classroom, and engages in paired and group activities that help build connections and learn explicit strategies to gain composure when upset.

When Jalissa asked Ms. Nguyen for a high-five, this was the beginning of her Strong Start, it was her personalized greeting. All twenty-one of her classmates would receive one. While she left rug time with Amara to re-center herself emotionally, she missed some of the full group routines that help build community and self-regulation practices such as "breathe and focus," where students complete a meditative breathing exercise or other community-building activities such as a dance-off between partners or chanting the classroom motto together or collectively setting goals. These "Strong Start" practices are most often joyous and fun. They are the lived experience of the "safety and connection" Design Principle.

Ms. Nguyen's classroom was physically designed to reduce stress. It smelled of lavender, avoiding harsh fluorescent lights. Only natural light from large windows and warm-toned table lamps gently illuminated the space. When Jalissa had a big feeling and yelled at Lorenzo, there was a dedicated space, called the "Centering Space" in the back of the classroom for her to regain her composure and reflect on her emotions and actions. Jalissa, Amara, and Lorenzo were also reflected in the space as their family photos filled the walls, not store-bought mass-produced visual teaching aids. The physical classroom environment was handmade by the students and Ms. Nguyen because the learning science suggests that a warm and welcoming space minimizes stimuli that may overwhelm or trigger students, making it harder for them to achieve their learning state.

Student Experience: "Boost Practices"; Time, Love, Connection (TLC); and Structured Recess

Boost Practices

- Increased Support
- Immediate Response
- Tailored Intervention

A majority of children's needs are met with CARE and its elements—greetings, breakfast in the classroom, and community-building. But some students and circumstances need deeper support, and that's where Boost comes in.

Boost comprises three elements: increased support, immediate response, and tailored intervention. A guiding belief within the model is that some students will communicate through extreme behaviors, and a nonpunitive system of support intentionally builds regulation and relationship skills while still prioritizing student safety. These are supports that are targeted for young people who need additional support beyond what the CARE model provides at the school level.

Two examples of Boost activities support learners: first, a practice called Time, Love, Connection (TLC), a once-daily connection with a trusted adult; second, an activity called Structured Recess.

Sensing that they might be missing a critical number of students who can often fall through the cracks at school, the school team made use of a student-facing survey to better understand how children were feeling at school. They learned from this survey that some children were feeling disconnected and didn't feel as though they had an adult who cared for them. Or, they didn't feel as though they had a close friend at school.

This led them to create TLC, a practice where for three to five minutes each day a child has a check-in with a trusted adult. TLC is part of the learning environment design aimed at a subset of children, like Jalissa from the chapter opening, who need to receive unconditional, consistent, positive attention from an adult who is not their current teacher. TLC is typically a three-to-five-minute noncontingent, positive interaction that learners receive even if they display challenging behavior. Research shows that an impartial adult can more naturally focus on an unconditionally positive connection.[8]

How did Senor Freddy become Jalissa's TLC adult? Earlier in the fall Jalissa took a survey where she identified Senor Freddy as a trusted adult; she knew that he loves soccer, and because her favorite cousin plays soccer, this became an entryway to build a relationship.

The theory behind the TLC design was that when students feel connected at school, their learning and social and emotional outcomes improve.[9]

For instance, Bunker Hill, a school adapting components of the Whole Child Model into their own, increased English language learners' (ELLs') sense of belonging this year through innovations around implementing Strong Start. After reviewing their Panorama data, Principal Jennifer Tompkins noticed that "our ELL scholars did not feel Loved, Challenged, and Prepared" despite a 17 percent schoolwide increase in their Loved, Challenged, and Prepared Index. "We identified as a school that we needed to determine how we could change this to ensure *all* scholars had a wonderful experience at Bunker Hill."

With the goal of both empowering their ELL population and increasing their connectedness to the school, Bunker Hill created "Strong Start Leaders," a group of ELL students who lead Strong Start in their classrooms and during all-school Town Halls.

These efforts are paying off. Tompkins says, "Our ELL students now exude confidence and feel connected to their community! We know this through observation and survey results. As a leader, knowing that students are not only learning but proud of who they are and what they can contribute to their peers and school community makes this work even more rewarding!"

Now, let's look at a second Boost practice designed to help teachers respond well to challenging behaviors. The Van Ness team understood that serving children with trauma and multiple adverse childhood experiences meant that young people would present difficult and "big behaviors." This became extremely clear in those first days of school during recess.

As with the other elements of the Whole Child Model, structured recess is one way to reinforce consistent behavioral changes—learning self-regulation and practicing playing safely are habits that need to be developed in children and adults, and structured recess is a way to build those mind-muscles. In a supervised and facilitated group, students can reflect on their behavior from the previous day, practice playing safely in a small-group structured environment, and plan how they'll interact safely with a larger group at recess the following day. They are also able to play cooperative games together, learning to collaborate and problem-solve in partnership.

Student Experience: "Family Circle"

The third component of the student experience within the Whole Child Model is "Family Circle," which is heavily inspired by the work of the Flamboyan Foundation.[10] Family Circle encompasses a series of practices designed to ensure that families from all backgrounds feel valued in their role as equal partners in contributing to their children's development and growth.

There are four core components of Family Circle. First, there is proactive relationship-building. Each student's family receives an initial relationship-building opportunity, such as a home visit, with the highest-need students prioritized for early and potentially multiple interactions during the summer months. The school may also employ innovative strategies to build authentic relationships with families outside the school setting.

Second, ongoing, two-way communication is a key component. The school prioritizes proactive, reciprocal communication that occurs both school-wide and on an individual level. Teachers actively reach out to families using various methods, such as text messages, app messaging, weekly newsletters, and websites, to keep parents informed and engaged. The school leader also plays a crucial role in disseminating information through multiple channels, including opportunities for families to engage in dialogue with the leader directly. Caregivers are encouraged to communicate freely with the school, fostering an environment of open exchange.

Third, family-to-family community-building is an essential practice within a diverse community. The school, parent organizations, and community partners work together to engage families in meetings that focus on both parenting education and community building. Attendance is encouraged across all identity groups to foster relationships and connections that bridge differences.

Finally, partnering with families on academics and on social and emotional supports is a crucial aspect of Family Circle. Its implementation varies based on the student's grade level. In pre-K to first grade, students participate in goal and data-driven parent conferences, where teachers discuss academic, social, and emotional goals for the child with their families in a one-on-one setting. Additionally, families of second to fifth graders attend academic parent-teacher team (APTT) meetings twice a year, following an initial conference.

THE BLUEPRINT: SCHOOL AND SYSTEM ELEMENTS

The final pieces of the learning environment design puzzle are the school and system elements, discussed in Chapter 2. School and system elements are the structures, resources, and decisions that enable the student experience (See Figure 3.3). These decisions sometimes live at the school level, the system level, or some combination of both.

We've identified in the following table ten key school and system elements that must be carefully considered and planned for as schools and systems make decisions around how to bring their learning environment designs to life:

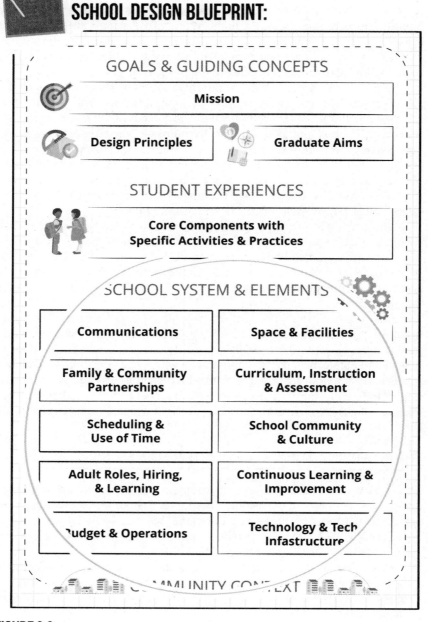

SCHOOL DESIGN BLUEPRINT:

GOALS & GUIDING CONCEPTS

Mission

Design Principles

Graduate Aims

STUDENT EXPERIENCES

Core Components with Specific Activities & Practices

SCHOOL SYSTEM & ELEMENTS

Communications	**Space & Facilities**
Family & Community Partnerships	**Curriculum, Instruction & Assessment**
Scheduling & Use of Time	**School Community & Culture**
Adult Roles, Hiring, & Learning	**Continuous Learning & Improvement**
Budget & Operations	**Technology & Tech Infastructure**

COMMUNITY CONTEXT

FIGURE 3.3

School & System Elements	How Each Resource and Structure Supports the Student Experience at Van Ness Elementary
Curriculum, Instruction, Assessment	■ The curriculum ensures that students are meeting DCPS standards *and* the graduate aims articulated in the school Blueprint. ■ Pedagogically, teachers are supported to ensure that all learning and assessment consists of exploration and discovery through play, repetition, and in-depth investigation into relevant and relatable content.
School Community & Culture	■ The school's community ethos is that student *and* adult culture matter and reinforce each other; all systems and procedures are created to ensure students, families, and staff feel safe, welcome, valued, and connected. ■ Through the Family Circle component of the Whole Child Model, the school creates purposeful interactions for families of diverse backgrounds to engage through special events and other group activities.
Adult Roles, Hiring & Learning	■ Hiring is the most critical activity, and everyone—from teachers to the custodial team to front-office staff—must share the school's ethos in the importance of student well-being and the belief that adults influence student experience through every interaction. ■ Weekly professional development and one-week intensive summer training ensures that everyone who interacts with children has rigorous and ongoing training on the Whole Child Model; teachers are provided meaningful opportunities for practice and attain leadership responsibilities for shaping the direction of the school.

(*continued*)

School & System Elements	How Each Resource and Structure Supports the Student Experience at Van Ness Elementary
Schedules & Use of Time	■ The schedule is designed to maximize support for students and align to principles of learning science (e.g., recess comes before lunch whenever possible, children have movement breaks throughout the day); the first six weeks of the school year are dedicated to learning systems and routines academic content is purposefully scaffolded throughout this period. ■ The schedule prioritizes consistency as predictability supports a sense of comfort and safety; within the schedule students have time for community building, content area instruction, deep work time, breaks, and play.
Community & Family Partnerships	■ Within the Whole Child Model, "Family Circle" practices are designed to ensure that families are engaged as partners in learning; relationship-building between home and school is proactive and frequent, and family-to-family community-building is supported to help build connections across lines of difference. ■ Teachers and staff utilize the practices and methods of the Flamboyan Foundation to support skill-building in how to cultivate authentic, student-centered relationships with caregivers.
Space & Facilities	■ The physical environment is a component of the Whole Child Model, and every classroom is designed to maximize the neurosequential experience from regulation to reasoning; the approach to lighting, smell, physical layout, and classroom decoration are all codified for teachers to personalize and create accessible environments for learning.

School & System Elements	How Each Resource and Structure Supports the Student Experience at Van Ness Elementary
Technology & Tech Infrastructure	■ Technology is used in classrooms to support increased levels of customization so that students can be working on content that's at their level of challenge and to help the teacher work with small groups of students when needed throughout the day.
Budget & Operations	■ Working hand in hand with the district, the school's budget is crafted to support teachers and staff to learn and improve within the Whole Child Model; social worker and psychologist positions are "given" or included on the budget. ■ Each year, leaders allocate funds to support a welcoming physical environment, invest in staff learning and culture, and support staffing structures that allow for strong implementation of CARE and Boost strategies.
Communications	■ Communications between school and home are frequent and two-way; caregivers and students complete surveys about their experience of the school community.
Continuous Learning and Improvement	■ The school continually evolves the Whole Child Model by running continuous Design Cycles of learning, envisioning, building, and testing new ideas as problems and opportunities arise; as they collect data from students and caregivers, the staff regularly reflects on the impact of their work and make adjustments in course.

School design requires holistic thinking about how all of these elements interplay. Often, we make innovations at the edges of these elements in incremental ways that will never break the gravitational pull of traditional, industrial learning.

Van Ness shows us how acutely important it is to have a cohesive learning environment design that over time helps to build critical conditions such as Clarity, Coalition, and Culture.

Since Robinson-Rivers' departure, the Whole Child Model has continued to thrive at Van Ness Elementary under the leadership of Maquita Alexander. As the new school leader, Alexander has not only sustained the model but has also worked to deepen its implementation and engage more educators in the learning process, ensuring a smooth transition for incoming teachers who join the Van Ness Elementary community.

Principal Alexander explains, "When I stepped into the role as Principal, I was committed to carrying forward the Whole Child Model because students deserve to be seen and loved and feel safe at school. The skills the model explicitly teaches—self-regulation, self-advocacy, and problem-solving—are skills that students need to be successful not just in school but in life. Under my leadership, the Van Ness team continues to invest in and refine the Whole Child Model by adding paid professional development after school led by Whole Child Model staff trainers, and we hold staff wellness sessions led by a trained mental health provider for new and novice teachers."

Chancellor Ferebee is building upon DCPS's history of community-based design by advocating for funding and resources to support several key initiatives. These include redesigning DCPS service models, empowering staff and leadership to engage both internally and externally, and meeting communities where they are to provide holistic education for each child.

In the next chapter, we venture to the cornfields of North Dakota, where we look at the Design Cycle, the iterative process of refining the learning environment design, at the heart of the community design process.

Our next guiding question is: *How* do school communities bring these extraordinary and equitable experiences to life?

CHAPTER 4

Northern Cass | Hunter, North Dakota

Key Points

- Northern Cass School District seeks to transform learning to be more customized by developing a competency-based learning model. Engaging students, families, and teachers throughout the design process has built conviction and clarity around the school's vision.
- They utilize the "Design Cycle" to guide and support their innovative efforts. This cycle is the engine of the design journey, enabling communities to learn, envision, build, and try new ideas in small ways before expanding them.
- One of the district's key innovations is called "Studios," which are project-based, competency-aligned learning experiences where students explore topics that interest them. Their model honors the Leaps of Customization, Relevance, and Rigor.

In the beautiful expanse of the cornfields of North Dakota, the learners at the Northern Cass School District are astonishingly motivated to learn, choosing to take on increasingly more rigorous and demanding work, while discovering their true passions and ambitions for life. Northern Cass High School learners are the hardest-working people in the school building.

The Van Ness design journey exemplified the power of alignment and cohesion in creating a fully integrated design. By establishing a strong foundation rooted in understanding the community's context and generating a shared, community-specific mission, student outcomes, and Design Principles, the design team successfully shaped an extraordinary learning environment at Van Ness. This process demonstrates the critical role that overall vision work plays in every community's long-term design efforts, ensuring that the resulting design is tailored to the unique needs and aspirations of the community it serves.

But once a school community has articulated these goals and core concepts in a Blueprint, how do they make it come to life? How does the innovation process unfold on a daily basis? What does the journey of turning a novel idea into reality look like in practice, from one day to the next? This chapter is an exploration of the Design Cycle, a set of continuous activities that refines a community's ideas and leads to better implementation and improved experiences and outcomes for learners.

Northern Cass School District is a small, rural district in Hunter, North Dakota. The student body is 98 percent white, with 2.5 percent eligible for free or reduced lunch. In the 2023–2024 school year state assessments, students scored above the state average: 64 percent proficient or advanced in science, 58 percent in math, and 58 percent in English Language Arts. More than 57 percent of high schoolers took at least one college course.

The district began its design journey before adopting the Design Cycle framework. To illustrate the framework and utility of the Design Cycle, we will examine how the design team applies it to develop a key student experience called Studios. This approach is helping to accelerate their efforts toward competency-based learning, shifting away from the standardized, synchronous methods of industrial-era education. Implementing this significant change in the school community's approach to learning will require considerable progress in three critical areas: Active Self-Direction, Customization, and Relevance. These elements are crucial for learners to succeed in the 21st century, and the Design Cycle will guide the team through this essential transformation.

"I sat in the back of the classroom and slept the whole time," reflects Matthew Donovan, a senior at Northern Cass High School. "I already knew what I wanted to do, and English class wasn't helping me. It was boring. I was ready to quit school."

Matthew's sentiments are familiar to most of us. He's a learner who wants to use his hands. He wants to be engaged in learning today that clearly connects to his interests and future pathways. Unfortunately, the traditional design of schooling that governs nearly all learning environments doesn't honor the Leap of "Relevance." Like many young people have reflected, particularly during the pandemic closures of 2020–2021, the disconnect between school and the real world is so vast that many of them no longer see the point in attending.[1] It's clear that school today isn't meeting our learners' needs. The educators at Matthew's school faced a dilemma: they could double-down on industrial-era learning and punish him for sleeping in class, or they could see Matthew's experience as a critical data point for why schooling needs to change.

Thankfully, they chose the latter. Tom Klapp, Beth Head, and Luke Bush, who make up the Personalized Learning Team at the Northern Cass School District, have been on a multiyear mission to revolutionize learning for their students. They are designing learning environments that honor each learner's capabilities and align with the principles of how people actually learn. Klapp recognized that students like Matthew needed a different approach to truly thrive.

"I like working with horses and was interested in blacksmithing," Matthew recalls. "I knew that Mr. Klapp does [blacksmithing] at home in his spare time." Klapp encouraged Matthew to try a new opt-in learning experience for high schoolers called Studios, self-directed, interdisciplinary, project-based learning modules that span six weeks within a semester. Learners attend Studios in place of two academic classes that they are threading together as part of the interdisciplinary core. Matthew, just a moment away from dropping out of school altogether, decided to give it a try. He loved it.

Within the first six weeks, Matthew was reading about the history of blacksmithing. He purchased blacksmithing equipment. Matthew's unique Studio brings together math, English, and history. He discovered that he has an entrepreneurial spirit, and as part of his project he set up a business selling his goods. He primarily sells horseshoes to farmers but also makes smaller goods like coat hooks.

"Studio helped me figure out how to run my business," he says. "I can actually use these skills in the real world."

Matthew developed other prized skills of entrepreneurship too: communication. He reflects, "I have gotten so much better at public speaking and expressing myself. Telling people what I need, for instance. Or communicating with my client about their horse's needs. This is really important because not every horse is the same."

He's aware of his personal growth. Many people around Matthew have told him that his disposition has changed. He's a lot nicer to be around. "I can actually sit down and talk to somebody without getting in a full-blown argument now," he says. What's fascinating to see in this story is that Matthew didn't spend his Studio time in anger or behavioral management. He spent his time intently studying something that inspired him and developed a whole suite of skills to complement his future ambitions.

Studios are having an impact beyond the school walls. Matthew has a plan for his business after graduation. He is currently doing an internship on his family farm. His friends have taken internships at John Deere working in mechanics. Another friend of Matthew's is a hunting guide, taking kids on guided hunts teaching them the foundations of the sport and how to be safe.

Mr. Klapp says of Matthew, "The evolution has been amazing to see. Matthew has turned into a nice future graduate of Northern Cass and a good young man. It's cool to see that he's walking away from high school with a plan. I can't say that I [had a plan] when I left school. I'm envious of Matthew!"

Northern Cass didn't create a Relevant and Self-Directed learning environment overnight. It has taken years of iteration, learning, failing, and trying again for them to refine these student experiences that empower learners. Matthew is just one story of many that illustrates the power of a relevant, self-directed learning experience for students that still achieves what school is designed to do—graduate competent young people who can thrive.

COMMUNITY AND LEADERSHIP CONTEXT

One of the most persistently challenging realities that rural communities face is talent drain: young people leaving their communities behind in search of work and other opportunities.[2] But what if a school district viewed itself as a window to the rest of the world and all its possibilities? **What if a school's purpose was helping students find the right path for them, rather than ranking and sorting all students under a rigid, one-size-fits-all mindset?**

Dr. Cory Steiner has the disposition of a former basketball coach. His voice is warm, clear, and commanding, and he has a motivational ring to every word. He began his career as a coach, and after realizing the joy and purpose he found in supporting young people, he became a social studies teacher. That led him to assistant principal and then principal, and for the last nine years he has been the superintendent of the Northern Cass School District.

Dr. Steiner is from North Dakota. He graduated from a school with twelve other students. He loved school, he had wonderful teachers, and this was his motivation to become an educator himself. Steiner had what many learners in rural communities don't have: a living representation of what he could become.

Dr. Steiner's experience as a father, teacher, and school leader has deepened his belief that every learner is different. Educators see this reality up close every day, but the traditional design of school doesn't allow for this obvious diversity. As a result, in the best of cases, most school districts are, in Steiner's words, merely "fine."

But the educators at Northern Cass don't accept that "fine" is good enough for their learners. Every learner has the potential to change the world. This belief is what compelled Dr. Steiner to shake things up. He did not want it to be business as usual at Northern Cass anymore. Working hand in hand with the Personalized Learning Team (Klapp, Head, and Bush), he helped set the tone for the district: "students" would be called "learners" to reflect their active participation in the process, and "teachers" would be called "educators," their job being to facilitate the process of learning, not solely disseminating information.

Dr. Steiner also had a compelling theory about what was holding not only Northern Cass back from being a truly extraordinary system but all schools: standards-based progression. Steiner knew that the only way to get his system out of this industrial-era rut was to refocus everyone's energy away from what learners *did* and toward what learners *know*.

Under his leadership, the Northern Cass School district was now on a journey toward competency-based education.

EARLY INNOVATIONS TOWARD COMPETENCY-BASED LEARNING: PURSUING GREATER LEARNER CUSTOMIZATION

One of the critical design features of industrial-era learning is its synchronicity. All learners focus on the same content, at the same time, and are assessed at a predetermined date. As a result, early in Northern Cass's design journey they focused on actualizing the idea of learning *progress* versus learning *pace*. Fortunately, this customization was possible due to a 2017 district petition to the state of North Dakota requesting a waiver on seat time policies (you can read more about this in Chapter 11). Dr. Steiner wasted no time in taking advantage of this precious legislative gift.

His team began creating an online school for eighth grade learners who wanted to advance more quickly through the curriculum and take online high school courses when they were ready. This seemed promising and was aligned with the spirit of the new waivers. In year one, thirty-five learners signed up for the opportunity. In the second year, only eight learners signed up.

"It wasn't great," Dr. Steiner recalls, "it was a disaster."

When they asked the children what went wrong, they heard familiar refrains that educators in 2020 would hear during the pandemic school closures.

"'We do not want to learn in a weird room on computers all day,' is what they told us," Steiner recounts. "They missed their teachers. They missed their friends. They missed being in an active learning environment."

In response to the learners' experiences with online learning, the design team set to work to create an in-person model taking the best elements of the self-paced curriculum and incorporating them into the classroom learning environment. Making learning and assessment more asynchronous—such as allowing learners to take assessments when they are ready—allows for content to be available at the pace of the learner. They were tweaking the industrial-era model quickly and began seeing some progress.

But as all discontents with industrial-era learning know well, once you start solving a problem, another arises. This time, the problem was one of the key external motivators of the whole system: grades.

Dr. Steiner and his team realized that grades (and relatedly, test scores) were getting in the way of transformative innovation. At the end of the day, learners were motivated by the grade. Learning itself was structured to produce a grade. Moreover, colleges wanted applicants with good grades.

So the team had *another* innovative idea: let's get rid of grades, something everyone is habituated to, and instead give learners a number one through four indicating their level of proficiency.

"Well, in the beginning of the grades thing, parents were absolutely furious," Steiner says. "I had parents crying, calling me up, parents coming to my office screaming at me. One guy was red in the face, 'My kid can't go to college. . .grades worked for me. You're ruining my kid's future.'" It was clear that the "Conviction" and "Coalition" conditions weren't strong yet. The broader community needed to be bought in; they needed the same fervor of belief that was animating Dr. Steiner. There was clearly work to be done.

These early days of change weren't all smooth sailing. The Northern Cass team had mastered two steps of any innovation cycle: building and trying.

What Dr. Steiner and his team needed most in those early days were tighter protocols for learning, better engagement of community voices, perspectives, and aspirations at the very center of the changes they sought to make. They found that to make the Leaps away from industrial-era learning, they most needed to align with their community on the purpose of schooling. What were they there to do? What was the promise of a diploma from the Northern Cass School District?

Developing the Portrait of a Learner

At the end of the 2017 school year, the high school hosted annual senior slideshows. This was a time for learners to share their future plans with the community and thank caregivers and teachers for helping them get there. Every year, when the fifty or so seniors would present slideshows, Dr. Steiner noted the disappointed community response when hearing plans for the graduates.

Northern Cass teachers noticed this too. They observed so many learners whose needs were not getting met and who felt disconnected from the school community. Some learners shared that school was a waste of time, when they could go make money *now*. The teachers realized that they had spent years and years putting information *into* kids. They were spending no time observing what kids could do and asking kids what they wanted for themselves.

This made Dr. Steiner and his team of educators wonder, "What would it look like to create a system where young people could have maximum exposure to all sorts of careers, activities, and pathways such that they knew what they wanted to do after school and, more importantly, what they *didn't* want to do?"

But where would they start this journey? They couldn't just dream up an idea (like the online class) and implement it right away. There was something deeper that they were missing.

Dr. Steiner had a key insight: we need to have a vision of what a successful Northern Cass learner looks like. Do we even know what we're trying to build in our young people?

Fortuitously, Dr. Steiner was in North Dakota, a state that was beginning its journey toward what they called "personalized learning" in 2018. In October of that year, KnowledgeWorks, an organization that partners with states and schools to align policy and practice to advance personalized, competency-based learning for learners and educators, had convened North Dakota educators around the central question that Dr. Steiner most needed to answer: When a learner receives a Northern Cass diploma, what is the promise behind that piece of paper? What habits, skills, and attributes do they possess that will help them thrive in a volatile and uncertain future?

The Northern Cass team had a hypothesis about what they most needed to do. But unlike the online class or the change to the grading system, they weren't going to just develop a document and share it with the community. They needed to go to the community and hear their voices directly.

Dr. Steiner convened a team to solicit feedback. They wanted to learn the habits, skills, and attributes students needed to be successful from those who are often the last asked: learners and their caregivers.

"We brought parents and learners together into the gym and all sorts of small group engagements and focus groups in town around 2018," recalls Tom Klapp, director of the Personalized Learning Team.

"They didn't say high GPA; they didn't say Harvard. They said, 'We want our kids to be good people, who have skills to do whatever they want to do,'" remembers Dr. Steiner.

This fired up the Northern Cass design team. What would it mean to cultivate good people? Which skills would they need in order to flourish? Certainly they learned that kids would have to be adaptable in this new world, different from the ones their parents and grandparents were raised in.

Dr. Steiner and his team heard from parents that they wanted their children to have skills to navigate real choices in their lives—they were not thinking about specific plans but the skills to determine which plans were best for them. As the design team learned from their community, they were also taking in facts and figures about all the unknowns that their young people would confront in the world after school—which industries would still be standing in the future, what skills did kids need now to prepare them? Similar to what the Van Ness team learned, the future of work was speculative. Schools would need to prepare young people for jobs that didn't even exist.

As the Northern Cass design team processed this information, they began envisioning what learning could look like in their district. The team called these burgeoning ideas a "choice-ready model"—college, career, military. This model would provide experiences to make informed choices about the future, not just what learners wanted to do, but also help them identify what they didn't want to do; the design team wanted them to be able to make informed decisions about their own future.

As they took in what they were learning from research, employers, and hearing from their own learners and caregivers, the design team envisioned what this ideal graduate might look like. A Northern Cass learner would be accountable and show responsibility for all their choices by following through with commitments. Importantly, learners for the future would need a learner's mindset—flexible and willing to put in extra effort when challenged and always striving to improve. In all, the design team identified five attributes:

- **Accountability:** Able to show responsibility for all choices and follow through with commitments.
- **Communication:** Clearly share thoughts and opinions so others can understand.
- **Adaptability:** Think deeply to find solutions to difficult problems.
- **Leadership:** Develop abilities in themselves and others to make a positive impact at school or in the larger community.
- **Learner's Mindset:** Be flexible and willing to put in extra effort when things are difficult and striving to always improve.

But simply writing down beautiful aspirations doesn't make it so in a school. The design team knew they needed to put ideas into action. This led the team to build and try a new version of senior slideshow—Capstone. The main idea was similar, but instead of reporting only their future plans, learners would reflect on how they lived into the attributes of the Portrait of a Learner.

"We butchered it right away," Steiner reflects. "Kids were saying things like 'I was accountable this year because I didn't skip many classes.' It was actually a mess."

The educators realized something: they had listened to what kids thought mattered most, but they hadn't involved them in defining these attributes in a tangible way. The learners hadn't been asked to make these attributes personal.

"Once we realized that, we went back to the drawing board," says Steiner.

When they engaged young people to define these attributes, insights emerged. From a learner sharing their thoughts of suicide came a distressing realization for the design team: for young people communication went deeper than just the ability to write an essay. They also needed to be able to communicate with each other, to share about their experiences openly, and to make it safe "to not be okay all the time."

"By learning from our young people, we were able to create support that we didn't know we needed," recalls Steiner, "and now we have high school learners running social-emotional working groups themselves. This came out of a community design orientation to the work."

As the learners began to internalize the Portrait of Learner, even more compelling stories began to emerge. During Capstone one year, a long-time special education learner who had felt marginalized for a long time reflected on why he didn't have the close friendships that he yearned for. He shared with the group that "I hadn't earned them yet." He continued therapy and went to college, which for him was the right path.

The Northern Cass design team was learning from the community and empowering young people to envision and build new experiences. They were testing ways to challenge the standards-based curriculum progression in their march toward competency-based education. However, Dr. Steiner noticed something about the changes they were pursuing—they lacked specificity.

Eureka! Designing the "Studio" Learner Experience

As part of his own professional learning and development, in 2021, Dr. Steiner joined a leadership cohort called the Learner-Centered Leadership Lab hosted by Transcend and the Lindsay Unified School District (you will read more about this program in Chapter 10). To this point the design effort toward competency-based learning had focused on Leaps toward Customization and Active Self-Direction, but Dr. Steiner wanted to re-engage on outcomes. Through this cohort experience and their relationship with Building 21, an organization that helps schools become competency-based, Dr. Steiner and his team would take another step on their design journey.[3]

This time, they would apply competency-based solutions to an issue in their community—credit recovery—because a small group of high schoolers were at risk of not graduating with just eight weeks without the proper credits. This is how one of the most important student experiences at Northern Cass came to be—Studios.

Dr. Steiner brought his challenge to the cohort of superintendents to problem-solve. He knew he wanted those eight students to graduate. He also shared with them the Portrait of a Learner aims; he wanted these learners not only to graduate but to demonstrate accountability, adaptability, and leadership, no matter how many weeks they had left as Northern Cass learners.

Klapp had learned a valuable lesson from other innovations: we can't simply apply what we think the solution is; we need to understand what we've learned from our young people. Klapp oversees the running of Design Cycles in the district. He and his team coach educators and learners as the district moves toward competency-based learning.

Part of that lesson learned was from the Leaps Student Voice Survey, a validated tool specifically tied to a school's current progress on ten key experiences of extraordinary and equitable learning (see Chapter 1 for deeper detail).

Klapp recalls, "The Leaps survey was a gut-punch for us; collectively only 30% of learners believed that their learning was relevant. It was even lower when we disaggregated for high school. That was hard to take. When you unpack it, kids aren't seeing school as something that is really meaningful, partially because they're not seeing how school is connected to the outside community. Relevance was the Leap we truly needed to make, and that is completely aligned with our competency-based vision."

So the design team, taking insights from learners and pulling in information from partnerships that North Dakota had helped to leverage, decided to solve a problem in front of them with the neediest learners.

Learning from other competency-based learning environments, the team came to the idea of a learning experience called "Studios." Studios are self-directed, interdisciplinary, project-based learning modules that span six weeks within a semester. Learners attend Studio in place of two academic classes that they thread together as part of the interdisciplinary core. Learners develop their given topics, using competencies as their guide to reflect on their strengths and areas for growth.

This was the innovation the design team tried with the credit recovery seniors, which solved for relevance and provided a unique solution for the most in-need students.

"The results were remarkable," Dr. Steiner beams. "I was absolutely amazed by what these young people created."

For example, a learner who never communicated well in writing got an article published in a local magazine. He loved farming but in the traditional, standards-based curriculum he could not explore the challenges and opportunities that modern farmers were facing in a broad sense. To complete his Studio, he interviewed dozens of local farmers, researched innovations in farming techniques, and cold-called newspapers to pitch his idea. The culmination of the project was the published magazine piece and a high school diploma.

Another learner from the credit-recovery cohort needed credits in film studies. She was a talented singer and decided to create a documentary, compose music for it, and present on the technical processes that made it all possible.

"In the senior Capstones that year, we heard the Studio recovery learners saying, 'This is the first time that I finally feel like a good student,'" Dr. Steiner remembers.

The small test of this Studio approach with a group of high-needs learners was a success. Klapp and his personalized learning team knew that they needed to build out this idea and test with even more young people. They decided to offer Studio as an elective for all high schoolers in the next iteration of the Design Cycle.

Maya, one of the first high schoolers to volunteer for Studio, reflects on her thinking when Klapp brought the opportunity to learners. "I prefer quality over quantity when it comes to learning. Klapp sold it to us as more teacher interaction. I don't like my peers; I get along with teachers. So this sounded cool. Honestly, I was struggling in the classes I was in. Constant workload and not getting anywhere. I thought a change would help out."

And it has. Maya is completing one of her favorite Studios to date. She is painting a mural representing New Deal politics and illustrating whom it included and excluded in American society.

Another high schooler, Nicholas, was receiving special education services and advocated for including Studio in his individualized education plan (IEP). "I had an IEP meeting, so I asked to do it. It's so helpful; it's like, not traditional learning at all. Right now, I am doing a history Studio on the impact of the space race in the 20th century."

Nicholas says that Studio saved schooling for him. "I was going to give up on school this year actually. But I decided to give it one more try. Without Studio, I was done with school."

Another high schooler, Nora, recounts her own transformative experiences with Studio. "I was really struggling with English 9; I just couldn't comprehend it. It was worksheet after worksheet; then we'd do a quiz. Great teacher or not, the setup just isn't that great."

Nora was encouraged by Maya's experience, so she gave Studios a try. One of her favorite projects combined English persuasive writing, physics, complex mathematics, Newton's laws of motion, and gravity. She explored the accuracy of action scenes in movies, from car crashes and explosions to fight scenes. She learned that most Hollywood scenes are nonsensical fiction, something she had suspected, but now she rests confidently in the knowledge that she knows *why*. This Studio helped her to hone her interest in science, filmmaking, and production. She now has a solidified goal for her life, and school helped her to do it.

The experiences of these interdisciplinary Studios at Northern Cass are unlocking curiosity, motivation, and helping learners envision career paths that may seem unattainable and unknown for young people growing up in rural America.

Active Self-Direction is one of the most elusive experiences of school. Because our schools are so teacher-centered, thoughtfully designed and implemented Studio models can shift teacher-led classrooms to ones where young people are meaningfully growing in their agency, building on their own knowledge and interests. Motivation is a key science of learning principle; it is possible to motivate through relevant, rigorous, authentic learning that learners had a hand in shaping for themselves.

HOW THE DESIGN CYCLE GUIDED AND SUPPORTED NORTHERN CASS'S DESIGN JOURNEY

In the early days of Northern Cass's design journey, Dr. Steiner and the design team had all the Conviction that school needed to change for learners. They even had ideas about how learning could change. But what they were missing was a process to help discipline and guide their efforts from one innovation to the next. They needed a process they could use to systematically try to learn from their ideas in bite-size ways that would add up to their vision for a fully competency-based learning system.

The engine at the heart of the community design process is the *Design Cycle*. Every community's design process is unique to their context and needs, but every community's journey consists of a series of large and small "turns of the cycle" (revolutions) through which a community will iteratively strengthen the design of their learning environment and tend to the conditions that support innovation along the way.

As you'll recall from Chapter 2, in the four phases of the Design Cycle, communities learn, envision, build, and try together over time.

Teams will cycle through all four steps of the Design Cycle many times, but they don't have to always go through this cycle sequentially. We will lay out the Northern Cass case example more linearly than it happened in real life in order to illustrate the distinct actions taken in each part of the cycle.

In the following sections, you will explore three focused Design Cycle iterations, or "turns of the cycle," as Northern Cass refined its Learning Environment Design vision. This vision is grounded in competency-based learning and aims to advance the critical Leaps of Customization, Relevance, and Active Self-Direction. Each turn of the cycle represents a significant step forward in creating a learning environment that better serves students like Matthew, Maya, and Nora.

These revolutions show how Northern Cass progressively integrated more ideas and Design Cycle activities over time, strengthening the design of Studio to align the learner experiences to their Portrait of a Learner. As they applied what they learned, they developed novel solutions to solve tangible learner challenges. Through all of these revolutions, the design team and the community strengthened their Community Conditions, including Clarity, Conviction, and Coalition.

First Turn of the Design Cycle (October–December): How Might We Pilot One-to-One Conferencing Within the Studio Model?

The Northern Cass design team now had a viable, Leaps-aligned student experience with Studios. The innovation had been a success with a high-needs group of learners needing credit recovery, and high schoolers were flocking to the experience too. The model itself helped to cultivate all of the Graduate Aims (Portrait of a Graduate) that the community had developed. But if they were to create a whole system designed for competency-based learning, the design team knew that even the youngest learners needed access to these kinds of experiences cultivating the Leaps of Relevance, Customization, and Active Self-Direction.

Klapp and His Personalized Learning Team knew that high school shouldn't be the very first time the learners experience this kind of learning environment. Studios had been so successful, why not expand access to *all* middle schoolers, with some modifications?

The Studios experience is a continuum of the Active Self-Direction Leap. In high school, learners are furthest along the continuum. Increasingly, more learners are participating in Studios and using the competency framework to identify which competencies they want to work on for credits to graduation and are meeting with an advisor to help create a six-week project that will demonstrate these competencies.

For middle schoolers, the personalized learning team modified the experience to include six week, ready-made experiences that learners can choose from rather than the learner-designed projects. Learners explore diverse topics. For instance, in "Fortress Fantasia," a student researches medieval warfare, castle construction, and designs a model castle that can withstand attacks and natural disasters. Another project, "Dollhouse Designer," challenges a student to build a fully furnished dollhouse meeting a fictional client's needs.

The middle school Studios experiences would need deeper development and design. Three smaller learner activities lay at the heart of the Studio model: a one-to-one conferencing structure, goal-setting, and assessment. They set out to tackle one-to-one conferencing first. They knew that competency-based learning requires a community that makes the Leap from Passive Compliance to Active Self-Direction. One way for educators to support learners in taking ownership over their learning in a fully competency-based classroom is to have them set their own goals and check-in on their progress through brief one-to-one conferencing. But how do you ensure effective teacher/learner conferencing within a learning environment where educators and students alike are accustomed to the synchronization and one-size-fits-all design of the industrial model?

The design team had learned from its early innovations that standing up ideas in whole without deliberate cycles of learning and testing created solutions that might be great in theory but suffered from lack of cohesion, community buy-in, or the building out of specific practices to truly support effective implementation.

With that knowledge, the design team set out to discipline the practice by utilizing tight Design Cycles of learn, envision, build, and try.

They had four learning questions they asked teachers to answer in this turn of the cycle:

- Is this conferencing protocol an effective way to check in with learners and help them set goals? (Outcomes)
- To what extent are you able to build relationships/rapport using one-to-one conferences? (Attitudes)
- How much time do you need to conduct one-to-one conferences with my learners? (Feasibility)
- What routines need to be in place to conduct one-to-one conferences? (Feasibility)

By the end of this cycle, the design team needed to know: *Can we design an efficient and effective structure for conferencing, and if so, what knowledge support will teachers need to implement this practice across Studios?*

With that, the cycle was ready to turn.

First, they set out to learn. They did "inspiration visits" to schools and other learning models that utilized one-to-one conferencing. They took inspiration from the Greenfield Model, developed at Achievement First Charter Schools; from Genesee Community Charter School; and from Casco Bay High School in Maine. These learning environments purposefully design the kinds of hands-on, Relevant, Active Self-Direction that Northern Cass is aiming for. They were inspired by what they saw, and those experiences increased their belief that they were headed in the right direction. These inspirational visits deepened their Clarity and Conviction.

After they saw what conferencing could look like, they began to Envision how they might pull it off themselves. How would educators test this new idea of one-on-one conferencing within a classroom of thirty learners? What would nonconferencing learners do? What do you actually talk about with young people in a conference? Can you effectively build relationships in such a short space?

These kinds of questions are essential during the Envision phase of the Design Cycle. Envisioning consists of three parts: ideation, refining, and landing. This brings order to the "spaghetti at the wall" nature of brainstorming that is fun but can also lead to competing visions and ideas. The design team took time to imagine and discuss all the ways that one-on-one conferencing could look. Perhaps they would need two teachers in the classroom, one conferencing the other facilitating the larger group. What might learners want to discuss in these conferences? How many times would it be feasible to conference with learners over a six-week period? How does conferencing enable the big vision of competency-based learning for all?

During the Envision stage of the Cycle, they brainstormed several approaches together before finally landing on an idea to try: they would pilot a four-question protocol with learners for ten minutes with five learners in succession, scheduled over six weeks.

Now that they landed a set of ideas, it was time to Build what they needed. They started with drafting many learner interview protocols, before landing on four key questions for students:

- What's something you're proud of this week?
- Think of a time during learning when you do not get as much done as you would like. This might be during independent work time or on computers or in small groups. What prevents you from achieving what you hope to achieve?
- What could you do to work better or more effectively?
- What's your goal to work more effectively over the next week?

Now, they were ready to pilot these conferences with two Studio teachers. They set the timers for ten minutes, conducting five learner conferences in succession, and then jotted down quick reflections when they finished. They decided for this first run that while conferences were happening, the rest of the class would be engaged in independent work.

After six weeks, it was time to come together to make meaning of what they just tried.

They found that teachers relished the time to have conversations with learners, as the traditional school day doesn't allow for this kind of interaction.

Teachers saw how even ten minutes with students individually goes a long way toward fostering the Connection & Community Leap, as well as the foundations of trust that strengthens Community Conditions.

But they also noticed there were adjustments to make. First, teachers were talking more than listening. The pilot teachers wondered how learners could direct more of the discussion, crucial to cultivating the Active Self-Direction Leap at the heart of competency-based learning, their big vision. Next, they realized that learners would need to bring themselves to the process. What did *they* care about? How did learners assess their own learning and growth? What did they aspire to?

Finally, they reflected that five conferences each session was too many. Three was likely the right amount.

From this first cycle, after discussion and meaning-making together, they surfaced new learning that would start the cycle anew:

- **Learning 1:** They would aim to meet with each learner at least three times over six weeks to check in on how Studio was going for them.
- **Learning 2:** Learners needed to reflect before the conferences to make the ten-minute discussion as meaningful as possible.
- **Learning 3:** They would execute three conferences each session, and when possible, a second teacher would support the full group, while the other teacher leads the conference.
- **Learning 4:** The lead Studio teacher would host the conferences given their direct daily relationships to learners. They wouldn't leverage administration or substitutes.

- **Learning 5:** Goal-setting needed to be part of the one-to-one conference protocol to promote practicing Active Self-Direction and the skills of communication and learner's mindset, two of their Graduate Aims.
- **Learning 6:** They would need to expressly teach goal-setting.

With that, they had the makings of another turn of the cycle. This time, they would run conferences with the adjustments they agreed upon, and they would add another critical competency-based feature: goal-setting.

Second Turn of Design Cycle (January–March): How Might We Add Goal-Setting as Part of One-to-One Conferencing So that Learners Can Practice More Active Self-Direction?

After the design team successfully piloted one-to-one conferencing, they learned that young people needed to be more reflective and active agents within the structure. As a result, they set out to add a component to the conference: goal-setting.

Disciplined Design Cycles are critical for this stage in design, as they allow teams to come up with new ideas, test them deliberately, and learn from what worked and what didn't. Too often, approaches to change in school focus on the product. The product becomes the solution. But by running the Design Cycle, the process of generating and testing solutions becomes the focus.

The team began their test of goal-setting in the same way as conferencing: they looked outside of their context to learn from other places. They were most excited by the approach taken at the Forest School, outside of Atlanta, Georgia. Rather than make goal-setting an isolating experience, the Forest School uses the idea of a "running partner" where two learners work together to express their goals, develop a plan to meet them, take action, and reflect and revise together.

The Northern Cass team Envisioned how they might test this for themselves in smaller, more bite-size ways. First, they realized that they couldn't assume that learners knew what goals were or how to set meaningful ones. So they imagined that to get to their big design vision of Competency-Based Learning, they really had to inculcate these skills with kids. They also knew that while making plans is something we all sort of do, the discipline and skill of making plans for a measurable, transferable, and ambitious goal is its own effort. So they worked together through how they might teach that as well. All of this was extremely important because in this round of the cycle they wanted for learners to be more self-directed. This meant that teachers needed to talk far less, and learners needed to talk far more.

From this Envisioning, they landed on some key things that they needed to Build to try goal-setting. The first two mini-lessons for learners on what goals are and how to make them meaningful were fairly straightforward. But they also built lessons on emotional resilience, helping learners to cope with obstacles and understand what's happening in the brain when we persevere through challenges. To facilitate this student learning, the team needed to train and support teachers to give meaningful feedback that was actionable, specific, and kind.

Now they were ready to Test. They were ready to execute goal-setting as part of the conferencing experience. After six weeks they surveyed the learnings.

Here's what they found:

- A 14 percent increase in learners affirmatively responding to "In my Studio, I have goals for my learning," from 63 to 77 percent
- A 9 percent increase in learners answering affirmatively, "Adults coaching me in Studio encourage me to work in my own way," from 58 to 67 percent
- A 10 percent increase in learners answering affirmatively to, "What I learn in Studio is connected to my Portrait of a Learner competencies," from 60 to 70 percent
- And only a 1 percent increase in response to, "What I learn in Studio is often connected to life outside the classroom"

From this turn of the Design Cycle the team learned even more than they had bargained for.

Rather than relying on their gut or anecdotal evidence alone, they had results from every middle schooler to guide where they most needed to test. They made progress in goal-setting, but it was clear that Studio needed to do two important things: connect to competencies so that learners could understand how they were growing and create more offerings that would provide the Relevant connections that learners were craving.

Third Turn of the Design Cycle (April–May): How Might We Pilot an Assessment Framework that Offers Learner "Voice and Choice" and Leverages Conferences and Goal-Setting?

The next big challenge the design team faced with Studios was ensuring that these experiences were cultivating the Portrait of a Learner vision that the community came to early in their Design Journey—accountability, communication, adaptability, leadership, and learner's mindset.

The design team set out a learning agenda:

1. How might we use our Portrait of Graduate competencies as a reflection tool, not a checklist for learners?

2. Are we creating authentic growth experiences around our Portrait of a Graduate aims?
3. Are we allowing "voice and choice" in Studios?

Like in previous Design Cycles, they set out to Learn from lots of different competency rubrics. There were many ways they could assess learner growth. They could take a survey approach, they could conduct interviews or small focus groups, or they could administer more formal assessments.

As they Envisioned how to approach assessment, they were reminded of the Leaps. Ultimately, their goal was to develop Active Self-Direction and reflective thinking, both critical for the big aim of Competency-Based Learning. They debated how different assessment types might honor or violate these aims. Ultimately, they choose a simple format: Glows/Grows mapped directly to the Graduate Aims all of the learners were familiar with.

They Built a simple reflection template to aid learners in assessing their own progress. Learners would choose one to three competencies from the Portrait of a Learner framework that they felt most aligned with their Studio. For the Science Olympiad Studio, one learner chose "Problem Solving and Design: Stage 4: I can articulate a clear problem statement and success criteria for solutions."

Finally, they were ready to Try this assessment reflection tool in six-week pilots with learners. From this, they learned a lot, not just from learners but teachers too. Some teachers reported that important mindset shifts were happening for them as a result of these Design Cycles. Learner relationships were improving, and there was more positive and two-way communication with learners. For some educators their mindsets went from "I don't have time for one more thing" to "This is worth it!" The Design Cycle was serving to deepen teacher Clarity about what they were ultimately striving for, and Conviction that these innovations were important and would yield deeper student learning.

The Glow/Grow self-assessment rubric also yielded important learning. The teachers found that "glow/grow" was "low-risk language." Glow/ grow wasn't sending the message to kids that they weren't good at something. Rather, they were learning that there are areas all of us can continue to improve and focus on. This was the essence of their Graduate Aim, "Learner's Mindset."

The Design Cycle is a powerful tool within the community-based design process. Each turn of this Cycle enables communities to reground in the Learning Environment Design, as they test new ideas to strengthen their original vision. This helps communities thwart one of the biggest challenges of fundamental change: holding vision in tandem with the current context.

The cycle requires that communities look inward—reflecting on their goals, their strengths, their weaknesses, or learner's experiences at school—and outward, by looking to other innovative models and practices that they can borrow and adapt for their vision. At Northern Cass, they were able to learn from many different approaches as they strengthened the design of Studio to apply to their middle school learners. They were able to brainstorm systematically before landing on ideas to test in short cycles.

This kind of testing is typically missing on the ground in school change. The desire to impact student learning right now means we race to implementation before learning experiences have truly been iterated upon and tested in the current environment.

Northern Cass continues its long march toward redesigning one of the most rigid aspects of industrial-era learning: assessing learning around what children know, not what they completed. For struggling learners, in fact all learners, mastery is more likely when learners are directing the process (with lots of support and guidance) toward what interests them and they believe is relevant. Linking that mastery and competence as the standard for graduation versus grades or other measures.

Many communities have sought to bring this approach to their schools but haven't had a mechanism for building out what is required to make this fundamental design shift alongside teachers and learners. The Design Cycle enabled the Northern Cass team to refine their learning environment design to better serve learners. They began to see students who never spoke up, speaking more boldly and sharing their hopes and dreams. Teachers saw how conferencing helped to strengthen Connection & Community, even as the Leaps they named were Relevance and Active Self-Direction.

Conditions for Community Design are strengthened when communities can practice, fail quickly, and try again. Design Cycles build resilience, trust, and widen the Coalition in ways that are critical for bringing the vision to more and more teachers and learners.

Sage Hayes, a middle schooler, reflects on a recent Studio rotation, "'Craft For Life' is one of my recent favorite experiences. It is different rounds of crafting projects, like crocheting, felting, and tufting. We went through them, figuring out what we liked and what we didn't. For my final project, we could do any craft, so I crocheted a blanket. I like using your hands, and I actually learned something new at school!"

She reflects on what she learned about herself, "I have a lot of work to do on perfectionism. I had to learn a new skill and be okay with what I made, even if it wasn't all that pretty. This was huge for me."

Elena Hudson, who also tried Craft for Life, chimes in, "I was so skeptical about crafting. My mom crafts, but I don't. This affirmed that crocheting is *not* for me. I don't have the patience for it, but I tried it. I absolutely confirmed that I am a sports person."

Hugo Stone participates in a math acceleration Studio on a personalized platform. "The program is super-useful. It has helped me work on my accountability. I've always been pretty good but time management is something I have grown in, since I have to go at my own pace."

In the successive turns of the Design Cycle Dr. Steiner and his team worked to go to the community and solve tangible problems along the way. Design Cycles are now part of the fundamental DNA of Northern Cass. This continuous cycle of learning, building, envisioning, and trying is creating new solutions that are changing learners' lives and reengaging them in the lifelong journey of education.

What Dr. Steiner and his team of educators are creating for Northern Cass is beyond "fine." It is extraordinary and equitable for all kids.

CHAPTER 5

Brooklyn STEAM Center | Brooklyn, New York

Key Points

- The Brooklyn STEAM Center (STEAM) provides rigorous career and technical education (CTE) for high school students across six career pathways (including computer science, design engineering, and culinary arts).
- STEAM was designed through a community-based process involving educators, industry partners, and students to align to New York City's labor market needs.
- The design Blueprint helped them create a cohesive environment that mirrors real workplaces. Their model honors the Leaps of Rigor, Relevance, Active Self-Direction, and Anytime/Anywhere Learning.

Not only do scholars from the Brooklyn STEAM Center graduate with an advanced Regents High School Diploma, but they can build computers, secure a network against invaders, design and build liveable homes, produce documentaries, and fabricate restaurant-quality meals—they can do all of this at extraordinarily high levels that enable them to earn sustainable incomes in one of the most expensive cities in the world. Learners are screaming out for relevant, real-world experiences, and at STEAM, they are receiving world-class training in the same building as industry professionals.

Picture the most futuristic work environment you've ever read about in *Wired* magazine. Entering STEAM, you would be forgiven for thinking that you walked into a high-tech startup, but these spaces are classrooms with polished concrete floors, cutting-edge equipment, and shared spaces for collaboration. The large industrial building is one of many in the vibrant Brooklyn Navy Yard where employees are bustling from meeting to meeting. The ground floor of the building has restaurants that represent the diverse background of the community—a bagel shop, a pizza stand, and a taco restaurant. STEAM is on the third floor, a stone's throw away from this large structure of about eighty businesses that directly link to STEAM programming, such as their Culinary Arts pathway. Inside STEAM is a high-energy atmosphere where young people are always *doing* something—building computers, cooking, or working with industry-graded machinery. There are lockers for scholars' belongings, snacks on deck, glass-fronted classrooms, and a community whiteboard throughout that functions as the community bulletin board.

What sets STEAM apart is its innovative and comprehensive learning environment design, which is revolutionizing our understanding of career technical education (CTE). In this chapter, we return to the concepts of learning environment design (supported by the Blueprint) and Community Conditions (see Chapter 2). We see how the largest school district in the country partnered with local industry to create an innovative, impactful, and immersive learning environment that is producing transformative outcomes and experiences for juniors and seniors in Brooklyn, New York.

As with Northern Cass, STEAM uses the Design Cycle to architect and continuously improve their model. This chapter highlights unique lessons about how to design CTE pathways geared toward advancing the economic mobility of students. This model is a powerful disruptor in our current moment. It helps to point a way through some of the thorniest tensions that exist in PK–12 education. It shines a light on the country's unsettled relationship to "blue-collar" work, especially in the age of generative artificial intelligence (AI) and rapidly advancing technology. The educators at STEAM have created a successful, joyful, rigorous, relevant, and responsive learning environment that is on the march to expansion in New York City and beyond. What are the guiding concepts of this model? What do young people experience? How is Brooklyn STEAM charting a new way toward workplace learning in the future?

When Natalya Tulloch graduated from the Brooklyn STEAM Center, she was immediately employable as a web designer. She could have been making the average salary of a web designer in New York of around $85,000. By her senior year, she had gained an Occupational Safety and Health Administration (OSHA) certification, as well as programming credentials in Hypertext Markup Language (HTML), Cascading Stylesheets (CSS), and Python. She could build a computer and knew how to make her own Ethernet cables. She also had experience as a product manager, owing to a rigorous project that she completed as a student within the Computer Technology program. While still in high school, Natalya traveled to China as part of the Americans Promoting Studies Abroad Program. She was able to put her burgeoning Mandarin to use and learn about how quickly technological advancements were happening. Natalya graduated with more advanced employment opportunities than many four-year college graduates.

She decided to attend Stony Brook University, rather than go straight to the workforce. For her and her family, this was an informed choice. While at STEAM she had earned so many college credits that she was able to graduate a year early. She had also taken advantage of the STEAM model's approach to professional skill-building. She saw the financial options up close before making her decisions and was able to create a budget for herself while still in high school.

Relevance, one of the ten Leaps mentioned in Chapter 1, is something students and caregivers have been demanding for a long time. Insights from the science of learning development suggest that learning experiences that are relevant increase student motivation—the willingness to start, put in mental effort, and persist even in the face of challenges.[1] The STEAM Center's learning environment provided powerful motivation for students that they will carry into a range of contexts in the future.

In college, Natalya took advantage of both work and enrichment opportunities. She worked with the IT department, helping the team fix computers, aiding other students in fixing and advancing their laptops, and protecting research computers on campus, all skills that she learned in high school. The income from this work, combined with her hefty scholarship, allowed her to save up and move out of her parents' home and cover tuition. She graduated from college debt-free and took a job at Dell.

As an Afro-Caribbean woman working in STEM, Natalya understands the importance of building and maintaining a network. She credits her time at the STEAM Center with helping her cultivate the soft skills needed for team engagement and working with others across varying lines of difference.

"I know how to manage the entire process of product development, like documentation, mapping stakeholders, developing product use cases, calendaring how long a feature takes to create, and how to check in with people without micromanaging," Natalya reflects. "So many people in my bracket at work are still learning to balance it all. But I've done it before."

As a child, Natalya knew early that she wanted to work with computers. She watched movies, she read articles, she followed the latest developments in the industry. But as an African-American child living in Brooklyn, she didn't have the natural connections or benefit of proximity to the booming tech industry. STEAM helped to fill in these gaps with an intentional instructional design that exposed students to budgeting and investing using real-life scenarios that they would encounter.

Natalya left the two-year experience at STEAM with confidence, experience, employability, and the will and skill to achieve her wildest dreams.

COMMUNITY AND LEADERSHIP CONTEXT

In 2014, the Civil Rights Project released a report stating that New York City's public schools were the most segregated in the country.[2] The report found that 60 percent of white and Asian students in New York City in 2010–2011 attended schools that the researchers named as "multiracial," while only 25 percent of Black and Latino students did. For New York state leaders like Dr. Lester Young, who currently serves as the chancellor of the Board of Regents for the University of the State of New York, these numbers were unacceptable and posed a significant threat to the state's future. Along with other leaders, he worked with the State of New York to put out a request for proposal (RFP) for schools and models aimed at desegregation. Could New York State make meaningful progress toward desegregation by stirring innovative school models? One of the big ideas that came from that experimental approach was for the city to pursue socioeconomic and racially diverse CTE programs.

CTE was coming back into public consciousness. For a long time, these programs were not considered viable pathways for many learners. In the worst incarnations, CTE was used as a funnel for low-income students, students of color, and special needs learners, for whom college was deemed off the table. In the 1980s, when studies showed that college graduates make over one million dollars more in their lifetime, the national ethos changed to "college at all costs."[3]

Today, the societal impact of this college-or-nothing mindset is harshly felt by students and families. Most young people take on debt for college or lack the experience to choose majors with appropriate future financial dividends. Families are also experiencing the hollowing out of the CTE infrastructure as access to high-quality, rigorous, and reliable programs is variable. Many high schools simply don't have the resources, human capital, or connections that it takes to support excellent work-based programs.

In response, the State Department of Education, locking arms with New York City Public Schools (NYCPS), the Brooklyn Navy Yard, and highly innovative school leaders, helped to lay the foundation for the Brooklyn STEAM Center.

One of those innovative school leaders was Kayon Pryce, the founding principal of STEAM. Expanding opportunity for all students and working to create rigorous CTE was at the heart of Pryce's educational philosophy. When he was a high schooler in New York City (NYC) schools, his guidance counselor encouraged him to only apply to career and technical programs. But Pryce didn't get the sense that his counselor saw his creativity and drive; he was placed in programs that matched the counselor's low expectations for what Pryce could achieve. The implicit message from the counselor in that meeting was "People like you just aren't college-bound."

People like Pryce, who was from a recently immigrated Jamaican family, Black, and receiving special education services, were often tracked into career pathways. There simply wasn't an expectation that college was in the cards. Today, Kayon Pryce is *Dr.* Kayon Pryce. He began his career as a teaching apprentice with NYCPS. He worked in several CTE programs across the city before leading his own classrooms and eventually rising to become the Senior Director of Career and Technical Education in the District. Dr. Pryce went from being a student who experienced low expectations by some educators to helping found one of the most innovative, work-based programs of its kind in the country.

STEAM opened to students in 2017 and is based inside the largest building on the Brooklyn Navy Yard, a 300-acre facility that is home to 550+ disruptive businesses and industries. Brooklyn STEAM is a joint endeavor between the NYCPS, the Brooklyn Navy Yard Development Corporation, and eight diverse public high schools in Brooklyn. Dr. Pryce and the design team set out to create a program that would provide a tangible pathway to economic mobility and wealth creation for young, predominantly Black and Latino eleventh and twelfth graders.

Since its inception, STEAM students have earned more than $1 million in earnings for paid work-based learning experiences and more than two thousand industry certifications (noninclusive of OSHA10 certifications).

The STEAM model exemplifies the collaborative spirit of a community-based design process. Dr. Pryce is not a lone visionary creating a school that would happen *to* the Brooklyn community. Rather, he was one of several leaders around the table coming together to design this new learning environment *with* the Brooklyn community, NYCPS, and New York State officials.

To initiate the planning, a team came together to participate in the inaugural Transcend and New Schools Design Collaborative; a ten-month journey with educators from across the country helped to reimagine and redesign their schools. One result of participating in the Design Collaborative was a strong initial vision for the STEAM model: student learning would be relevant, hands-on, rigorous, and informed by current industry standards; students would leave the program with skills and tangible opportunities that could lead to middle-income careers. Even with this solid vision, the team underwent many rounds of the Design Cycle (see Chapter 4 for a deeper exploration of this cycle) at the heart of community-based design to learn, envision, build, and try new student experiences.

In the Design Collaborative, the design team learned about the current state of CTE. They took inspiration visits together to other school communities and workplaces to generate key elements of the design. They learned from older approaches to career-technical education to understand tried-and-true practices like project-based learning, where students work on a complex question, problem, or challenge over an extended period, gaining knowledge and skills by investigating and responding to an authentic, engaging, and complex question or problem. This initial research helped to articulate a robust vision for what the STEAM model could be. The team envisioned the specific professional and industry skills that students would develop. They also began to chart the pathways that the school would offer—from culinary arts to construction. Through iteration the team began to articulate the design of the learning environment, captured in the Blueprint, which enabled them to open their doors in 2017. Through engagement in a community-based design process and utilizing the Blueprint and Design Cycles, STEAM has become a remarkable model of CTE that can be shared in communities everywhere.

THE BLUEPRINT: OVERVIEW OF BROOKLYN STEAM'S LEARNING ENVIRONMENT DESIGN

In this section we walk through the three prongs of the Blueprint: Goals and guiding concepts, student experience, and school and system elements. We describe the design choices that the STEAM design team made to cultivate a Leap-filled model that honors the science of learning and development.

THE BLUEPRINT: GOALS AND GUIDING CONCEPTS

SCHOOL DESIGN BLUEPRINT:

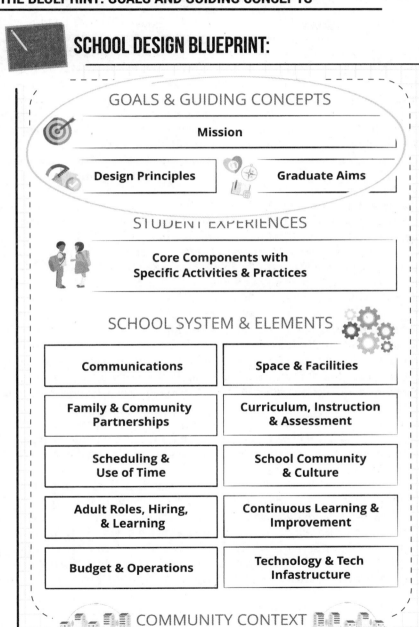

Developing the Mission, Graduate Aims, and Design Principles

In 2016, Dr. Pryce joined the Transcend + NewSchools Venture Fund School Design Collaborative, the ten-month, cohort-based program convening educators from school districts and charter networks around a shared vision to reimagine the design of school. The STEAM design team researched the science of learning and development, visited other CTE models, and engaged in iterative Design Cycles to strengthen the design of the STEAM learning environment.

The team consisted of Pryce, a representative from NYCPS, and principals from one of the eight Brooklyn high schools who would be sending their learners to the Navy Yard for half-days during their junior and senior years. Members of the team were not novices to CTE. They understood the basics of a work-based program, but they were determined to reverse the negative attitudes that caused many districts to divest from this kind of learning.

"Many CTE students are meant to feel that they are less than," says Dr. Pryce, "and that's just not the case. We knew that we needed to develop programming that was an option of first resort, that young people were excited by, and, crucially, that could provide a ladder to middle-income jobs."

The design team learned a lot about the specific work landscape of NYC. They learned that 50 percent of all jobs in the last decade between 2005 and 2015 were what is considered "middle-skill," meaning the position requires experience beyond a high school diploma but less than a four-year college degree. Employers in NYC needed these middle-skill workers but lacked the adequate talent pipelines to fill hundreds of high-demand, well-paying jobs. For many structural reasons, young people of color and low-income households are locked out of these quality income careers that could provide tangible pathways to economic mobility and invaluable social capital needed to access even more opportunities.

The mission and purpose of the Brooklyn STEAM Center would be about opportunity and advancement, not exclusion from college-going learners.

In time, the team came to an inspiring mission to ground their efforts:

The Brooklyn STEAM Center provides a tangible pathway to economic mobility and wealth creation for young New Yorkers from a diverse range of socioeconomic and educational backgrounds, by preparing them, through project-based learning in a real-world environment, with the technical, professional, career and financial skills to create their own futures. With a focus on building their own identity, agency, and social capital, scholars are prepared to adapt across their careers in the 21st-century economy.

Just like the Van Ness Elementary School team, they didn't stop there. Once they had a sense of the mission, their Graduate Aims came into focus. Because this was a work-based model, industry-specific skills were a must. The team set out to learn from real industry professionals about the kinds of attributes they were looking for and the kinds of professionals that succeeded in many of the most high-demand industries. What would learners need to work on an insured construction site? What would learners need to operate film equipment as camera people on one of the hundreds of television shows and movie sets anchored in New York City?

Damiano Mastrandrea, the senior director of Pathways & Partnerships at STEAM, recalls, "One of the biggest benefits of being colocated at the Navy Yard around industry professionals is that our sense of industry skills is informed by the latest and greatest needs of those industries and their credentialing requirements. It allows us to have a sharp sense of what these industry needs are, so that our programming can be responsive as things change."

The team also understood that employability is based on more than technical skills alone. They dove into research on skill development and ultimately adapted the MHA Labs Skill Building Blocks framework.[4] These Building Blocks comprise thirty-five core social, emotional, and cognitive skills that STEAM design team deemed important for college, career, and life success. The team learned from current trends that the future of work is likely to be highly collaborative in nature. Verbal communication matters for young learners as they will need to interact with colleagues, share their knowledge, and communicate disagreement with skill. Many work-based programs of the past took this kind of "soft skill" development as innate. But the STEAM design team understood that these skills would need to be practiced and reflected upon in authentic work environments for true learning to occur.

The design team arrived at four Graduate Aims shown in the following table:

Graduate Aim (Student Outcome)	Definition
Industry Skills	A wide range of technical skills relevant to a learner's chosen pathway; this includes credentials required for work in that industry.
Professional Skills	Thirty-five social, emotional, and cognitive skills deemed critical for college, career, and life success in the 21st century.
Identity & Agency	Learners develop a deep awareness of: who they are, what they care about: their interests and values, and where their strengths lie.
Social Capital	Learners activate a growing professional network of relationships and contacts they can rely on for future support and connections to access career development.

The STEAM team worked to articulate the corresponding Design Principles that would define student experiences at the center.

As they continued to build out the Blueprint, the STEAM design team came to four highly descriptive and actionable Design Principles in the following table:

Design Principle	Description	Why This Principle Matters
Learning by Doing	Young people thrive in a hands-on setting, where they are able to be active participants in their learning, with all new skills immediately applicable in a project setting. These projects are industry-informed, through the review and support of the Industry Advisory Council, and rooted within real-world learning.	Hands-on learning allows for meaningful encoding. People learn best when new learning is experienced in memorable ways and is related to prior knowledge. In addition, people learn best when they practice challenging but doable skills at frequent, focused intervals and across diverse contexts, which is made possible through project-based learning.
Workplace Immersion	The best career preparation is industry-relevant and responsive to the real world, changing to match new trends in industry and society. Young people should have the opportunity to meet real-world work expectations in a learning environment that is constantly iterating to keep up with the speed of change in the world of work. The feedback loop from the shop floor to the classroom should be hours, not years. Industry leaders will choose to invest in preparing the next generation of the workforce when given the opportunity. Through workplace immersion, scholars are set up with the technical and professional skills and credentials needed at this moment in the local industry ecosystem.	Creating an immersive experience through workplace learning lays the foundation for a school and industry community, within which scholars can feel a sense of belonging. People learn best when they feel connected to, as well as accepted by, the people and environment around them. Industry investment, made possible by proximity, allows the curriculum to be constantly informed by the current trends and needs of the industry, with industry voices contributing to curricular decisions.

Design Principle	Description	Why This Principle Matters
With, Not For	Young people should play an active role in designing their learning experience. All experiences at the Brooklyn STEAM Center should be developed with scholars, not for them, from the community culture to the learning environment to the work products.	When people can maintain a sense of control, they can develop agency while having the autonomy to weigh in on what and how they learn. Being an active contributor to the community of which you are a part, and seeing yourself reflected in the community's norms, builds a sense of belonging that supports learners' ability to thrive.
Equitable Access	Young people should have the opportunity to pursue careers that will provide economic advancement and the ability to create wealth.	The STEAM Center seeks to respond to the reality of inequitable career outcomes for young people in New York. Middle-skill jobs, which require education beyond high school but not a four-year degree, make up the largest part of New York's labor market—50 percent of all jobs in New York in 2015. Key industries are unable to find enough sufficiently trained workers to fill these jobs. For a variety of reasons, young people of color and those from low-income households are often locked out of high-demand, quality income careers that provide tangible pathways to economic mobility.

By not articulating Design Principles, many learning environments fail to align their experiences and their goals. For instance, if a program aims to have students "prepared with the hard and soft skills needed to work in an authentic workplace" but students remain in one classroom with one instructor and never engage in authentic workplace projects, they are unlikely to achieve these aims. The Design Principles help a design team audit their vision and the reality of what young people actually experience.

The STEAM design team now had the foundations of their model. They had a contextual mission that was particular to the realities of New York City. They had Graduate Aims with tangible and measurable student outcomes that encompassed cognitive, social, and emotional development. And they were equipped with the Design Principles to ensure that the student experiences they created would have the greatest possible chance to provide extraordinary and equitable learning for all.

Supporting all of this work were the Conditions that made it possible: a) a Culture of innovation that was committed to a design that embraced the context of New York City; b) Capacity in the form of a physical location that housed the school at the heart of real-life postsecondary learning opportunities; c) a Coalition of partners that supported young people's dreams for their future, and especially, d) an ever-emerging Clarity of design that continues to evolve.

THE BLUEPRINT: STUDENT EXPERIENCE

SCHOOL DESIGN BLUEPRINT:

GOALS & GUIDING CONCEPTS

 Mission

 Design Principles

 Graduate Aims

STUDENT EXPERIENCES

 Core Components with Specific Activities & Practices

SCHOOL SYSTEM & ELEMENTS

Communications	**Space & Facilities**
Family & Community Partnerships	**Curriculum, Instruction & Assessment**
Scheduling & Use of Time	**School Community & Culture**
Adult Roles, Hiring, & Learning	**Continuous Learning & Improvement**
Budget & Operations	**Technology & Tech Infastructure**

 COMMUNITY CONTEXT

Six Career Pathways at Brooklyn STEAM

The students at STEAM spend their afternoon school hours on the Navy Yard campus. In the morning, they attend one of eight Brooklyn public high schools, such as Medgar Evers College Preparatory High School and Bedford Academy. STEAM classes are an add-on experience where students earn an Advanced Regents High School Diploma, with a special CTE designation, earn up to fourteen elective credits on their transcript and an optional credit for an internship course.

During the application process in their sophomore year students learn about the six industry pathways offered at the school. They ultimately choose one pathway to focus on, but this early exposure helps them ask questions and make informed decisions.

Mastrandrea recalls, "I like to call how we developed the pathways the 'triangle' approach. Typical CTE programs look at labor market data and then they look at what's feasible in the local education system; curriculum development is two-sided. But young people are very intelligent, and they know what they want, so we asked them to give input."

Young people formed the third side of the input that informed the learning environment design at STEAM. The STEAM design team attended open-enrollment school fairs and spoke with students at partner schools. They asked students what they most wanted to get out of a CTE program, and they heard back things like fashion, computer science, and culinary arts. By listening to young people and their partner schools, the design team deepened their understanding of the community's aspirations.

They also developed an Advisory Council of industry professionals that shares job requirements, co-constructs projects, and opens doors to scholar visits so that scholars learn the most relevant hard and soft skills. Having current industry professionals as part of the ongoing design process ensures that the design remains current and relevant, which is essential for a school designed to equip learners with skills to immediately enter the workforce. By looking outward to labor research and engaging industry professionals they were able to contextualize the vision of the school so that it was most responsive to the needs of learners in NYC. Unlike industrial-era learning design which seeks to homogenize the content and experiences of learners, this design approach is informed by, and responsive to, specific, authentic learning environments.

As they assessed the offerings of the Navy Yard, considered student input, and summarized their analysis of the NYC labor market, the design team developed six industry pathways:

- Computer Science: Full stack development
- Computer Science: Cybersecurity/penetration testing
- Construction technology
- Culinary arts and hospitality management

- Design and engineering
- Film and media

The design team knew that the success or failure of STEAM would rely on the ways in which students *experienced* the pathways. Would they rely on theoretical learning alone? Or, would they be hyper-focused on creating the most industry-aligned work spaces possible? It was an easy answer for the design team: the more real the design of the learning environment, the better.

The advantage of being co-located on the Navy Yard Campus was that students would have access to real, operable industry work environments. From fabrication companies to toy developers to the kitchens of all the restaurants that dot the Yard, work-based learning could happen in workplaces.

So, the design team envisioned that work-based learning would be a key learner experience. They also heard from potential STEAM students that learning should be hands-on, practical, and relevant. Students wanted to work on real problems that they might face at work. They wanted to be trusted with real life. A project-based learning approach engages students in relevant problem-solving and decision-making processes as they make their way through their industry pathways.

Four core practices, shown in the following diagram, support each of the six industry pathways: project-based learning, progress check-ins, work-based learning, and post-secondary planning.

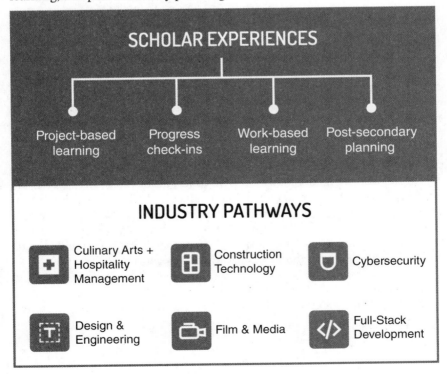

These core practices also show how the Design Principles come to life in student experiences. The principle of "Learning by Doing" animates the instructional approach of project-based learning, where students aren't only gaining knowledge by reading a textbook but by doing immersive, rigorous, hands-on work. The principle of "Workplace Immersion" shows up in the work-based learning core practice.

Student Experience Deep Dive: How the Core Practices Are Applied to the Design and Engineering Pathway

In this section we look at one career pathway—design and engineering—to see how the core practices come to life in the student experience. You will see how various components of the Blueprint, Leaps, and insights from the science of learning and development all come together in these student experiences deepening Community Conditions along the way.

Joshua Cruz was a founding member of the STEAM faculty and the school's first Design and Engineering instructor. He began his partnership with STEAM not as a teacher but as an industry advisor, helping the design team to bring their vision to life. Before becoming an instructor, Joshua was an architect with years of experience at small firms in New York City and had experience as a design and engineering consultant helping businesses launch new products. Joshua was motivated by diversifying the world of design and engineering. He went to college with students from mostly rural and suburban communities, but many Brooklyn natives like himself had a hard time breaking into the world of design and engineering. The opportunities, especially for low-income or marginalized students, aren't as plentiful. Joshua believed that STEAM was filling an important role for learners in New York City. He was fully committed to developing this new learning environment.

"At the core, design and engineering is about solving problems," Cruz reflects, "it's all about how you tackle the different challenges that arise from ideation to manufacturing."

Problem-solving and helping learners persevere through obstacles are at the heart of the design and engineering curriculum at STEAM. In the working world, designers and engineers have clear and distinct roles—designers typically interfacing with clients, while engineers work closely with manufacturers. The design choice to offer the entire continuum of learning works to expand "Equitable Access"; one of the four Design Principles states that young people should have the opportunity to pursue careers that will provide economic advancement and the ability to create wealth.

Cruz applied the four core practices—project-based learning, progress check-ins, work-based learning, and post-secondary planning—to create a curriculum that provides students broad and well-rounded exposure to the field. They will practice the hard and soft skills required to be successful in the highly collaborative and competitive industry.

Project-based learning is an instructional approach that the STEAM design team identified early in their community-design process. The goal of project-based learning is to engage students in deeper learning experiences that help them develop content-matter knowledge as well as industry and professional skills, two of STEAM's Graduate Aims. This instructional approach has solid validation from the science of learning and development as a helpful tool for breaking down tasks into discrete actions and sequenced increments, which manages cognitive load, one of the principles of Cognition.[5] This is essential for design and engineering as the work is always multistep. Additionally, project-based learning helps foster collaboration and teamwork, which can set students up early for professional success.

One of the rigorous and complex projects that students undertake in design and engineering is how to design and build a shoji lamp from scratch. This is not an IKEA lamp. Students start with a blank page sketching myriad potential designs. One student, Dante Mohamed, narrowed down from ten initial designs to just three. Each of the designs offered something different aesthetically and technically. Did he want bold illumination? Or more subtle and warm? Should he use triangles, circles, or squares for the light screens? How did the shape influence the movement of light? These are the kinds of questions that students are grappling with as they test different designs. Students execute all parts of the lamp's production from sketching to drafting the structural elements to 3-D modeling to constructing the wood base. By the end of the project, students have a functioning product.

Yoanna Donalds, a former student recalls, "I really enjoyed this project. I think the whole class did! We learned about craftsmanship and the technical parts of measuring and cutting wood safely. I still use the techniques I learned to this day in college as a design major hoping to work in 3D art and graphic design. This taught me how to be more patient with myself and with others. Since it was a tedious project, it took time for us to understand what we were supposed to do and get it correct. I also learned how to manage my time efficiently because we had a deadline to get this work done. Having those skills really helps me now that I'm in college and working. Knowing how to use my time wisely is really important."

The second core practice that students experience in the design and engineering pathway are progress check-ins conducted throughout the year, where students and teachers meet to discuss progress, reflect, and plan for the future. In Design and Engineering, these check-ins have dual-purposes: they allow the instructor to understand the students' day-to-day experience, and they serve as one touchpoint for long-term, post-secondary planning.

Cruz found that these check-ins were also a powerful way to monitor his students' emotional well-being and help them deepen their awareness of self and how they engage with others—central skills undergirding the Identity & Agency Graduate Aim of the school.

Progress check-ins also play an invaluable role in learning by honoring several science of learning and development principles all at one. Metacognitive thinking—that is the ability to observe, evaluate, and adjust one's own learning process—is often at the heart of these meetings between teachers and students. How well did you collaborate with others? Why? What could you have done differently? What will you do in the future if a problem like this arises? This kind of learning about how one learns is critical for young people today as they find themselves needing new skills throughout their lives. It also deepens learners' self-understanding of their strengths and areas for growth.

The third core practice, work-based learning, is another learning science related practice to augment student experience. Work-based learning achieves several Leaps at once (Relevance, Connection & Community, Rigorous Learning, Active Self-Direction) by placing learners in authentic contexts where they can practice skills and receive high-quality feedback from experts. The work opportunities are varied and relevant in the Navy Yard and in New York City broadly. Students may participate in a jewelry design program, a toy-making internship, or internships at a 3-D printer manufacturing company, all located in the Navy Yard. This kind of hands-on learning is invaluable because of the hard skills gained but also the social connections and social capital that students are able to build upon.

The post-secondary landscape for design and engineering students often requires college or more specialized programs, the fourth core practice of this pathway. Students at STEAM can leverage relationships they have built to gain this specialized experience. For instance, Daniel James Carter, while a student at STEAM, worked at Armada on the Navy Yard. While in college for mechanical engineering he also had an internship with this company, which helped him get into a weekend training program. That experience then led to him being hired for an apprenticeship program at Nanotronics, a tech company focused on using machine learning and AI to create software and hardware to streamline the production and inspection of superconductors. The experiences at STEAM helped to pave a way for Daniel James Carter within a notoriously challenging field.

The core practices at the heart of the student experience at STEAM illustrate the power of a cohesive learning environment design. The Blueprint helps STEAM remain intentional even as it pursues rich Design Cycles (described in Chapter 4) that improve the model over time.

The Blueprint: School and System Elements

SCHOOL DESIGN BLUEPRINT:

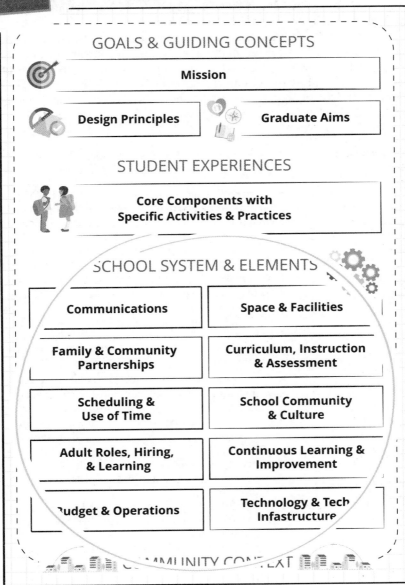

GOALS & GUIDING CONCEPTS

Mission

Design Principles   **Graduate Aims**

STUDENT EXPERIENCES

Core Components with Specific Activities & Practices

SCHOOL SYSTEM & ELEMENTS

Communications	**Space & Facilities**
Family & Community Partnerships	**Curriculum, Instruction & Assessment**
Scheduling & Use of Time	**School Community & Culture**
Adult Roles, Hiring, & Learning	**Continuous Learning & Improvement**
Budget & Operations	**Technology & Tech Infastructure**

COMMUNITY CONTEXT

The final pieces of STEAM's learning environment design puzzle are the school and system elements, which are the structures, resources, and decisions that generate the student experience. These decisions sometimes live at the school level, the system level, or some combination of both. Decisions at STEAM are weighed and decided among NYCPS, the Navy Yard, the eight participating high schools, and the school itself.

As part of the framework, there are ten school and system elements that can be used for decision-making and planning as learning communities articulate their design. At STEAM, students show up as professionals ready to work and learn, and all the school's system elements support this intent. In the following table, these school and system elements are applied to STEAM's model:

School & System Elements	How Each System Element Supports the Student Experience at the Brooklyn STEAM Center
Curriculum, Instruction, Assessment	▪ Every project, credential, product, and meeting is purposefully designed to mirror real-world work. STEAM's unique curriculum, developed over years, includes a series of projects that build upon one another and are grounded in things one would do in the industry. ▪ All pathways' curricula: align to industry relevant skills and credentials, include industry grounded projects, build professional as well as technical skills, involve industry, professionals coming into the classroom, and scholars going into industry environments, leverage the STEAM Center's unique environment of classrooms and work spaces that have been modeled on real industry specifications. ▪ The STEAM Center offers scholars an alternative route to graduation beyond the traditional requirement of passing five Regents. STEAM scholars instead can use the "4+1" option that allows them to graduate with four Regents exams and the completion of their course at STEAM, including passing the approved industry credential. They are also eligible to earn the Career Development and Occupational Studies (CDOS) endorsement on their diploma.
School Community & Culture	▪ Consistent with the Graduate Aim of Self-Direction, STEAM aims to have a student-driven school culture, encouraging student leadership of Town Halls and clubs, as well as having students serve as Ambassadors.

School & System Elements	How Each System Element Supports the Student Experience at the Brooklyn STEAM Center
Adult Roles, Hiring & Learning	■ STEAM turns industry experts into full-time teachers, side by side with experienced educators. There are at least two qualified teachers for every pathway, who are NYCPS employees and have a blend of industry and formal or informal teaching experience. ■ Candidates with industry experience are recruited into the profession by leveraging the Transitional A Certification and the Success Via Apprenticeship Program. Additionally, STEAM hires adjunct teachers directly from the industry to teach individual units or part-time. Over time, these instructors may elect to pursue full-time teaching. ■ Teacher development at STEAM takes two main forms: Weekly Professional Development sessions, led by STEAM leaders and instructional coaches, to build pedagogical expertise and maximize the impact of their instruction; support to ensure that teachers stay up-to-date in their fields.
Schedules & Use of Time	■ The STEAM Center is purposefully built to create career and financial pathways for scholars who traditionally do not have access to these experiences. To this end, the STEAM Center enrolls scholars from eight partner NYCPS high schools, chosen to yield an intentionally socioeconomically diverse student body. ■ The STEAM Center also coordinates with the eight partner high schools throughout potential scholars' ninth and tenth grade years. The eleventh grade entry point to STEAM requires that partner school leaders and guidance counselors deeply know their scholars and can: set scholars up for success through accelerating their credit-earning in ninth and tenth grades, encourage completion of a standardized STEAM application in their tenth grade year, collaborate with the STEAM Center to recruit middle school scholars who'd benefit from STEAM to enroll in the eight partner schools

(continued)

School & System Elements	How Each System Element Supports the Student Experience at the Brooklyn STEAM Center
	■ **Backbone Coalition:** The STEAM Center is guided and enabled by a partnership between the NYCPS and BNYDC. NYCPS operates the STEAM Center and employs STEAM staff. BNYDC is the STEAM Center landlord and brings access to an ecosystem of 400+ manufacturing, creative, and tech companies. A Steering Committee includes members from both NYCPS and BNYDC and operates like a governing board of The STEAM Center. The partnership between NYCPS and BNYDC is memorialized both through the lease for the STEAM Center space at the Brooklyn Navy Yard and through a separate MOU that guides the shared collaboration on the program.
Community & Family Partnerships	■ **Industry Advisory Council:** BNYDC is the core industry partner of the STEAM Center and has a dedicated staff that convenes the STEAM Center Advisory Council and organizes workplace learning opportunities for STEAM students. The Advisory Council is a league of advisors from businesses inside and outside of the Navy Yard and higher education institutions who provide insights, inspiration, and workplace learning experiences for each of STEAM's five pathways. The Advisory Council shares job requirements, co-constructs projects, and opens doors to student visits so that students learn the most relevant hard and soft skills.
	■ At STEAM the work environment is the classroom, not the other way around. The STEAM Center is immersed within a 400+ industry ecosystem, putting scholars in daily contact with industry professionals and making it near instant for an industry partner to pop into the STEAM Center to give feedback on a project and for a STEAM Center scholar to go to an internship after school.
Space & Facilities	■ The 30,000 square foot environment of the STEAM Center itself mirrors each pathway's real-world work environment. The spaces were designed with industry engagement, including defining the space specifications, reviewing architectural plans, and selecting equipment. The result is a learning environment industry professionals regularly ask to borrow for their own work.
	■ STEAM "classrooms" include a full sound stage, control room, editing booth, and screening room, a fabrication lab, a construction workshop, and a professional-grade kitchen.

School & System Elements	How Each System Element Supports the Student Experience at the Brooklyn STEAM Center
Technology & Tech Infrastructure	■ STEAM has very specific tech needs to ensure that all classroom spaces include the highest quality, industry-grade equipment necessary for learners to learn to use as part of their career preparation. This includes 3D printers, fabrication tools, and a green screen and sound stage. ■ Each classroom also has a class set of laptops, used for "Starter" activities at the beginning of class, for building a digital portfolio and updating their Employ-ability Skills Profiles (that document their industry certifications and workplace learning experiences), for completing surveys such as the monthly preflections to prepare for Progress Check-Ins, and, in some pathways, for coursework via Schoology. In Film & Media, there are many specific software needs including Adobe and other programs used for sound mixing. ■ As another crucial element of operating in the shared instruction model as a hub for scholars from eight different high schools, having access to the NYCPS tech infrastructure is important for functions such as collecting and tracking attendance and sharing student data.
Budget & Operations	■ STEAM gets its NYCPS funding through a tax levy funded School Allocation Memorandum (SAM) rather than receiving per-pupil funding. It supplements this funding with money through grants and other fund-raising. STEAM is in the process of working with the state to identify a funding model that will create more sustainable revenue for the program.

(continued)

School & System Elements	How Each System Element Supports the Student Experience at the Brooklyn STEAM Center
Communications	▪ Communication between the STEAM Center and the eight partner high schools is critical to ensure that both parties have the necessary information to best support the scholars they share. This happens through guidance counselor outreach and monthly principals' meetings where the STEAM Center principal and the principals of all partner schools get together at one of the partner schools to discuss ongoing business including scholar outcomes, transportation logistics, and scholars' admissions and retention. ▪ STEAM's newsletter and website strive to provide consistent updates to the full school community, as well as active use of Instagram. A robust support staff is also able to consistently do family outreach.
Continuous Learning and Improvement	▪ Due to the unique Graduate Aims of the STEAM model, the school needs to gather a rich set of data about scholars that is not typically gathered by high schools, including data around industry certification/credentials, how learners are performing in the workplace both during internships and after graduation, and how successfully they are building social capital. This requires new tools and data collection processes. STEAM also is committed to engaging in R&D work, choosing strategic pilot projects to improve the school and learning from those projects to constantly evolve and improve the model.

While most communities may not be able to design to the exact specifications of STEAM, they may be able to create on-site collaborations in medical complexes, aerospace fields, and other large industrial spaces where hands-on learning in a concentrated field is possible. These concentrated industry businesses on the outskirts of so many American towns can offer a way forward for creating more rigorous and relevant workplace learning.

Brooklyn STEAM is blazing a path ahead for what CTE can look like in this country. When these programs are intentionally designed to be responsive to in-demand industries, take into account student interests, and ensure that there are real jobs on the other side for learners, CTE can become a viable path of first resort for any young person.

CHAPTER 6

Intrinsic Public Schools | Chicago, Illinois

Key Points

- Intrinsic Public Schools was founded on the belief of advancing equity through personalized, relevant education. The cofounders cultivated strong conditions through a community-based process involving families, educators, and partners to meet students' diverse needs in flexible, customized ways.
- A central part of Intrinsic's model is the "learning pod" structure—large classrooms with multiple teachers working with students in different modalities based on their individual goals and needs.
- Their "EPIC" socio-emotional model, with experiences like "Choice Day," helps develop perseverance, identity, and curiosity beyond just academics. The model honors the Leaps of Customization, Whole-Child Focus, and Rigorous Learning.

At Intrinsic, tap any learner on the shoulder, and they can eloquently describe how their choices and experiences today are setting them up for life tomorrow. Young people own their learning in ways that will set them up to be in charge of their lives as adults. With a deep sense of self and knowledge of their interests and passions, Intrinsic learners know what they want from the world and, more importantly, how to attain it.

In previous chapters, we looked at the way the Blueprint elements work together to form a cohesive design. In Chapter 3, we assessed how the act of articulating a powerful learning environment design serves to strengthen a community's underlying conditions. In Chapter 4, we examined a school community's use of the Design Cycle, understanding how several "turns of the cycle" allow teams to continually strengthen their designs and by doing so improve student experiences and outcomes. In Chapter 5, we took a closer look at the school and classroom practices that create an innovative learning environment.

In this chapter, we look across the full community-based design process to see how all of the components come together over time. This chapter shows how a Leaps-aligned learning environment design was improved by continuous turns of the Design Cycle, deepened the Conditions for Community Design, and led to the successful implementation of a design with extraordinary, equitable experiences and outcomes for students. We look at two learning environment models at Intrinsic Public Schools in Chicago: the academic model and their socio-emotional learning model, which they call "EPIC."

Intrinsic Public Schools is a charter network located in Chicago, where 93 percent of the student population identifies as Hispanic. In the 2022–2023 school year, Intrinsic outperformed both Chicago Public Schools and the State of Illinois with graduation rates at 90 percent and postsecondary enrollment within twelve months of graduation at 92 percent. Their students also excel at the SAT, with the Belmont campus' average composite score at 891, outperforming surrounding neighborhoods.

Young people leave Intrinsic with a deep sense of purpose and clarity— confident from years of exposure to real-world working environments. Intrinsic graduates, predominantly from recent immigrant backgrounds, are enrolling in college and finding career opportunities at dramatically higher rates than their peers in Chicago Public Schools. They have the will and skill to navigate a postsecondary landscape that is more complex and volatile than ever before.

What about their school experiences at Intrinsic makes these outcomes possible?

Today Isaaq is a software engineer at Target in Minneapolis, Minnesota, and a graduate of the University of Chicago with a degree in computer science and psychology.

Isaaq came to Intrinsic as a ninth grader. Raised by a single mother, Isaaq praises her as one of his biggest motivators and influences; she said "yes" to every experience he wanted, and she encouraged him to seize opportunities.

Before Intrinsic, he attended another middle school in Chicago. There, he was bullied and had negative interactions with his teachers. He was passionate about math, but his teachers never encouraged his interest. He describes his first middle school as "your typical school experience, a teacher talking to you all day. In math, I asked a lot of questions. Finally, my teacher said, 'Enough! Enough with the questions.' And that's when I knew I had to get out of there."

Through word of mouth, his mother found Intrinsic Public Schools.

When he arrived in ninth grade, Isaaq was determined to take calculus before graduating high school; he understood even then that advanced math was an essential gatekeeper. But he was four years off the calculus track. Undeterred, Isaaq was so driven to achieve his goal that he pushed teachers and administrators.

In his words:

> When I got to Intrinsic, they said, "Keep the questions coming!" In eighth grade I wrote a goal letter to myself. "I will take precalculus my sophomore year." Obviously there's a lot of steps before that. You need to have taken Algebra I, Geometry, Algebra II, Trigonometry, and then you can get to Precalculus. That's like four years of content.

Not only did the Intrinsic educators encourage his insatiable curiosity in math, but the flexibility in the design of their learning environment allowed him to take three math classes concurrently (Algebra I, II, and Geometry), unheard of in a traditional curriculum that stresses sequential, paced progression. At Intrinsic students move through content as they develop new competencies, which made it possible for Isaaq to build an approach that would help him achieve his goal.

Isaaq's achievements would not have been predicted by statistics from the neighborhood he grew up in. As he will tell you, he has no doubt that the reason he is where he is today is the result of the Leaps-aligned experiences he had at Intrinsic—Customization, Relevance, Whole-Child Focus, and Rigorous Learning.

COMMUNITY AND LEADERSHIP CONTEXT

Ami Gandhi and Melissa Zaikos worked in Chicago Public Schools before founding Intrinsic. At Chicago Public Schools they loved their fellow colleagues and were extremely committed to the students. But like many longtime educators, they had seen how the churn of change produced one fizzled initiative after another. Year after year, they saw talented young people apply to a handful of Chicago's famed selective high schools. If a student wasn't admitted to one of these schools, their choices were often limited by proximity, and they were likely sent to a lower-performing high school (as defined by the district's School Quality Ratings). For these students, postsecondary opportunities drastically diminished, and their life pathways could be predicted by harrowing statistics. Gandhi and Zaikos believed that under the right conditions and with a school built around student and teacher needs, things could be very different for children in Chicago.

They also recognized that there were smart people working on hard problems in Chicago schools, but the traditional, industrial-era design of schooling was inherently limiting. Working at the district level, after many years in education, Gandhi and Zaikos could see the talented educators struggling to meet children's needs within a system designed to track and sort them.

In Gandhi's high school math classroom, she often wished she could clone herself. There was simply not enough of her to meet the needs of her learners. Sometimes, she'd want to be running a math talk while simultaneously supporting a group working on a Geometry project and another group of students who needed help solving proportions. But in Gandhi's reality, as with millions of other teachers, there is often only one person at the head of the classroom and thirty learners with varying needs. Gandhi imagined that if she had her own school, she would find a way to offer multiple learning experiences simultaneously in every classroom to meet learners at their level.

One day, that opportunity came. Gandhi and Zaikos decided to build a school—one that solved many of the challenges that teachers across Chicago face.

Intrinsic was founded on the belief of advancing equity through education. To do that, students needed access to far more customized approaches to learning, authentic experiences in the real world, relevant and rigorous course content, and, critically, all the enriching activities that make adolescence fun. They knew that Intrinsic wouldn't be another school where academics alone defined its spirit.

"I realized that school isn't designed to change," Gandhi reflects. "It isn't designed to be responsive when a child needs it most. It isn't designed to allow a teacher to apply their expertise to unique problems. **That made us wonder, 'What if we built a school that was designed to be flexible and change and expand based on what children most needed?'"**

From there, Gandhi and Zaikos began to envision a design that would be able to meet the needs of individual learners. Their "what if" came from a place of deep respect and value for learners' lives and their potential for growth. The school's name refers to people's innate tendencies to be curious and interested, to seek out challenges, and to exercise and develop their skills and knowledge, even in the absence of operationally separable rewards. Intrinsic was founded on the human development insight that attending to the drivers of motivation (value, self-efficacy, attribution, and mood) leads to people who are more motivated, confident, and successful. The cofounders set out to create an environment and a curriculum to match.

The cofounders also knew that a school is of, and should be responsive to, a local community. In the early days of the founding, they listened to families about what they most wanted for their children. They didn't attempt to sell the vision of Intrinsic to families; they solicited local wisdom to understand what the Belmont community most desired for its children. Parents and caregivers would come to have a continuous voice in shaping the school.

As educators who aimed to stay on the cusp of new thinking, Gandhi and Zaikos were well aware of the research within the science of learning and development. They knew that learning is best primed when people feel safe.[1] They focused on creating an environment where learners felt a sense of belonging: safe, welcomed, and valued by the peers and adults in their community. Because they didn't condescend to their students but instead elevated them, the cofounders wanted a system where students could set and monitor their own individualized growth goals and receive consistent and accurate feedback toward those goals. To address the "what if" question about curriculum flexibility and to respond to the inequities they had seen in their years of teaching in traditional school models, they knew they wanted to adapt classroom instruction to be personalized and rigorous, where learning is social and differences are valued.

As with the three prior design journey deep-dives, Conditions were the foundation for innovation at Intrinsic. Gandhi and Zaikos led the design process with a strong conviction in the design vision. By involving the local community, they built a strong and inclusive Coalition that was essential for advancing equitable outcomes. This approach ensured that diverse voices, experiences, and wisdom, which are often excluded from important decisions, were incorporated into the process.

THE ACADEMIC MODEL: HOW COMMUNITY-BASED DESIGN STRENGTHENED LEARNING

The "Learning Pod" Structure: The Heart of Intrinsic's Learning Environment Design

Intrinsic's school building is on the site of a former lumber yard. It is built in longhouse style with pitched roofs. Inside the school has a contemporary feel of gray concrete floors with an open second-floor of classrooms above a large flexible space below. There's movable seating on the ground floor, small couches, and nooks for students to work before school starts.

The classrooms themselves are large to facilitate the unique learning environment design. Launched with the idea of flexible space, the floor plan was designed to meet multiple needs at once. These spaces are called "pods," a shape and design that facilitates two to three teachers working at once to meet the needs of students in multiple learning modalities. In pods, students work independently and in a variety of student-to-student and student-to-teacher groupings based on their individual learning needs and goals. The academic model is a team-taught approach to providing customization. The pod design is special because it solves one of the most entrenched design challenges of industrial-era learning: four walls, one adult, and thirty children with diverse needs.

Eva, an Intrinsic high-schooler, reflects, "I think the pod structure is useful and helpful because there is so much support. I like to be able to learn from different teachers and support structures. It's very different from how my other school was organized."

However, physical design alone doesn't lead to extraordinary experiences and outcomes for all learners. Instructional design and teaching matters tremendously. It took various turns of the Design Cycle for the educators at Intrinsic to optimize this Leaps-aligned spatial design.

Let's look at a "turn of the Design Cycle" in a math pod.

Improving the Pod Structure: Math Design Cycles

In this flexible space, the teachers broke kids into smaller groups and then provided direct instruction. After the direct instruction, the students moved into independent practice during self-directed work time. The teaching and learning approach more closely resembled traditional math instruction than the envisioned flexible, multimodal instruction.

It wasn't just that this approach was "traditional"; there was also mounting evidence that it wasn't preparing students. Using the Design Cycle to learn and refine the design vision, the design team interviewed former students about what worked at the school and what didn't. Many of the students reflected that they struggled with college math and there were serious gaps in their knowledge. It was clear that the pod structure wasn't reaching its full potential.

Chris Lin, now assistant principal and a former physics teacher during these Design Cycles, reflects, "For a long time math education has been stuck in the past. We were acting like computer processes haven't completely and thoroughly changed the world. At the very least, we need to be willing to imagine what kids need to know now. It's critical thinking, it's problem solving, it's contextualizing."

Lin continues, "Think of it this way: no engineer is working out problems by hand. Computers do complex math, and soon artificial intelligence will advance beyond what we can imagine. Today the goal is for students to understand math and how it influences the world. A computer can't do that work for us; the math curriculum at Intrinsic needed to move students from computational to conceptualization to contextualization."

In his conception, young people need to understand what mathematical answers mean in the context of our society.

Learn

The math educators needed to be inspired for the model to reach its full potential. To facilitate this inspiration, the design team organized visits to observe math in action in schools already using innovative methods in the classroom. What they saw was something entirely different than what they were offering. Math, in schools like Long-View Micro School,[2] was shifting from a *purely* computational focus to a conceptual one. For a simplistic example, the Intrinsic teachers saw kindergarten students evaluate how to subtract conceptually, rather than simply memorizing the steps. These five-year-olds were saying things like, "Fifty-four minus twenty-nine? Fifty-four is really fifty plus four, and twenty-nine is twenty plus nine. So you can write it as $(50+4)-(20+9)$."

The Intrinsic math design team was floored. Children as young as five years old were building mathematical literacy that went far beyond memorizing the steps of computation. These were the kinds of discussions and progressions that the math pod needed to facilitate.

Envision

After learning from Long-View and others, the design team did some envisioning together. They decided to use a storyboarding technique to tell the story of a day in the week of an Intrinsic math student. How could they use the pod structure to build the kind of conceptual awareness that they knew mattered so much in a world changed by technology? Could they have a small group of students above grade level working in small groups with a teacher? Yes, they could. Could they break down math lessons to represent the highest order application for advanced students while meeting the needs of students who were following behind in computation? Yes, they could do that, too. Finally, could they utilize a personalized learning platform developed by Summit Public Schools[3] so that learners could track their own progress and unlock new math skills when they were ready? Absolutely.

Build and Try

"Once we started to build out a new pedagogical approach and put it into practice, refining, refining, and refining," Lin describes, "we really started living into the potential of the pod and were able to customize in powerful ways."

Self-directed learners like Isaaq were benefiting. Davis Chambers, now a student at the Massachusetts Institute of Technology, was "so-so" in math during his seventh and eighth grade years, but he began to flourish once the math pod was turbocharged. Before graduating, Davis Chambers took an independent quantum computing course and hosted morning workshops in math for undergraduate classrooms in response to a math teacher shortage at the school.

The highly innovative math model at Intrinsic uses six kinds of pedagogical environments that students flex among, depending on their individual needs. These environments are as follows:

- **Traditional instruction:** One teacher providing direct instruction
- **Intervention:** One or more teachers working with small groups needing additional support
- **Student-designed group projects:** Self-directed, educator-facilitated independent learning opportunities
- **Socratic style:** Small groups of discussion-based problem-solving experiences
- **Student group stations:** Small groups of students working together on a complex problem

For a student like Davis Chambers, who demonstrates advanced mathematical abilities, more time could be allocated to working in a small group setting with a similarly skilled peer on complex problem-solving tasks. Simultaneously, a larger group of students might receive direct instruction from a teacher on a specific math concept. Because Isaaq experienced this flexible learning model in high school, he developed the skills to form effective study groups, seek one-on-one support from professors and teaching assistants, and utilize various resources to ensure his comprehension of mathematical concepts and overall academic success in college.

The EPIC Model: The Iterative Design of "Choice Day"

EPIC Model: How Choice Day Came to Be

When we look at Isaaq's amazing outcome—a University of Chicago graduate in computer science—the temptation is to focus on just the curriculum or the degree. However, we can't attribute his achievements to one thing. To understand the enormity of Intrinsic's role in Isaaq's achievements, let's explore another element of this extraordinary and equitable learning environment.

In affluent communities, students are exposed to after-school clubs, unpaid internships, and other enrichment.[4] These robust community-driven opportunities offer ways for young people to develop communication skills, team-building skills to work with peers and adults, and so many other relationship-building skills that lead to career success. They are also ways in which young people pursue interests beyond the classroom to learn what inspires them.

But often in low-income, immigrant, and/or first-generation communities, those opportunities can be few and far between.[5] To build some of those communication skills for students with less access and opportunities, at Intrinsic, they have developed a socio-emotional model that represents their Graduate Aims called EPIC. "EPIC" is an acronym for the following:

- **Empathy:** Understanding the perspectives of others, building inclusive communities, and acting in kindness.
- **Perseverance:** Setting and pursuing goals proactively, adapting and building resilience in the face of obstacles, and becoming independent.

- **Identity:** Analyzing and taking ownership of one's life story and discovering and working toward a greater purpose.
- **Curiosity:** Seeking to continuously learn about the world and be cognizant of the limitations of one's own perspective and experience.

The EPIC model consists of five integrated components (Choice Day, Seminar, Advisory, Student-Led Conferences, and Exploration Experiences) designed to support Intrinsic students to authentically develop EPIC values. Together, the EPIC model supports students to cultivate their passion, strengths, and interests and to develop the relevant knowledge and skills needed to develop, evolve, and pursue their purpose. We will explore one of these experiences in more depth: Choice Day.

Choice Day, or "C-Day," is divided into two experiences: academic support and enrichment. These experiences help young people have a deeper understanding of self and gain more confidence to navigate a volatile, uncertain world where they need to be adaptive and creative. Students use a scheduling system to make choices about how they spend their time. The academic support is determined through a spreadsheet model linked to the learning management system. This allows Maureen Raffenetti and Greer Tagler, the C-Day managers, to help students decide where they spend their time. The managers provide students with data about their current learning progress. If a student is struggling in math, they can choose to use their time for math tutoring in a small-group setting. The system is designed so that grades and missing assignments act as a flag for the C-Day managers, triggering counseling and intervention with students. This kind of experience is important for students to learn how to make effective short- and long-range choices about their time, with the guidance of educators. Leaps like Active-Self Direction and Customization are highly honored in the C-Day experience.

"It's very much *on you* to make good decisions about how to spend your time," Jessica reflects. "This year my classes are very hard. So I do extra AP Biology. Sometimes I do quiz corrections or ask all my questions during office hours."

Her friend Eva seconds this: "When those grades drop, you gotta make better decisions!"

Enrichment activities and clubs, including competition teams, a Boyz II Men support group, high school/middle school mentors, basketball, softball, astrology club, chess club, and the like, are also part of C-Day at Intrinsic. The opportunity to pursue different interests makes it possible for students to form relationships with people around a shared interest versus only age or academic-level connections. Guest speakers come in and talk about careers, including nursing, real estate, culinary arts, and the building trades.

C-Day wasn't created overnight, nor was it invented at Intrinsic. Northside College Prep High School (a selective enrollment Chicago school) had been implementing "Colloquium" as part of their model for decades. Gandhi and Zaikos saw how motivated and *happy* the children were to have their interests present at school. Being the visionary that she is, Gandhi wondered how they might evolve this structure to more expressly align with their vision of EPIC development. How might they make a structure like this work in their school context?

Raffenetti, one of the C-Day managers, reflects on what makes Choice Day so unique: "When I was a kid, I never got to leave my high school. So many of our kids are going out, seeing, and being in the world—taking culinary classes, taking pottery classes, shadowing artists. And, every week they are forced to reckon with their choices. If we look in the system and see that a student is failing biology and the student never chooses that block, we [the coordinators] are going to help them choose to go to biology rather than another club block. We want kids to make mistakes at fifteen, not at twenty-five."

The introduction of C-Day to the Intrinsic staff was not easy at first. There was well-intentioned resistance. Many staff members warned that giving up an entire instructional day felt like malpractice. In a community with so many first-generation students, how could they not be focusing on all academics all the time? In teacher focus groups and small-group discussions, staff raised an issue they saw: the design of C-Day had to become more than a club day. The academic component of C-Day was shaped by teacher *and* student-caregiver input.

"We had a lot of trial and error to really figure out what to offer. It may seem as though something like 'Senior Library' is a good idea, until you see it in practice and children are just running everywhere and doing everything," Tagler, another C-Day manager, recalls.

So, the design team brought these challenges to teachers and students. How might we have a better grasp of the academic needs of students so that we can direct them?

"Mainly my job is staring at data," Maurreen laughs. "Seriously, I am constantly looking at where kids are in their grades and competencies and that is how we know where they are supposed to be each week."

The team had to build an advanced tracking system to make the complicated schedule work. Once a week, from 8:30 a.m. to 1:30 p.m. for fourteen weeks, there are hundreds of students moving in and out of the building. The design team had to build ways of tracking students and monitoring their progress, as well as assign students to the many active clubs that both students and teachers could propose to the community.

Over time teachers and students have come to revere C-Day as one the marquee experiences of Intrinsic. Because of its success and continuous iteration through the Design Cycle, teachers understand the value of C-Day, and young people look forward to it and are gaining perspective on their interests that are having long-lasting reverberations throughout their lives. It also expands the Intrinsic school community to include myriad business and stakeholder groups. Choice Day has expanded the walls of Intrinsic.

In the earliest iterations of C-Day, Isaaq formed a club to pursue and share his other passion: video games.

Isaaq knew a ton of his classmates shared his love for gaming, and he knew after school they were all playing at home alone in their rooms. In his words:

> I thought, why don't we come together and socialize and like spend time next to someone else, maybe build a relationship and maybe build some friendships and camaraderie in the video game community so we're not all on Isolation Island all the time.

So Isaaq started a video games club, which quickly became the most popular of the after-school activities, with up to one hundred kids in the pod once a week playing games. The beauty of the club was that it brought together kids who did not seize other opportunities (like student government) and kids who participated in sports but generally avoided other clubs; it was an activity that united disparate groups and interests around a common interest, led by a peer.

Isaaq looked at the size of the group and realized it needed some kind of system. He wanted to rank kids based on their wins, but he needed some kind of tracker. He had a vision for what he wanted this tracker to look like, but he didn't have the Excel or Google Sheets skills to really build it out, and everyone said it couldn't be done.

Undeterred, working with one of his favorite teachers, Erin Teater, Isaaq learned the coding skills to build a spreadsheet that could rank students' game play in real time, an Elo rating system borrowed from chess. He went to Intrinsic's "data guy," who told him, "I don't think this can be done, dude." He was discouraged. But he kept going. The "P" for perseverance in the EPIC model wouldn't let him stop. Here's how he described the experience:

> I kept working at it. I kept trying. And then one day, it was funny because I think I was just looking at it. I wasn't even intending to work on it. I think I was doing other homework. I just looked at it, changed a few things, and suddenly, everything started working. I was like, Wait a minute. So, I did some of my test cases. I wrote like someone's name, someone else's name. It showed up, and I was like,

what did they play again? Did it update?! It was an indexing issue. I figured it out! I learned a ton from this, mainly never to give up even when someone says it's impossible. Reach as far as you can, jump as high as you can, because you realize you may have jumped even higher than you would have thought.

I'd also like to give another little shoutout to those who helped me learn spreadsheets. Mr. Earnest, now Ms. Teater's husband, pushed me to learn different ways of framing the problem. The two of them would help me before and after school where I would arrive sometimes at 7 a.m. just to learn from Mr. Earnest or Ms. Teater and go through a lesson on spreadsheets. The two of them really went above and beyond for me.

That's the special magic of a purposefully designed learning environment that brings together rigorous academic discipline and a zest for hobbies. With the opportunity to follow his own drive and motivation, Isaaq developed perseverance and the courage to experiment, which made it possible for him to achieve the extraordinary goals he set for himself.

Intrinsic Public Schools shows us that the work of a community-based design journey doesn't stop once a school building opens or after the first year or even the fifth year. **Community-based design means continuous "turns of Design Cycle" to ensure that the learning environment design is responsive to learner needs.** Intrinsic doesn't stop at understanding the experiences of its current students, either, as many of the most insightful lessons have come from young people who are well into their lives after graduation. This school illuminates a posture that all schools can take: how to be an intentional learning organization.

In Part 3, we will lay out what communities can do to get started on their design journeys and sustain them over time.

III

How to Embark on a Community-Based Design Journey

Now that you have the key ideas of community-based design and the insight from the four examples that illustrate these concepts in action, this part details the specific steps communities take as they work to create extraordinary learning for all.

Chapters 7 and 8 describe the key actions you will pursue early in the design journey. Typically within the first year, you envision, build, and begin to test new learning environments with young people. You decide who will participate in your design journey and how. You examine your current reality and craft a vision for the future. You then take small steps toward this broader vision by piloting new student experiences. The insights you gain allow you to refine the vision and prepare the design team to bring more and more aspects of your vision to life.

Chapter 9 lays out how you will continue to progress on your design journeys after the critical first year. This involves continuing to bring the vision to life through taking additional student experiences through the Design Cycle and moving into broader implementation with more and more students. As communities do this work, they often update and refine their high-level vision. Altogether, this work fortifies the five Community Conditions.

You may feel conflicted about the idea of "testing" or "experimenting" with new approaches to student learning. It's a valid concern—we don't want to risk failures that could have lasting negative effects. That's why we ground all design choices in the science of learning, collect and analyze data, and rapidly evolve—sometimes even within a single class—based on insights from students.

CHAPTER 7

Launching Your Design Journey

Key Points

- The earliest stages of a design journey involve assembling a team to understand the current reality and future aspirations, build conviction for change, and plan next steps.
- Key activities in the first phases of this work include learning from and shadowing students, analyzing data, creating a Case for Change, and articulating a school and/or system-level vision.
- The vision includes the mission, Graduate Aims, Design Principles, and student experiences. It provides the foundation for teams to run Design Cycles to develop and test specific aspects of the vision in more detail.

Fall   *Spring*

Gear Up	**Map It**	Zoom In	Test-Drive	Look Ahead
Lay the foundation for your community design journey	Craft a high-level vision for the entire school or system	Craft a detailed vision for a specific aspect of the student experience	Try out the student experience	Prepare to continue the journey

This chapter outlines the common steps communities take during the early stages of their design journeys. **No two design journeys are the same. Every journey is responsive to Community Conditions, so the order and timing of these early steps can vary.** The first year or so of this journey focuses especially on strengthening learning environment design (supported by the Blueprint) and Community Conditions, using the Design Cycle you read about in Chapters 2 and 4.

143

Within this early stage of your community's journey, you will complete five key phases of work to improve design and conditions.

1. **Gear Up:** Lay the foundation for your community design journey.
2. **Map It:** Craft a high-level vision for the entire school or system.
3. **Zoom In:** Craft a detailed vision for a specific aspect of the student experience.
4. **Test-Drive:** Try the student experience.
5. **Look Ahead:** Prepare to continue the journey.

To better illustrate these activities and methods, we'll follow a fictional composite school district based on several communities we have worked with directly throughout Part 3. While inspired by real events, this community is not meant to depict any one school community in particular.

Our composite community, Elm Town Unified School District (ETUSD), serves twenty-five thousand students, prekindergarten through twelfth grade. Here are some community characteristics: 54 percent of students in the district identify as Black or African American, 22 percent identify as white, 13 percent identify as Hispanic, and 2.8 percent as Asian or Pacific Islander; on traditional standardized achievement tests their results vary by race; elementary schools in the district have the most diverse student populations, while the middle and high schools are overwhelmingly Black and Hispanic; since 2020, enrollment has declined by 2,000 students.

The board has hired a new superintendent, Dr. Wallace, with twenty-five years' experience to turn the district around. Dr. Wallace is interested in engaging her community in a community-based design process, an approach one of her superintendent colleagues is successfully undergoing. Despite her previous success in turning around other school districts, she has seen those gains disappear once she left, leading her to question the effectiveness of the top-down initiatives and tight management style she is known for. She is starting to reflect on her reasons for becoming a superintendent and feels that her impact has been hollow. The more Dr. Wallace learns about the industrial-era design of school, the greater her conviction grows that educators and young people are trapped in an ineffective and outdated design.

The Elm Town Board of Education has competing voices; some members are open to change and innovation, while others believe that schooling needs to "get back to the basics" and focus on raising achievement. Business leaders in the community want to hire local talent but find that students lack skills such as collaboration and conflict management. Dr. Wallace is surprised by this, as she thought businesses would prioritize technical skills above all.

Among her colleagues, Dr. Wallace has found a like-minded educator in Mr. Arthur, the district's head of instruction. With eight years of experience at Elm Town Unified and his own children enrolled in one of the elementary schools, Mr. Arthur brings a unique perspective to their conversations. Through their discussions, Dr. Wallace discovers his openness to trying new approaches and his reflective nature about past successes and failures. Mr. Arthur shares his experiences with the numerous instructional initiatives he inherited, which often faltered due to staff turnover or the tendency to revert to old habits during standardized testing season. Having previously experienced community-based design and completed training through an Institute, Mr. Arthur is well-equipped to guide the community through a new type of design process. Dr. Wallace believes he will play a crucial role in leading this transformative change.

The students of Elm Town are like students anywhere—they are kind, they are curious, and they have big dreams.

Let us reestablish the basic ideas of the community-based design journey: on a design journey, communities engage in a local process where young people, educators, administrators, caregivers, and experts come together to collaboratively pursue better learning experiences and outcomes.

"GEAR UP": LAY THE FOUNDATION FOR YOUR COMMUNITY DESIGN JOURNEY

Key Activities:

1. Assemble a small team to kick off the work.
2. Understand the current reality of the school/system and reflect on future aspirations.
3. Decide and plan for what's next.

In early fall, Dr. Wallace and Mr. Arthur will lay the foundation for their community design journey. This stage of the work has three main activities: first, assembling a small team to drive forward the foundation work; second, understanding their current reality as a school or system and crafting a vision for their future aspirations; and third, making decisions for the next stage of the work.

Laying the foundation has several benefits for your community. First, it helps tend to several Community Conditions at once. Dr. Wallace and her small team will spend time building their own Conviction that their school community needs to change through a process of community-based design. They will collectively deepen their Clarity about what a design journey will entail. And they will make key decisions about the Capacity (people, time, resources) they will need to dedicate to the journey over time. By tending to these Community Conditions, Dr. Wallace will work to ensure that she and her team understand the culture of trust within the community. They will also work to understand the instructional and operational foundations of their system.

"Gear Up" Activity 1: Assemble a Small Team to Kick Off the Work

The first activity that Dr. Wallace and her team will pursue is to determine who will be involved in this initial "lay the foundation" work, what they are aiming to accomplish, and in what timeframe they are trying to accomplish it.

Dr. Wallace has some early ideas about several key players for this initial work. First, she wants to engage the help of a "Design Partner" for her community's journey. **A Design Partner is someone who has the capacity to help the community through its design journey, by helping steward the process, surface design options and recommendations, and make connections to useful resources, capacity, and networks within and outside of the community.**

Dr. Wallace asks the head of instruction, Mr. Arthur, to play this key role. Mr. Arthur has the skills and mindsets for the work. He believes that learning needs to change and has experienced community-based design first hand in his previous community. More critically, he has received training from an institute and has been in his role for eight years. He has strong project management skills, making his team very effective at executing big projects. He has the time and the headspace for a multiyear process like community-based design. Finally, Mr. Arthur is very plugged into the innovation space. He is a member of several learning cohorts and regularly attends education conferences. Now, Dr. Wallace and Mr. Arthur need to figure out which schools will actually embark on the design journey.

Together, Dr. Wallace and Mr. Arthur decide to add a few more critical leaders to the foundation team: a high school principal, Dr. Li; the district's lead counselor, Mrs. Stewart; and the president of the parents' association, Mr. Baker. Dr. Li, the principal of Meadow Field, the district's largest high school, is driven to improve learning outcomes in a district facing declining enrollment. While not opposed to change, he remains cautious about new initiatives.

For the coming months this small team will engage in the second big "Gear Up" activity: understanding the current state of the district and ideating their future aspirations.

"Gear Up" Activity 2: Understand the Current Reality of the School/System and Reflect on Future Aspirations

This small but mighty foundation team will now take steps to understand the current reality of school within the system. They will work together to synthesize what they learn and begin to imagine future aspirations for their school system.

Understanding the current reality of the system is a critical early activity for communities. First, it builds Clarity for the foundation team about the state of student experience, teaching and learning, and Community Conditions. This phase of work will help to build the Conviction in others, beyond Dr. Wallace, that school needs to change in Elm Town Unified.

Mr. Arthur, the team's Design Partner, will play a critical role in this work. He will make a plan for how the foundation team will gather insights about the current reality of schools in the district. He decides that every member of the foundation team will learn together in the following ways over the next three months. They will:

- Administer the "Leaps Student Voice Survey" to ninth graders at Meadow Field High School, Dr. Li's school
- Shadow a student for a day
- Reflect on their Community Conditions
- Analyze student outcomes data

- Assess current and future trends in the world of work
- Create a "Leader's Initial Case for Change" articulating why the district needs to undergo community-based design

The **Leader's Initial Case for Change** is a document created by the foundation team that captures early reflections on the gap between the desired state of your learning environment and its current reality. This starting point encapsulates the Clarity and Conviction leaders bring to the design journey.

After engaging in Shadowing a Student for a day, they share their observations:

- They were all exhausted by 11 a.m. with very few sanctioned opportunities to talk with her peers, either discussing ideas or socializing.
- The elementary school classrooms were vibrant, offering diverse learning experiences, including direct instruction, small-group discussions, socio-emotional learning lessons, and recess; in middle school, classes were predominantly teacher-led, with limited opportunities for student-directed learning.
- In the high schools, a culture of strict behavioral management persisted, despite nearly all teachers and school leaders expressing a desire to nurture independent thinkers.

The Leaps Student Voice Survey also provided critical feedback from Meadow Field's ninth grade students. Here's what they said about their experiences:

- 53 percent of students answered affirmatively that they experienced a strong culture of Connection and Community in their school.
- 30 percent of students answered affirmatively that school felt Relevant to their life.
- 20 percent of students answered affirmatively that learning was Rigorous.

These results surprised Elm Town Unified leaders. This is a common reaction, as Shadowing a Student and administering the Leaps Student Voice Survey is typically an eye-opening experience for adults. There is often a noticeable chasm between what adults think is happening in schools and what young people report experiencing. This chasm is a critical starting point for community-based design because the data can help to dispel some false assumptions.

After these hands-on experiences, Mr. Arthur supports the team to draft the Leader's Initial Case for Change. They create a simple, bulleted list as their Leader's Initial Case for Change. These snippets will play an important role in this community's design journey:

- *Our city is diverse, but students experience less diversity as they progress through school; they deserve classrooms that reflect the community's diversity.*
- *Students are creative and have unique perspectives, but classrooms too heavily rely on direct instruction, which often silence their voices. We want classrooms where students can explore their own ideas and feel valued.*
- *The future of work is unpredictable and dynamic, but our classrooms remain rigid. Learning environments should better prepare students for the evolving nature of work.*

"Gear Up" Activity 3: Decide and Plan for What's Next

The final activity in the "Gear Up" phase of work is to decide and plan for what's next. At this stage, communities can select from multiple options, with the optimal choice being the one that aligns best with your Community Conditions. Most commonly you will decide to create a Journey Plan for the next phases of work.

Journey Plans can be important tools for foundation teams to articulate the pace, sequence, and participants within the community design journey. Some teams choose to go big: they start by articulating a vision for the entire school or system. Other teams choose to start small with initiatives or ideas that they already have in play. Some teams realize after this foundation setting that conditions need to be strengthened, so they invest time there. No matter what you do, you can keep moving forward on your design journey, always walking at the pace of your Community Conditions.

Use the following QR code to find some examples of Journey Plans:

The team at Elm Town Unified decided that they work best backwards planning from a vision. Dr. Li, the principal, and Dr. Wallace agree that the district should start their design journey within one of the Meadow Field High School feeder patterns. The foundation team agrees that the Community

Conditions are very solid in these communities and the feeder pattern is representative of the district as a whole. The school leaders of both the elementary and middle schools have displayed high Conviction that school must change, and they all recognize what community-based design will entail.

With this initial thinking, the foundation team is now moving to expand the team to include the elementary school and middle school principals. They also know that they will need other key supporters within these school communities. They want to hear critical information from caregivers and educators, such as, why are many white parents leaving the district after elementary school? Where are they sending their children, and why? They want to understand how teachers view their own instruction. Would they be willing to try more student-centered, hands-on approaches to learning?

Additionally, the group decides that Mr. Arthur (with the support of his district-level instructional team) will continue to be the Design Partner for the journey. With these critical decisions made, they are now embarking on the second phase of work we call "Map It: Craft a high-level vision for the entire school or system."

"Gear Up": What Just Happened?

- Dr. Wallace, the new superintendent, believes that her community should undergo a design journey; she knows that it's not enough that she holds this Conviction; other key leaders at the system level need to build their Conviction as well, so she recruits a small team known as the "foundation team" to kick-start the work.
- Mr. Arthur will serve as the community's Design Partner; he creates learning experiences for the foundation team to understand the current state of learning and student experiences at Elm Town Unified.
- Using what they have learned from shadowing students and administering the Leaps Student Voice Survey, the team synthesizes their thinking into a Leader's Initial Case for Change, a starting point for the community's design journey.

"MAP IT": CRAFT A HIGH-LEVEL VISION FOR THE ENTIRE SCHOOL OR SYSTEM

Key Activities:

1. Create new teams to lead the design journey.
2. Gain knowledge from your community, research, and practice.
3. Envision your school or system design.

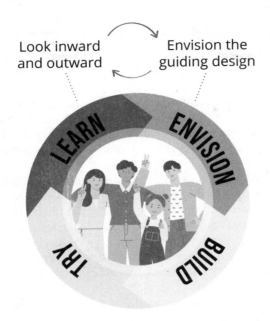

Look inward and outward

Envision the guiding design

In the "Map It" phase, the foundation team is set to expand and include more key players in community design. To do this, communities gather knowledge from various sources. For instance, the Van Ness Elementary foundation team from Chapter 3 learned about the science of learning and development, observed socio-emotional learning in schools, and reflected on current global economic trends. The "Map It" phase represents a "half-turn of the Design Cycle," where communities alternate between Learn activities and Envision work. For the Elm Town Unified team, this phase will culminate in the community envisioning a design for Meadow Field High School.

Communities that opt to begin their wider community design work by creating a guiding design for the entire school or system discover that this approach offers several benefits. First, it enables many more members of the community to participate early in the design process. This can really help galvanize Conviction and Clarity across the community, leading to a larger Coalition and a more diverse coalition. An entire school or system guiding design can provide a clear, inspiring foundation for years of change. It serves as a "North Star" to align the community on a shared vision of extraordinary learning for all, guiding every future step of the journey. Finally, having a guiding design ensures coherence as communities design various aspects of the student experience. It provides an overview of the entire "forest" while focusing on individual "trees."

To achieve this, the Elm Town team will take on three key activities as they make the half turn of the Design Cycle.

"Map It" Activity 1: Create New Teams to Lead the Design Journey

Mr. Arthur, acting as a Design Partner, will help the foundation team form a planning team and design team to drive the work and determine who else from the community will engage.

The planning team continues to steward the community through the "Map It" phase of the journey and often through the rest of the journey over multiple years. They set up the schedule, keep the Design Cycle turning, and make logistical decisions. The planning team typically includes the following:

- Any Design Partners supporting the work (in this case, Mr. Arthur)
- A project manager or co-pilot, who is not a superintendent or principal (Mr. Arthur chooses a strong project manager from his department)
- One or two school or district administrators (Dr. Li, Mrs. Stewart)

The design team acts as the "design decision-makers"—alongside anyone in a formal position of decision-making authority like the superintendent—and actively participates in the Learning and Envisioning stages of the Design Cycle from the start. Their role is to align on the guiding design vision. The design team typically includes the following:

- The planning team
- A heterogeneous team of administrators, educators, families, and students
- Multiple teams or clusters of stakeholders with more similar roles (e.g., a teacher design team, a student design team, a family advisory board, etc.)

You can find some examples of strong design teams by using the following QR code:

In addition to setting up these two new teams, Mr. Arthur will think about how to involve other members of their community in the design process. There are many ways to do this (the following QR code has guidance and examples). Most importantly, though, Mr. Arthur understands that the "community" for this design process includes students, families, educators, school administrators, district administrators, and local leaders.

Who Is Typically Part of a Community-based Design Journey?
At the heart of the community-based design process many people are coming together to work as a team. Each assembled team should reflect the unique community contexts and needs of its members.

Group	Example configuration
Foundation team: a small and temporary initial group of people who kick-start the process	**Size: two to five people** ■ One senior district leader with decision-making authority (e.g., a superintendent) ■ One school principal and two or three other key leaders from their campus
Planning team: a small group driving forward the process for the duration of the design journey	**Size: two to five people** ■ One Design Partner ■ One school principal and two or three other key leaders from their campus
Design team: diverse stakeholders advancing the school design vision	**Size: eight to twelve people** ■ Three or four students with unique lived experiences of school ■ Three or four school teachers and school-based leaders ■ Two or three student caregivers with varying proximity to school ■ Planning team members (see above)
Extended community group: key community members who will give input and play key roles in implementing the design	**Size: Twelve+ people, broadest group** ■ People who will experience the design in some way (e.g., young people, teachers, caregivers) ■ People who will approve and implement the design (e.g., board members, educators, funders)

Learners, families, educators, school staff, administrators, district staff & leaders, local community & political leaders

As the foundation team steps back and the planning team takes shape, the planning team will make preliminary decisions about which elements of the Blueprint (see Chapter 2 for greater detail) they aim to complete and agree upon during the "Map It" phase.

This step enables a community to assess aspects of the design journey they have already completed.

In Elm Town Unified, Mr. Arthur observes that the district already has a strong understanding of its Community Context, which they completed before launching the search for Dr. Wallace, the new superintendent. Additionally, they had engaged in a years long strategic planning process to develop a system-wide mission statement, Graduate Aims, and even Design Principles. This base of knowledge from the years of strategic planning implied that the design was well underway, but the results from the Leaps survey revealed gaps that took the foundation team by surprise—relevant learning, customization, and rigor had all been keystone concepts developed during the strategic planning years. However, the planning team realized that once the documents were written, schools were not given any support to implement changes that aligned with these new ideals. To remedy this disconnect, the planning team creates a workshop for the design team using and revising early drafts from the strategic planning work.

With this system-level clarity, the design team focuses on applying the Mission, Graduate Aims, and Design Principles at Meadow Field High School. They will identify a few key experiences to develop and test in detail. Instead of creating separate Goals & Guiding Concepts for both the system and school levels, the planning team decides that schools will work to contextualize and interpret the system-level version. From their experience, they know that having multiple priorities causes tension. They want Elm Town Unified to be on the same page, ensuring students have a cohesive experience from elementary to high school, where essential skills are nurtured throughout their experience.

"Map It" Activity 2: Gain Knowledge from Your Community, Research, and Practice

The second activity within the "Map It" phase involves gaining knowledge from the community, research, and practice. Informally, we divide these activities into two parts: "looking inward," which means learning from your community and what you have tried, and "looking outward," which means learning from research and practices beyond your community. Communities often find it useful and galvanizing to synthesize lessons learned into a Community Case for Change that describes the gap between the community's aspirations for the learning environment and its current state.

Mr. Arthur and his project manager, Mr. Esteban, create a list of opportunities for the design team to look inward and look outward in late fall and early winter. The following table shows some example learning activities:

Look inward	Look outward
Interview students and families—meet one-on-one or in small groups with student and families to learn about what they want from the learning environment and their experience of the current learning environment	*Explore local and broader trends*—examine trends in areas like science and technology and the economy and employment, and consider how students are currently being prepared—and need to be prepared—to thrive in and transform the world they'll be graduating into
Shadow a student—accompany a student throughout their day, sometimes including outside of school, to get a different vantage point on their current experience	*Understand the science of learning & development*—engage in a concise review of current research to consider where your learning environment is aligned—and could better align—with what is known about how learning and development best occurs
Administer the Leaps Student Voice Survey—learn in a broader and more quantitative way what students say they experience on Leaps dimensions like Relevance, Customization, and Connection & Community	*Understand and leverage the Leaps*—use resources tied to the Leaps to learn about the different ingredients that make an experience Relevant or Customized, for example, for young people, and virtually tour schools that have made tremendous strides in making a given Leap
Conduct classroom observations—observe classrooms with a set of look-fors—whether Leaps Look-fors or some other framework—to make meaning together of what you are seeing in the student and adult experience	*Conduct in-person and virtual inspiration visits*—explore learning environments (or even other types of environments) that exemplify or inspire aspects of learning that your community values
Unpack learning outcomes data—examine together the patterns of student achievement in the various outcomes your community values	*Explore the Innovative Models Exchange*—explore Transcend's online platform of models that help communities make various Leaps, as another way to draw inspiration and be able to access implementation supports if the community wants to adopt or adapt those models

You can find tools to conduct these activities in your community by using the following QR code:

The Elm Town Unified design team finds these activities energizing and cathartic, as they are accustomed to dealing with the most urgent needs of school. Educators on the Elm Town design team express in reflection meetings led by Mr. Arthur, "This reminded me why I chose this profession!" After shadowing students or observing other schools, team members begin to realize how disengaged students can easily slip through the cracks, how their current focus on rote skills lacks rigor, and how their school shares responsibility for student motivation but is not designed to support it for young people. Teachers on the design team are invigorated by these activities, which bring them back to their sense of purpose.

This moment is crucial to assess the strength of Community Conditions. Earlier in the journey, during the "Gear Up" phase of work, the superintendent and a few colleagues shared these initial experiences and insights. During the "Map It" phase, this Conviction expands to the diverse design team because more stakeholders are involved in the process. This demonstrates how community-based design radiates outward, creating energy and building momentum as more people are involved. This is not a top-down change driven solely by Dr. Wallace. If she had simply written her vision in a memo, shared it with district department heads, and started holding schools accountable, she likely would not see the same level of Conviction and Coalition that she is building now.

By interviewing parents and students, "looking inward" provides the design team with valuable insights that will shape the team's design ideas in the Envision process:

- Elementary-aged students report that they feel cared for and loved by their teachers, but perceptions change as students enter middle and high school.
- Overwhelmingly, middle school students report that math class is their least favorite subject. They do not feel successful; they describe math as "extremely boring," state that it produces deep anxiety in them, and state that they complete worksheets or book work every day without opportunities to complete "fun projects."

- Caregivers report that they want school focused on more real-world skills and tasks such as finances, common household tasks, and even taxes.
- Young people report that they want more flexibility to move at their own pace in school; once they understand something, they would like to move on or they would like more time when they are struggling.
- Caregivers of late elementary and middle school students report concern that their children seem to struggle so much with math, they are worried that their children will be less competitive in the job market given how important they perceive math skills to be for higher-paying STEM careers.

By "looking outward" and exploring local and global trends, the design team learns the following:

- Careers in science, technology, public health, business, engineering, and mathematics (STEM) are among the fastest-growing and highest-paying jobs; these fields heavily rely on advanced mathematical skills.
- In an age of increasing artificial intelligence, many careers are likely to evolve and new roles are expected to emerge; AI specialists, data scientists, cybersecurity specialists are expected to be in-demand fields of the future.
- Gig work, also known as the "gig economy," a labor market characterized by short-term contracts or freelance work instead of permanent jobs, will likely dominate in many sectors by the time most of the district's students enter the workforce.

Finally, the design team looked closely at student learning outcomes across the district. Here is some of what they noticed:

- 60 percent of white third graders are proficient in math; 33 percent of Black third graders are
- 26 percent of Black third graders are proficient in reading, compared with 59 percent of white third graders
- The graduation rate for Black students is 79 percent, 89 percent for white students
- The SAT average for Black students on evidence-based reading and writing (EBRW) is 454, math is 439; for white students EBRW is 600, math is 550.

Mr. Arthur, with the help of his network of Design Partners, also arranged for the design team to participate in live and virtual "inspiration visits." During one of the most impactful visits, design members visited a cybersecurity firm for a day. As with insights gained from looking inward, educators often report that visiting learning environments beyond schools resets their understanding of the workforce. During the visit, design team members were amazed to see how workers collaborate—their assumption was that cybersecurity specialists worked alone. Instead, they found teams of colleagues collaborating on security policy development, security assessments and audits, and security architecture design.

The design team interviewed several cybersecurity specialists to gain insights into the skills they considered most valuable for their profession. Interestingly, when asked which skills they wished they had learned more thoroughly in school, many of the experts highlighted communication and teamwork abilities, beyond the standard technical proficiencies. The specialists emphasized that effective communication is crucial in their field, as they often need to explain complex technical concepts to nontechnical stakeholders, collaborate with diverse teams, and clearly articulate cybersecurity risks and strategies to leadership. They also stressed the importance of teamwork, as tackling cybersecurity challenges often requires coordinated efforts across multiple departments and disciplines.

Again, this feedback surprised the design team, who had initially assumed that the specialists would prioritize highly technical skills. What they learned from these interviews underscored the importance of incorporating opportunities in the design for students to develop strong communication and collaboration skills as often and early as possible. Educators also asked the specialists how they developed their technical skills. Some said they had attended a high school with a cybersecurity career technical education (CTE) pathway, while others mentioned enrolling in a postsecondary cybersecurity program. A few specialists reported completing an online program, and some said they started with fewer qualifications at the company and then learned on the job. As a result, many of the specialists wished their high school had offered a similar program to help them avoid the out-of-pocket costs they incurred after graduation.

After several weeks of research and learning, Mr. Arthur and Mr. Esteban take the first steps to synthesize a Community Case for Change, an artifact that captures the community's aspirations and commitments. They create an initial draft, which is then heavily refined by the design team. This collaborative process leads to a sharpened vision that the entire team feels invested in and proud of.

To ensure that the Community Case for Change effectively represents the diverse perspectives within their community, the team engages in multiple rounds of sharing and feedback with a wide range of community members. They actively seek input from various stakeholders, including students, parents, educators, and community leaders. Through this iterative process, the team incorporates the insights and ideas gathered from the community, refining the document to reflect the collective vision and values of the many voices they have heard.

The final version of the Community Case for Change is a testament to the power of collaboration and inclusive decision-making. It stands as a shared commitment to the community's aspirations and serves as a guiding light for the transformative work ahead. Mr. Arthur, Mr. Esteban, and the design team feel confident that this artifact authentically represents the hopes and dreams of their vibrant community.

You can find some strong examples of Community Cases for Change by using the following QR code:

"Map It" Activity 3: Envision Your School or System Design

The Learn/Envision Design Cycle "dance" continues in the third and final key set of activities within the "Map It" phase: envisioning your school and/or system design. This activity helps a design team to build more clarity about the community's aspiration for each section of the Blueprint.

System-Level Vision

SCHOOL DESIGN BLUEPRINT:

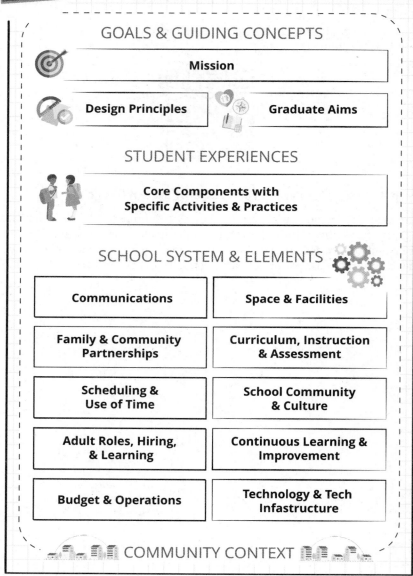

FIGURE 7.1

Dr. Wallace, Mr. Arthur, and the Elm Town Unified design team take a tailored approach responsive to their Community Conditions. First, they decide to update existing aspects of the Blueprint (See Figure 7.1) rather than drafting them all from scratch using the Goals & Guiding Concepts from prior strategic planning sessions to understand Community Context, a grounding component of the Blueprint. They use this same research as a starting point to articulate an updated Mission, Graduate Aims, and Design Principles for the system.

Mr. Arthur hosts many Envision discussions with the design team. In those meetings they have big and small discussions—*What kind of world did we learn our graduates will be entering? Given that, what kind of experiences should we be aiming to create for them?* From all this discussion, Mr. Arthur distills a vision for the whole system in Figure 7.2.

MISSION

Elm Town Unified School District is committed to empowering all students to become adaptable, collaborative, and innovative problem-solvers ready to thrive in an ever-changing world.

DESIGN PRINCIPLES

| **Active Self-Direction** | **Customization** | **Relevance** | **Rigorous Learning** |

GRADUATE AIMS

| **Team Players** (Growth Mindset & Communication) | **Adaptable Futurists** (Vocational Knowledge & Skills) | **Independent Thinkers** (Responsible Decision-Making & Critical Thinking) | **Community-Minded** (Work Across Lines of Difference & Collaboration) |

EXPERIENCES

| **Blended Learning** | **Project-Based Learning** | **Multi-Tiered-Supports** | **High-Dosage Tutoring** | **Circle Practice** | **Community Projects** |

FIGURE 7.2

The image illustrates one approach for a community to visualize its desired school system. The design team values this consolidated vision of the system represented in a single image. The revised Graduate Aims and Design Principles are largely consistent with the strategic plan but now include more evidence and detail to support the design of experiences, grade-level expectations, and assessments. However, two notable changes emerged: the elevation of "Team Players" as a critical Graduate Aim and the prioritization of "Relevance" as a key Design Principle. This high-level vision will serve as the foundation for various Design Cycles implemented across the community's schools.

Dr. Wallace believes that the school system requires a cohesive vision that incorporates the community's input and experiences while maintaining consistency among individual schools. When she joined Elm Town Unified, she observed a misalignment between the understanding of district administrators and that of school leaders and educators about the community's mission and the experiences necessary to achieve it. By engaging the community in the design process, Dr. Wallace aims to realign the schools and the district, ensuring that all stakeholders work collaboratively toward a shared purpose.

In this phase, a Design Partner like Mr. Arthur is invaluable. He functions similarly to HGTV interior designers, who act as leaders and facilitators in a home design process. In this stage a Design Partner can help the community access a wide range of resources and examples for each Blueprint section. Design partners also collect community input, synthesize it into "what we heard from you" and "here are options that often work for households with your preferences," and then gather more feedback. This process leads the community to a design vision that aligns with their context and aspirations, without requiring everyone to have extensive knowledge of every design possibility. Community design teams often find this Design Partner support reassuring, as they want to drive their design vision but do not want to invest the time in synthesizing everything and creating every decision from the ground up.

Not all communities approach the process like Elm Town. Communities may choose to create the Blueprint components from the ground up. For instance, after conducting extensive student and family interviews, analyzing outcome data, exploring trends, and making inspiration visits, a design team might attempt to draft a set of Graduate Aims for the guiding design vision. These Graduate Aims describe the outcomes they want all students to achieve. When drafting Graduate Aims, communities often find it beneficial to refer to the Graduate Aims of other communities with similar contexts and aspirations. The fact that many communities have gone through this process can be a significant advantage for the next community embarking on the journey.

You can find strong examples of Blueprints by using the following QR code:

School-Level Vision

Now, Elm Town has various smaller design teams operating at the school-level. These design teams will play a critical role in building and testing various student experiences aligned to the system's vision. To facilitate this work Mr. Arthur and the big design team made some key decisions:

- First, they would pursue Design Cycles within feeder patterns so that there is coherence between elementary, middle, and high school change.
- Improving experiences and outcomes for students in math is a major priority given what they learned from students and parents and by looking at current and future trends in the economy and society.
- Finally, they would run early Design Cycles in Dr. Lin's (a member of the main design team) high school feeder pattern, with elementary, middle, and high school design teams working concurrently.

To kick off work at the school level, Mr. Arthur supports a middle school design team to Envision a "Day in the Life" of a student. Given the student experiences drafted at the system level, what would a middle schooler's day look and feel like? What would the schedule entail?

You can find strong examples of "Day in the Life" narratives by using the following QR code:

After the middle school team has a high-level vision of the school day, they will "Zoom In" on a specific aspect of a student's day. This involves crafting and testing a particular part of the design vision in greater detail.

In the next chapter, we will follow the design team working at the middle school level to run Design Cycles in math instruction.

Map It: What Just Happened?

- The Elm Town Unified design team, building on previous strategic planning work, Envisions a guiding vision of the school system. They have clarity around key elements of the Blueprint: Mission, Graduate Aims, Design Principles, and Student Experiences.
- The design team creates a Community Case for Change that describes what the community wants for their students and shows the gap between that vision and the current reality. The Case for Change is documented using information gathered through extensive interviews with students and parents (which builds Conviction) and research on local and global trends (which builds Clarity).
- Mr. Arthur and the design team decide to splinter into school-based design teams so that schools can run Design Cycles trying student experiences that they have aligned on within the Blueprint; Design Cycles are now ready to begin at multiple schools.

CHAPTER 8

Deepening Your Design Journey

Key Points

- After creating a school and/or system-wide vision, the design team develops a more detailed vision for a specific part of the student experience using community insights and research.
- For example, in developing an innovative math experience, the team undertakes a full turn of the Design Cycle: Building, Trying, Learning, and Envisioning. This same process occurs for other prioritized experiences that the team develops.
- Design teams then prepare to continue their journeys by setting priorities, goals, and engaging key community members for upcoming phases.

Roughly in the first year or so you will continue working through the five key phases of work to improve design and conditions:

1. **Gear Up:** Lay the foundation for your community design journey.
2. **Map It:** Craft a high-level vision for the entire school or system.
3. **Zoom In:** Craft a detailed vision for a specific aspect of the student experience.
4. **Test-Drive:** Try the student experience.
5. **Look Ahead:** Prepare to continue the journey.

This chapter will cover the Zoom In, Test-Drive, and Look Ahead activities with Elm Town Unified.

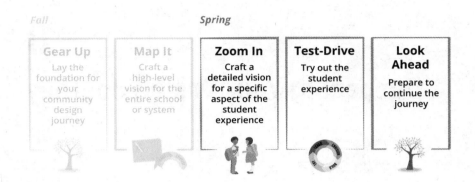

Fall   *Spring*

Gear Up	Map It	**Zoom In**	**Test-Drive**	**Look Ahead**
Lay the foundation for your community design journey	Craft a high-level vision for the entire school or system	Craft a detailed vision for a specific aspect of the student experience	Try out the student experience	Prepare to continue the journey

"ZOOM IN": CRAFT A DETAILED VISION FOR A SPECIFIC ASPECT OF THE STUDENT EXPERIENCE

Key Activities:

1. Plan and begin student experience design work.
2. Gather knowledge from your community, research, and practice.
3. Envision part of the design.

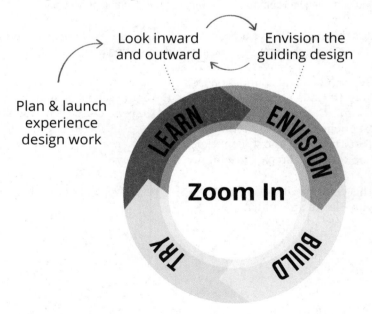

The third key phase of work in getting started on a community-based design journey requires teams to "Zoom In" on a specific aspect of the student experience. Creating a detailed design vision for part of the student experience is like crafting a school or system design vision. It involves a half-turn of the Design Cycle, focusing on learning and envisioning to develop an initial design vision.

After completing this phase of work, communities will have crafted a real Student Experience within the Blueprint with young people. This section outlines the key activities and practices that constitute the part of the Student Experience being designed, as well as the Goals & Guiding Concepts it aims to achieve. Additionally, communities will have even more refined thinking about the School & System Elements of the Blueprint needed to make the Student Experience real. School & System Elements provide details on aspects such as curriculum, scheduling, staffing, and adult roles that allow each activity and practice to be implemented and ensure compatibility with the overall design.

To revisit the HGTV metaphor, this phase of work can be compared to creating a detailed Blueprint of a new kitchen renovation (See Figure 8.1).

SCHOOL DESIGN BLUEPRINT:

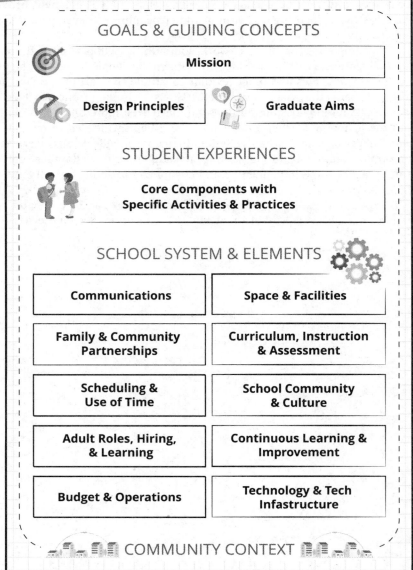

GOALS & GUIDING CONCEPTS

Mission

Design Principles   **Graduate Aims**

STUDENT EXPERIENCES

**Core Components with
Specific Activities & Practices**

SCHOOL SYSTEM & ELEMENTS

Communications	**Space & Facilities**
Family & Community Partnerships	**Curriculum, Instruction & Assessment**
Scheduling & Use of Time	**School Community & Culture**
Adult Roles, Hiring, & Learning	**Continuous Learning & Improvement**
Budget & Operations	**Technology & Tech Infastructure**

COMMUNITY CONTEXT

FIGURE 8.1

Like all phases of work, "Zoom In" strengthens Community Conditions. By forming more specific design teams and engaging many community members in designing a specific part of the Student Experience, communities build a stronger and wider Coalition. They also enhance Clarity and Conviction among many community members regarding the design vision for this student experience. The community's Capacity for executing design work grows, especially within the design team, and the culture of learning and innovation flourishes.

In Elm Town Unified, Mr. Arthur helps his middle school design team enter this phase by leading a group reflection around these three questions, designed to help the team get specific about *what* to test first in their context:

- What part of the student experience must be redesigned to achieve our Graduate Aims and Design Principles?
- What "signature experience" can we design and pilot to indicate the changes we plan to make in our multiyear design journey?
- What bold but feasible "big bet" could we start with to begin progressing toward our guiding vision?

The middle school design team comes to the conclusion that redesigning the math experience from elementary through high school will have a significant impact on student experience and the life trajectories of students. From student interviews and achievement data, they conclude that math is a significant hurdle beginning in late elementary school. Many families notice how difficult math becomes as caregivers struggle to help their children and math achievement scores plummet in high school. This has a significant impact on the reputation of the district's high schools. Caregivers expressed concern during the "Map It" looking inward activities that their children would have low math achievement scores on tests like the SAT. As a result, many families looked to place their children in private schools or homeschool settings by the end of middle school.

It became clear to the design team that math learning experiences needed to change. They were not the only part of the learning environment in need of redesign. But they needed to start somewhere and they had momentum with the math teachers in the Meadow Field feeder pattern.

Like in the previous phase, "Zoom In" consists of three major activities.

"Zoom In" Activity 1: Plan and Begin Student Experience Design Work

Mr. Arthur now works to create a new, smaller design team that has more expertise in math. Mr. Arthur; Mr. Esteban, the project manager; and Dr. Dexter, the middle school principal will work hand in hand to assemble a middle school "math experience design team."

The new middle-school-based math experience design team, named "Pi Pioneers," will include the following:

- Dr. Dexter, the middle school principal
- Mr. Buckley, the math department team leader and ninth grade math teacher
- Mrs. Gann, sixth grade math teacher
- Mrs. Wood, seventh grade math teacher
- Several middle school students in advisory roles

System-level (district) support will consist of the following:

- Mr. Arthur, who will continue as the Design Partner
- Mr. Esteban, who will serve as project manager and will support Mr. Arthur
- Ms. Feld, the district-level math specialist
- Dr. Wallace, the superintendent, who will not attend regular meetings, but will be a Pi Pioneers cheerleader and regularly informed on the group's progress

You will notice that students are back in the design process. Within community-based design, the role of young people is particularly important, and their voices and experiences can show up in myriad ways throughout the journey. For this phase of work, the Pi Pioneers want students close, so they will directly advise the math experience design team.

In some cases, such as in Northern Cass (Chapter 4), young people serve in an advisory capacity during the design decision-making process. However, in other instances, they can take on a more active co-design role, particularly when their lived experiences and unique perspectives are crucial to the design. For instance, in a high school designing a series of "rite of passage" experiences, a student co-design team played a vital role in ensuring that the design was authentically honored and aligned with their various backgrounds and cultural traditions.

To explore more examples of "experience design teams" in action, please refer to the QR code.

With this planning clarity, the Pi Pioneers can begin the math experience design work.

"Zoom in" Activity 2: Gather Knowledge from Your Community, Research, and Practice

The second activity within the "Zoom In" phase of work mirrors work done in the "Map It" phase. It involves gaining knowledge from the community, research, and practice, but this time is focused on a specific part of the student experience. For our Elm Town Pi Pioneers, it will be middle school math.

Again, Mr. Arthur and his project manager, Mr. Esteban, create a list of opportunities for the math design team to "look inward" and "look outward," but this time specifically focused on math.

To explore Look Inward/Look Outward learning activities focused on math, please use the following QR code:

For this phase of work, the Pi Pioneer team is especially excited to learn from innovative math instruction happening across the country. Mr. Arthur is able to use professional development funds to visit Long-View Micro School in Texas and organize a virtual visit with Intrinsic Schools in Chicago (Chapter 6). Both are renowned for their Leaps-aligned math learning environments. Long-View increases rigor by focusing on math discourse and has several projects a year where students apply math skills. Intrinsic has created a multimodality model where students are able to go deeper in content and get individual attention on what they need. These experiences prove catalytic for the Elm Town educators. They witness extraordinary rigor happening in math classes. Students in these learning environments have a clearly honed vision of themselves as mathematicians, confident to discuss and *debate* math solutions in class.

The Pi Pioneers are also interested in hearing from students themselves. They want to know about how students experience math, know how competent they feel with math, and more deeply understand students' ideas around Relevance.

Here are a few things they heard directly from young people:

- **Lack of relevance:** Students struggle to see how math relates to their future and want to learn practical skills like personal finance. The content is often too easy or too difficult, and they do not receive targeted support.
- **Negative self-perception:** Many students believe they are not "math people" due to past challenges.
- **Lack of customization:** Students cannot get help on specific concepts or learn at their own pace.
- **Uninspired instructional methods:** Math class is repetitive, with teachers lecturing at the front of the room and little opportunity for group work or projects.

In addition to the inspiration visits, the Pi Pioneers also "look outward" by engaging in current research and thinking around math instruction. First, they explore ed tech tools to better understand what's available for more customized instruction. They spend hours together assessing platforms like Khanmigo, created by Khan Academy to provide one-to-one guidance to students and support teachers in instructional planning; Zearn, a platform that teaches and assesses on grade-level content and provides scaffolds for students; or Dreambox, a platform that provides scaffolds and adapts learning for every student.

Together they explore current points of debate in the math field and within their own school community. They talk about issues such as the role of AI—*how might generative technologies enhance their instruction?* They discuss the racial and gender disparities they discover in their school data, which reflect national trends that worsen over time.

The design team does not want to start from scratch; most communities should not have to. So, they explore the Innovative Models Exchange, a free platform that provides a wide array of Leaps-aligned learning models for communities to adopt or adapt as needed. Models, programs that fundamentally reshape the educational experience, are key ingredients that can speed up a community's design journey. Rather than starting from a blank page, the Pi Pioneers decide to take inspiration from three existing models and adapt those practices for their unique context.

To see more learning models on the Innovative Models Exchange, use the following QR code:

"Zoom in" Activity 3: Envision a Part of the Design

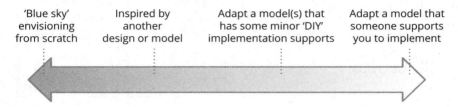

'Blue sky' envisioning from scratch | Inspired by another design or model | Adapt a model(s) that has some minor 'DIY' implementation supports | Adapt a model that someone supports you to implement

Now, Mr. Arthur will support the Pi Pioneers to Envision part of the design. This activity helps the math experience design team to get clear about what students are doing and what they will encounter within the learning environment. This stage is often a back-and-forth process where the design team applies what they have learned to design choices in the Blueprint. The Pi Pioneers have decided to do their Envision work toward the right side of the spectrum shown earlier because they have seen in the earlier activity that there are several existing options that could meet their aspirations and could likely be adapted for their context.

The team moves to create opportunities for Relevance and increase Rigor (insights they have gleaned from the Leaps Student Voice Survey and student and family interviews)—and they hypothesize that by providing greater Customization in its math experiences they can maximize how useful the content feels and the depth of critical thinking.

From all of their learning, the Pi Pioneers come away with one big insight around math teaching and learning: they must create math learning environment designs that utilize multiple modalities for learning. Their task is bigger and deeper than merely adopting a new curriculum (though that will be important) or bringing in a few discrete lessons that have real-world applications. They will need to Envision math instruction as a collection of cohesive learning experiences responsive to the skills and abilities of individual students, similar to the math learning environments at Intrinsic.

Mr. Arthur leads the Pi Pioneers through several rounds of creating and refining their ideas. They Envision the following framework as their approach to new math learning environments: multimodal math learning environments.

BLENDED =
MULTIPLE
MODALITIES

Whole-Group Instruction	Small-Group Instruction	Online Learning
Teacher-led instruction using high-quality instructional materials.	Teacher provides targeted instruction to a small group of students.	Students use online learning software to work independently in the classroom or computer lab.

Peer Learning	Independent Learning	Goal Conferencing	Tutoring
Students work together (on- or offline) to learn, work on projects, and create work products.	Students work alone to learn, work on projects, create work products, and take assessments.	Students set goals and discuss progress with teachers or peers.	Students work with a peer, teacher, or tutor to learn, work on projects, and create work products.

Through their research and meaning-making they have come to a shared understanding that redesigning math is a matter of blending many different experiences. Sometimes whole-group instruction is exactly what's needed; other times students need direct tutoring. By embracing multiple modalities the Pi Pioneers believe that they can meet the system's Design Principles of Active Self-Direction, Customization, Relevance, and Rigorous Learning.

But how does such a big vision come to be? These are all significant design ideas that the Pi Pioneers will need to scale down to develop at least one activity or practice with sufficient detail to be effectively tested with students. After all, each of the modalities has their own frameworks, curricular tools, and teaching practices.

After several rounds of ideation, the Pi Pioneers decide to first implement math goal conferences, where students receive one-on-one or small-group support in setting goals and discussing progress. The experience design team believes that they need to begin by nurturing students' "math identities," which refer to their self-perceptions regarding their abilities in the subject. Drawing from the science of learning and development, they recognize that identity plays a crucial role in how students approach learning. During student interviews, the team observed that many students held a fixed mindset about their math abilities. The Pi Pioneers have a Graduate Aim to cultivate a growth mindset among students, encouraging them to view their math skills as something that can be developed and improved through effort and practice, rather than as fixed traits. By helping students set goals, tracking their progress, and reflecting on their work, the team hopes students will see that they *can* learn math and be great at math.

In the following section, we will accompany the Pi Pioneers as they enter the fourth phase of their community design journey: the "Test-Drive." During this phase, the Pi Pioneers will pilot and refine their idea of math goal conferences. The team will gather feedback and data to assess the effectiveness of the conferences and make necessary adjustments to improve the experience for students. This practice represents one element of the Pi Pioneers' broader learning environment design of integrating blended math learning throughout a student's academic journey, combining personalized support, technology-enhanced instruction, and engaging, real-world applications of mathematical concepts. By piloting and refining the math goal conferences, the Pi Pioneers seek to create a strong foundation for their larger vision and ensure that their approach effectively meets the needs of their students.

"Zoom In": What Just Happened?

- Mr. Arthur shepherds a new math-focused experience design team (the Pi Pioneers) through ideation to Envision a multimodal math learning environment design that integrates personalized support, technology-enhanced instruction, and direct instruction.
- They determine they do not need to build new math learning models from scratch. They can borrow and adapt existing approaches tested and developed elsewhere; adopting models is a critical factor that can speed up a community's design journey.
- The Pi Pioneers prepare to pilot/test the first math student experience: Math Goal Conferences.

"TEST-DRIVE": TEST AND REFINE THE STUDENT EXPERIENCE

Key Activities:

1. Plan to test part of the student experience design.
2. Build what you need for the test-drive.
3. Test-drive.
4. Learn from it and update the design.

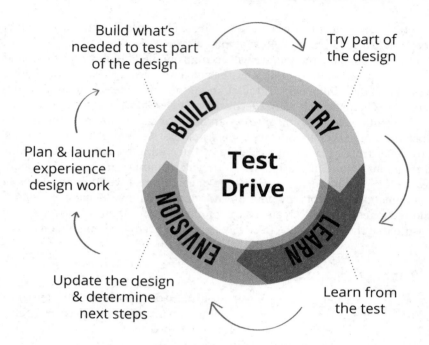

Build what's needed to test part of the design

Try part of the design

Plan & launch experience design work

Update the design & determine next steps

Learn from the test

By now, our Pi Pioneers math experience design team is in about March of the school year. They will spend the next few weeks of spring testing and refining part of their student experience design: Math Goal Conferences, which are one-on-one or one-on-two discussions with students about their math skills and needs.

The Design Cycle continues to guide this phase of work, but now the math team will complete a "full turn of the cycle." They will take the ideas developed in the Envision step and progress through the Build, Try, and Learn steps, ultimately returning to the Envision step.

This phase of work has myriad benefits for your community. By making a full turn of the cycle, communities strengthen their learning environment design and fortify key Community Conditions. Trying small or even large ideas helps communities to gain insights that will improve their design. Our Pi Pioneers may learn that they are exactly on the right track, or they may learn that the conferencing idea was based on a faulty assumption. Regardless, by completing a full turn of the cycle, our team will deepen its Clarity around their big idea. They will likely also increase their Conviction that school needs to change, purely by seeing what's unleashed in student motivation and growth in these conferences. In almost all cases, we have seen significant growth in the Capacity condition, as educators build critical knowledge, skills, and mindsets before and during testing new ideas.

Piloting ideas also provides essential insights into the steps required to implement the different aspects of the experience more sustainably and at a larger scale. For example, communities sometimes discover that teachers need more support than anticipated or that the engagement of families and caregivers plays a more critical role than expected. In design, communities are always grateful to "try it before we buy it."

Ultimately, through piloting/testing an idea most communities see that some meaningful changes in experiences and outcomes for students start to emerge, even when the ideas seem small. Depending on the experience being tested, communities can gauge growth by enlisting tools like the Leaps Student Voice Survey, classroom observations, assessments of learning, student and teacher interviews, looking at student work, or analyzing administrative data like attendance or suspensions. Testing an idea is a critical part of community-based design.

Now, let us follow our Pi Pioneers experience design team to see what it looks like to progress through the Design Cycle and achieve these outcomes.

"Test-Drive" Activity 1: Plan to Test Part of the Student Experience Design

Mr. Arthur and the Pi Pioneers math experience design team will begin to Test-Drive their Math Goal Conferences experience with an approach familiar to all educators: backwards planning.

Here are the steps and questions they will ask as they prepare to Try their idea:

1. The Pi Pioneers will start by looking to the end of the Design Cycle and ask, "What do we want to do or decide with this test?"
2. Next, they will look ahead to the Learn step of the cycle and ask, "What do we want to learn through this test that would inform those decisions and actions we want to take?"
3. Then, they'll look at the Try step of the cycle and ask, "What should we try, and with whom, that would enable us to learn those things?"
4. Finally, arriving back at the Build step, the Pi Pioneers will ask, "What do we need to compile in order to successfully execute this test?"

You can find planning tools and examples of strong testing plans using the following QR code:

Because the Pi Pioneers are trying a conferencing experience, they will be able to borrow and adapt materials from Northern Cass, which leads conferences with students as one experience within its Studios learning model. Mr. Arthur, the Design Partner, helps the team gather the testing plans and other prebuilt materials to adapt them for the pilot.

The Pi Pioneers decide on the following goals for their Math Goal Conferencing Test-Drive:

- Decide if this form of math conferencing should be part of the vision for multimodal math going forward.
- Understand how to set customized goals with students and monitor progress over time.
- Share evidence of improved experiences and outcomes, if they occur, with other community members to build clarity and conviction in the design vision.

"Test-Drive" Activity 2: Build What You Need for the Test-Drive

Mr. Arthur and the Pi Pioneers are now ready to "build," largely adapting materials from Northern Cass's Studios model to test-drive the Math Goal Conferences idea.

Typically, you will need to develop three types of things:

- Materials for running the pilot, such as lesson plans, assessments, professional development (PD) sessions, and family communications
- Tools for gathering evidence from the pilot, including surveys, interview guides, observation rubrics, and data analysis tools
- Fertile Community Conditions for conducting a successful pilot, like Clarity and Capacity among teachers who will administer the pilots

Math teachers on the design team will select students to participate in a math conferencing pilot. The conferencing cycle will consist of three weeks:

- **Week 1:** Teachers will meet with each student to set personalized learning goals.
- **Week 2:** Teachers will provide students with a data report of their progress and discuss their advancement toward the set goals.
- **Week 3:** Teachers and students will reflect on whether the students achieved their goals or if they need to make adjustments for the next cycle.

After the third week, teachers will restart the conferencing cycle with the same students. Having prepared the necessary pilot materials, the math teachers on the design team are now ready to test-drive the math conferencing experience with real students!

To access a prototype AI bot trained on the Innovative Models Exchange and the Leaps, scan the following QR code:

"Test-Drive" Activity 3: Test-Drive

By mid-spring, the Pi Pioneers are three weeks into their six-week Test of the math conferences, and they are learning a lot from students, educators, and all the unexpected things that can happen day to day in a school building.

Two significant patterns emerge in this phase of work. First, teams often underestimate the preparation needed for educators and students to test the design with enough fidelity to learn what they need to learn. When some of the educators running the test were not part of the initial design team, more time and effort were required to align on what a strong test looks like and to build the necessary capacity to make it happen. Second, and this is no surprise to anyone who has worked in schools, all the issues that could have happened to the Pi Pioneers did happen. There was a fire drill, several students were absent, and there was a special assembly that completely knocked the scheduled off course.

However, the intentional planning was still important, and Mr. Arthur helped them prepare for necessary course corrections by providing two guiding questions:

- How can we learn what we intended to learn and make the decisions we need to make within the required timeframe?
- How can we ensure we are treating students and educators fairly as we make adjustments?

As piloting goes on, the experience design team meets weekly to talk about how the goal conferences are going. One teacher notices something they did not expect: students know what goals are in a general sense, but they do not know how to set them for a specific subject like math. Teachers find that they need to directly teach students how to create and analyze examples of SMART goals—goals that are Specific, Measurable, Actionable, Relevant, and Time-bound.

By the end of piloting, the design team has a lot of information to think about. They have great examples of SMART math goals from students at different levels. They have thoughts from the students who are advising the math experience design team. They even have other teachers in the school saying how motivated students seem to reach their goals.

The tests, while not perfect, create amazing learning opportunities for the design team, and they can already see students becoming more motivated. The real, clear goals are helping students believe they can make a big difference in how well they do in math. Seeing students' confidence in math grow is especially powerful for the math teachers.

Here's an example of some SMART goals created by students with the help of teachers in goal conferences by eighth grade pre-algebra students:

My Goals in Pre-Algebra

Duration: April 1–April 30

1. I will get better at adding and subtracting negative numbers by doing 20 practice problems each day for the next 14 days. I will aim to get at least 17 out of 20 correct on the quiz at the end of the unit.
2. I will learn how to solve equations with one variable by going to a study group with my classmates once a week for the next four weeks. By the end of the month, I will be able to solve at least 15 equations on my own.
3. I will do this by reviewing my notes for 30 minutes each night and asking my teacher for help when I do not understand something.
4. I will learn how to graph linear equations using the slope-intercept form by the end of this week. I will watch two online videos that explain how to do this and practice using the graphing tool for at least 30 minutes each day.
5. I will get better at solving word problems by doing one hard problem from the textbook each day for the next four weeks. For each problem, I will write a short paragraph explaining how I solved it.

Note: Taken from multiple student work samples, developed with teacher support in math goal conferencing.

"Test-Drive" Activity 4: Learn from It and Update the Design

Even as the test is still underway, the Pi Pioneers team is learning from the effort. During the planning activity of this phase of work, they aligned on four learning questions that describe what they most wanted to learn from the test to inform improvements to the design and other next steps.

These questions were as follows:

- **Usability:** Is it easy enough for students and teachers to do math conferencing consistently?
- **Experience:** Do students and teachers have a positive experience that aligns to the intended Leaps we most want to maximize (Relevance, Rigor, Customization)?
- **Outcomes:** Do the math conferences lead to the goals we want?
- **Scalability:** Do we have the resources to win at this idea across the middle school math experience?

As a reminder, here are the learning goals that the Pi Pioneers set during the planning stage:

- Decide if this form of math conferencing should be part of the vision for multimodal math going forward.
- Understand how to set customized goals with students and monitor progress over time.
- Share evidence of improved experiences and outcomes, if they occur, with other community members to build clarity and conviction in the design vision.

During this learning step, the Pi Pioneers will seek answers to these learning questions and reflect on their goals using evidence gathered through the tools they compiled earlier. They decide to use multiple evidence-gathering approaches such as student interviews, end of unit tests, teacher debriefs, and observations.

Here's what they learned:

- 90 percent of participating students reported improved Community & Connection, especially with their teachers.
- Students needed direct instruction to understand what SMART goals look like and how to craft them.
- Educators found it extremely challenging to facilitate 10–15 minute discussions with individual students within a class period, even when other students had work to complete.
- Students loved achieving their goals and felt motivated to craft more ambitious goals building on prior success; they answered positively that they believed they could grow their math skills, critical to developing positive math identities.

■ Scheduling for even five conferences over six weeks was challenging; educators in the pilot reported that meeting with all 125 students would not be scalable in the current school schedule.

As they complete a full turn of the Design Cycle, the team will update their design idea (Math Goal Conferences) and determine next steps.

For common next steps, use the following QR code:

A common next step after a test is to prepare for another round of testing. The following chapter will explore how to determine when you are ready to move from testing part of the design to committing to it through more extensive implementation.

The Pi Pioneers determined from rounds of piloting that Math Goal Conferences were a powerful experience for boosting student confidence and building stronger teacher-student relationships. However, scaling these conferences across the whole of eighth grade would be impossible without changes to the schedules. The Pi Pioneers want to consider changing the schedule in the coming year, such that Fridays are used for conferences, independent work, and small-group instruction.

"Test-Drive": What Just Happened?

■ The Pi Pioneer design team steers Math Goal Conferences through a "full turn" of the Design Cycle, first determining the question they want answered in the first trial of the experience.

■ Students who participated in the tests showed increased motivation and confidence in math, bolstering their math identities.

■ Scheduling conferences for even five students was very challenging, and the team would need additional support in how to do this at a larger scale; to solve scalability issues, the team aims to try a new schedule on Fridays that allows students to move between conferencing, small-group instruction, and independent work.

"LOOK AHEAD": PREPARE TO CONTINUE THE JOURNEY

Key Activities:

1. Set priorities and goals, and engage key people for the year ahead.

"Look Ahead": Set Priorities and Goals, and Engage Key People for the Year Ahead

The fifth phase of work within the first year or so of the design journey involves preparing to continue the journey in the coming year. Typically design teams find it useful to set priorities, develop more detailed plans, and engage key people who will be required for the journey ahead.

Remember that Mr. Arthur has been running multiple Design Cycles at three schools. For the sake of clarity, we explored just one Design Cycle at the middle school. In reality, communities may be running several Design Cycles across multiple content areas and schools. The process is designed to go at the pace of a community's conditions. Mr. Arthur's task will now be to consolidate the learning and help the various design teams to reground in the vision of the design—empower all students in Elm Town to become adaptable, collaborative, and innovative problem-solvers, ready to thrive in an ever-changing world. In this phase of work, the system-level design team and the experience design teams will reflect together: *Where are we trying to go in our design journey, and what progress have we made so far?*

This is a critical moment to step back, synthesize all of the evidence of progress in design, conditions, implementation, experiences, and outcomes, and celebrate wins with your community. Design journeys are hard work, and change can be painful. It's important to seize as many opportunities as you can to celebrate progress and honor the contributions of various community members to that progress. In this process of taking stock, communities may surface challenges in moving toward the vision, such as the departure of a key leader, a need for additional funding, or a lack of clarity and alignment around key parts of your design vision.

Mr. Arthur brings together the broader system-level design team (which is inclusive of many of the educators on experience design teams from the school level). Together they will answer the question: *What should we prioritize to keep moving forward at a pace that aligns with our current conditions?*

The design team deliberates and decides on the following:

- Continue testing and refining the student experience designs they started crafting and testing this year and implement them when ready, and begin designing and testing additional components of the student experience.

- Piloting changes to the Friday schedule to accommodate the math goal conferencing student experience.
- Prioritize specific conditions alongside the design work, such as fundraising, enhancing leadership capacity, improving team culture, or transitioning from external to local design capacity.

For the priorities the community agrees on (usually the planning team at this stage, with input from others), they specify aspirations and goals for the year. These should be tied to the progress you want to make in design, conditions, implementation, experiences, and outcomes.

Examples of these priorities, goals, and the components described next can be found in sample community Journey Plans by scanning the following QR code:

After the design team has set priorities and goals, they will then develop more detailed plans. Mr. Arthur supports the team to do the following:

- Divide the upcoming year into a set of "rounds"—usually tied to schools' quarters—where they can set goals and plan activities within each round.
- Plan what evidence of progress is most important to gather and what "baseline data" needs to be collected in the near term.
- Align on key dates that they can get on calendars before everyone spreads out for the summer.

With increased clarity through these plans, the Elm Town design teams will be well-positioned to make the most of the summer and start the next phase of their journeys strong in the fall.

Finally, Mr. Arthur and the design teams will start to consider the people who should be involved in the upcoming stretch of the journey, by identifying the roles and teams they will need to drive each priority forward. This usually includes a priority owner or planning team for each priority, as well as various design teams, testing teams, advisory groups, and others depending on the priority.

With clarity and alignment on these three elements before the summer break, the Elm Town Unified design teams will be ready to do the most critical thing they can to improve learning experiences and outcomes in their community: continue making progress on their journey.

How to sustain and deepen the design journey after the critical first year or so is the focus of Chapter 9.

"Look Ahead": What Just Happened?

- Mr. Arthur, the Design Partner, and the Elm Town Unified design teams haven taken in all their learning from the year and are setting plans for the summer and coming school year.
- They have formally reflected on their North Star Vision and make key decisions about what aspects of the design they want to continue with in the future.

Advancing and Sustaining Your Design Journey

Key Points

- Successful communities sustain their design journeys through deepening their conditions, including a strong and diverse coalition that is invested in maintaining momentum.
- As communities progress, they develop more and more student experience components, iteratively improving designs, conditions, implementation, and outcomes.
- Design teams also periodically refine the overall vision to ensure relevance and effectiveness. Since context is constantly evolving, the design process is an ongoing, iterative activity.

For many communities implementing changes in school design, the period between the first year and subsequent years can be a significant gap where things fall apart. There are plenty of stories about ambitious change initiatives in schools and school systems that begin boldly but then fizzle out when it comes to sustaining and expanding the change beyond the initial small group of champions.

Communities often struggle to sustain change initiatives due to two main factors. First, high turnover rates among district and school leaders can diminish momentum. Without consistent leadership, it becomes challenging to maintain focus and commitment. Second, many schools rely on supplemental funding to initiate change, but these funds often prioritize early stages rather than the "critical middle" phase of sustaining and deepening progress. Once initial funding ends, schools may struggle to secure resources for ongoing staff, professional development, and materials needed to fully integrate the changes. As a result, promising initiatives can fade over time.

These challenges lead to a frustrating cycle of "initiative-itis" in many communities, with change efforts starting and stopping frequently. Leaders often feel stuck making modest tweaks to an outdated industrial model before leadership changes disrupt progress. These patterns are among the strongest forces keeping schools trapped in industrial-era learning that does not fit our present or future, even when young people need better and we all want better.

However, there is reason for optimism. Many communities are successfully navigating these obstacles and finding ways to sustain and deepen their design efforts. By leveraging the skills and momentum gained during the initial stages of their community-based design journeys, more communities can maintain progress. One key strategy is to involve a broad coalition of stakeholders, including teachers at all levels, to ensure the change effort can endure beyond the tenure of any individual. This approach is not just theoretical; we have witnessed numerous cases where design journeys have continued despite the departure of key leaders, thanks to the advocacy of others invested in the process.

Here, we outline the key activities communities undertake to maintain and deepen their design efforts over time. These activities are an extension of the community design process, as the Design Cycles to iteratively improve their designs, conditions, implementation, and, ultimately, their learning experiences and outcomes.

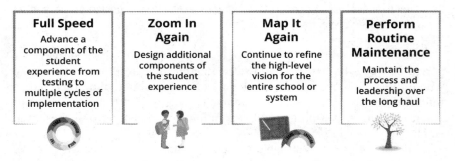

Full Speed	Zoom In Again	Map It Again	Perform Routine Maintenance
Advance a component of the student experience from testing to multiple cycles of implementation	Design additional components of the student experience	Continue to refine the high-level vision for the entire school or system	Maintain the process and leadership over the long haul

You will complete four phases of work over time:

1. **Shift from "Test-Drive to Full Speed":** Advance a component of the student experience from testing to multiple cycles of implementation.
2. **"Zoom In Again":** Design additional components of the student experience.
3. **"Map It Again":** Continue to refine the high-level vision for the entire school or system.
4. **"Perform Routine Maintenance":** Maintain the process and leadership over the long haul.

This set of activities enables communities to progress toward extraordinary experiences and outcomes for young people while fertilizing the soil of their community's conditions. This helps sustain and deepen the design journey and ensures the continued coherence and relevance of their overall design vision. We'll describe each of these work streams, including offering QR codes with open-source tools and resources you can use in your own journey.

In Chapter 7, Dr. Wallace and the dedicated educators of Elm Town Unified completed the first year of their community-based design process. Students who participated in the initial learning tests are already reporting that they feel more capable and able to accomplish the big goals they set for themselves. Educators are reinvigorated by their jobs and believe they play a crucial role in transforming learning for the students they serve.

Throughout this chapter, we will continue to follow implementation at one middle school within Elm Town Unified. However, Mr. Arthur, the district's head of instruction and Design Partner, facilitates multiple Design Cycles across the district. As the design journey advances, he will guide the district to scale its design initiatives from the initial pilot schools to a district-wide transformation.

SHIFT FROM "TEST-DRIVE TO FULL SPEED": ADVANCE A COMPONENT OF THE STUDENT EXPERIENCE FROM TESTING TO MULTIPLE CYCLES OF IMPLEMENTATION

Key Activities:

1. Plan and launch a phase of implementation.
2. Build what you need for implementation.
3. Implement.
4. Learn from it.
5. Update the design and plan next steps.

To recap from Chapter 7, in the first year or so, the Elm Town Unified School District embarked on the early stages of their community-based design journey. Dr. Wallace, the superintendent, was eager to build off of work that she had inherited from her predecessor. Years of strategic planning followed by leader turnover had left Elm Town with lots of false starts but provided a lot of information for Dr. Wallace to build from.

Elm Town's design teams, led by Mr. Arthur, developed an overall vision for the school system's design. They focused on math and created a vision for math-related experiences for middle school students. They selected one practice, math goal conferencing, to test and refine through multiple cycles of

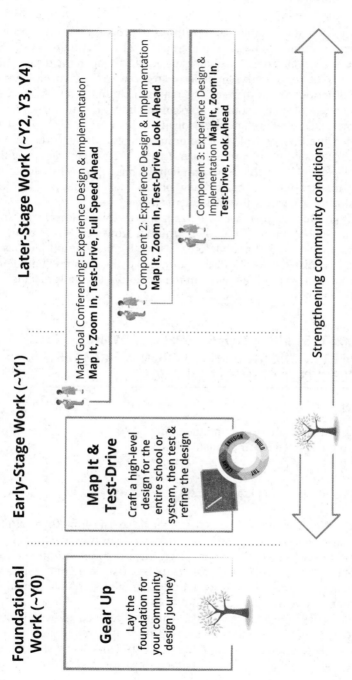

Foundational Work (~Y0)

Gear Up

Lay the foundation for your community design journey

Early-Stage Work (~Y1)

Map It & Test-Drive

Craft a high-level design for the entire school or system, then test & refine the design

ENVISION BUILD TRY TEAM

Later-Stage Work (~Y2, Y3, Y4)

Math Goal Conferencing: Experience Design & Implementation **Map It, Zoom In, Test-Drive, Full Speed Ahead**

Component 2: Experience Design & Implementation **Map It, Zoom In, Test-Drive, Look Ahead**

Component 3: Experience Design & Implementation **Map It, Zoom In, Test-Drive, Look Ahead**

Strengthening community conditions

Note: while whole-school/system design usually begins with a concentrated stretch, communities often return to it over time to update the design vision, build additional elements aligned to it, etc.

Learning, Envisioning, Building, and Trying. This allowed them to continuously update the vision.

In the ongoing pilot of math goal conferencing, if the results consistently show positive experiences and outcomes for students and the community conditions are favorable, the community will transition from the small-scale conferencing to the larger-scale implementation.

This may seem like a small transition, but for each component of the experience designed, there typically comes a moment or series of moments when the community decides to shift from a workshopping mindset—where it would not be too difficult to abandon an idea—to an implementation mindset. To sustain implementation in this new, committed mindset, the community builds communication, professional development, prioritization, and additional supports that make it more challenging to reverse course. While it's always possible (and advisable) to continue revising the design, at this stage, the community feels confident in their commitment to implementing the initiative consistently and sustainably.

When a community reaches this transition point, they will adjust their Design Cycles from being testing-focused to implementation-focused, utilizing the five sets of activities depicted in the picture shown earlier.

Transitioning from the "test-drive" to "full-speed" strengthens:

- *Student experiences and outcomes:* At this point, changes in experiences and outcomes should be consistently observed and tracked. During testing, you will likely have seen some progress in experiences and outcomes, but mostly at a smaller scale and in service of learning, iteration to the design, and building conditions. With implementation there is still focus on learning and iterating and building conditions, but the main emphasis shifts to ensure strong experiences and outcomes in this specific part of the student experience. As before, you'll have various tools to help you gauge progress, from surveys to assessments to observations to student work to interviews to administrative data, and more.
- *Implementation:* As the name suggests, this cycle is where you focus more on the important link between design and conditions and experiences and outcomes: good implementation. You'll set goals for both how much implementation happens (number of classrooms, grade levels, schools, etc.) and how well it's implemented (how closely it follows the design).
- *Design:* Even though making changes to the design is not the main focus anymore, it's still an important part of this phase. With each round of implementation, you will learn new things about the design vision and support needed to make it work on a larger scale, more consistently, and more sustainably. Sometimes this will require only small tweaks, but other times, you may need to make bigger changes. This happens when

you find that the original design and supports do not work well enough for the wider range of teachers and students or do not allow for enough consistency or sustainability.

■ *Conditions:* Strengthening conditions is still crucial in this phase. Through implementation, you'll continue investing in Conviction, Clarity, and expanding the Coalition. You'll focus heavily on building Capacity for quality and consistency, and nurture Culture as the design idea shifts from "something we are trying" to "how we do things here."

In Elm Town, Mr. Arthur and the design teams are ready to continue moving through the Design Cycle to achieve these results.

After a summer break of rest and learning, Mr. Arthur is back at the middle school with the Pi Pioneers. The majority of the team from the previous year has remained, with one member expressing renewed enthusiasm and commitment to seeing the vision through for the benefit of all students. Despite some turnover, there is sufficient continuity to bring new design team members up to speed and continue the work. Dr. Wallace and Mr. Arthur continue to expand the broader Coalition of stakeholders to support the design journey.

In the first year, the Pi Pioneers envisioned a bold learning environment design for math instruction. This design contains multiple modalities of teaching and learning. See the following image to recall what this experience design team envisioned:

BLENDED = MULTIPLE MODALITIES	Whole-Group Instruction	Small-Group Instruction	Online Learning
	Teacher-led instruction using high-quality instructional materials.	Teacher provides targeted instruction to a small group of students.	Students use online learning software to work independently in the classroom or computer lab.
	Peer Learning	**Independent Learning**	**Goal Conferencing**	**Tutoring**
	Students work together (on- or offline) to learn, work on projects, and create work products.	Students work alone to learn, work on projects, create work products, and take assessments.	Students set goals and discuss progress with teachers or peers.	Students work with a peer, teacher, or tutor to learn, work on projects, and create work products.

To review, Mr. Arthur and the Pi Pioneers could not take on such a bold vision in one step. During the "Zoom In" and "Test-Drive" phases of work in their first year, they decided to start with "Math Goal Conferencing" where students receive one-on-one or small-group support in setting goals and discussing progress. From all the team had learned by looking inward at their own school and looking outward to research and other learning models, they knew that they had to begin by building students' math identities—their self-perceptions regarding their abilities in the subject.

The first rounds of testing Math Goal Conferencing produced significant insights and gave the team confidence that they were on the right track. They learned that students and educators needed support to craft SMART goals for a content area like math. But once they got the hang of it, students loved watching themselves achieve their goals, which bolstered their growth mindset and self-perception that they could improve in math. On the operational side of the tests, there were challenges to solve for. Educators found it difficult to host conferences during class time even when students had work to complete. In the first year and within the first few months of the new school year, the Pi Pioneers set out to iron these wrinkles. By early fall, the team was ready to launch a phase of implementation.

"Test-Drive to Full-Speed" Activity 1: Plan and Launch a Phase of Implementation

Transitioning from the test-drive to full-speed implementation means bringing the student experience to a larger group of learners. First, the Pi Pioneers set goals for the desired student experiences (the Leaps) and outcomes (what students should know and be able to do). The team also sets targets for the scale (number of classrooms and timeline) and fidelity (how closely the experience follows the design). Finally, they consider how to collect evidence, monitor progress, and make adjustments as needed.

The team collaborates to make other important decisions, such as assigning roles to individuals involved in this early implementation phase. This includes identifying the educators and students who will participate in the experience, as well as the support staff responsible for building capacity, collecting data, and providing additional assistance.

At the middle school, Mr. Arthur and the Pi Pioneers decide that they will implement Math Goal Conferencing for all seventh and eighth grade students during an elongated Friday math block of one-hundred minutes. This required change to one of the key System Elements: scheduling. This change in scheduling brings the new experience to two hundred and fifty students from the initial five. This will require professional development and support for the two seventh grade math teachers who are not on the experience design team. Implementation is all about expanding access to experiences for students and thoughtfully supporting more adults to change their practice from industrial-era experiences to extraordinary ones.

Implementation planning is common in school and school systems. As mentioned in Chapter 2, system leaders and educators frequently engage in some version of the Design Cycle: Envisioning, Building, Trying, Learning, and Iterating. However, in community-based design, the desired changes are often more ambitious. The coalitions are usually broader and less top-down, which creates a greater need for input and deep stakeholder engagement throughout the process. Community-based design also typically flexes between implementation and the design vision, as the community continues to explore the ways to achieve Leaps in this aspect of the student experience at a larger scale.

"Test-Drive to Full-Speed" Activity 2: Build What You Need for Implementation

After planning, the Pi Pioneers will build what's needed for implementation. Mr. Arthur will assist the team to borrow, adapt, or create the necessary materials to run the implementation and review the results. Similar to the Test-Drive in the first year, communities will need to build three types of things:

- Materials to run the implementation, such as lesson plans, assessments, PD sessions, and family communications
- Tools to gather evidence, including surveys, interview guides, observation rubrics, and data analysis tools
- Strong conditions to conduct a successful implementation, like Clarity and Capacity among teachers who will administer the new experiences

Just like in the "Test-Drive" phase, "building" materials can be loosely interpreted as "build, adapt, or borrow." Mr. Arthur is particularly adept at helping his design teams strengthen their skills by adapting materials versus starting from scratch. As a result, various design teams within Elm Town are able to progress through the Design Cycle more efficiently.

The Pi Pioneers will spend much of their working time together in the fall building materials and supporting the seventh grade teachers who will be implementing goal conferencing.

"Test-Drive to Full-Speed" Activity 3: Implement

By early November, the Pi Pioneers are ready to bring the Math Goal Conferencing experience to all seventh and eighth grade students. This includes supporting educators and others to implement the design, monitoring progress and supporting course corrections along the way, and navigating unexpected challenges or changes to the plan. They spent the better part of late summer and early fall building all the necessary tools and providing professional development to teachers who were not part of the initial testing phases. They also asked their math curriculum specialists and ed tech companies to be a thought partner in the best data to focus on to set goals within their programs.

"Test-Drive to Full-Speed" Activity 4: Learn from It

Toward the end of the cycle, the Pi Pioneers are learning from this phase of implementation and using that information to update the design of Math Goal Conferences. As before, Mr. Arthur will play a significant role in helping the team to synthesize insights about outcomes, experiences, usability, and scalability, and use those lessons to determine what should be prioritized next.

In Elm Town, the Pi Pioneers have a lot to be proud of. Dr. Wallace decides to spend an entire day observing seventh and eighth grade math classes at the middle school. She shares with Mr. Arthur that these are some of the most engaging classrooms she's seen in a decade. Students are able to share with her specific and customized goals that they have developed in math, speaking about their strengths and areas for growth in profound new ways. She observes a different energy in these middle school math classes; students aren't just complying, they are excited to learn. As a result, the math teachers share, class averages on unit tests have gone from 62 percent to 79 percent.

Here's what the Pi Pioneers learned from this first round of Math Goal Conferencing implementation:

- **Outcomes:** Class averages on end-of-unit tests increased by an average of 10 percent; 60 percent of students met their declared SMART goals.
- **Experiences:** In the Leaps Student Voice survey, students report feeling like math is more relevant now (a surprise to the Pi Pioneers); seventh-graders especially reported that they preferred having conferences in groups of two, rather than one-on-one.
- **Usability:** The tools developed for the Goal Conferencing needed more options and examples for students who learn differently; these students also needed greater support in monitoring their progress over time with increased visual rewards, like stickers.
- **Scalability:** Scheduling the conferences over a nine-week period for two hundred and fifty students with the additional Friday time was challenging, but possible. Teachers all report using morning advisory time, lunch time, and some after-school study hour time to complete all conferences if students were absent or needed additional time. Educators like the new math schedule but want to continue to tweak the schedule. Educators also observe that some students needed more frequent touchpoints than others, and they want to customize the experiences even further.

In general, the evidence collected during a "learn from it" implementation cycle can vary in its nature and implications. Sometimes, the data will be more formative, leading to incremental changes. Other times, particularly at midyear and end-of-year points, access to more summative data may allow a team to draw larger conclusions. For instance, through the Leaps Student Voice Survey, students might report stronger Connection & Community, or annual math assessments show improved results. These are some of the most thrilling moments in the design journey, when communities witness their efforts yielding tangible results and meaningful change for a growing number of students.

"Test-Drive to Full-Speed" Activity 5: Update the Design and Plan Next Steps

To close out this phase of work, the Pi Pioneers make updates to the design of Math Goal Conferencing and plan for next steps. There are four clusters of work that they will tend to now:

- Revising the design
- Fertilizing the community conditions soil
- Making improvements to existing implementation rounds
- Continuing to lay the groundwork for further implementation, scaling at the pace of conditions

The Pi Pioneers will update Math Goal Conferencing in the following ways based on information collected from implementation:

- Seventh grade conferences will be conducted two on one, as seventh graders overwhelmingly reported positive experiences with having a peer of their choice as a goal buddy.
- Eighth graders will be given the option to participate in either one-on-one or two-on-one goal conferencing settings.
- They will utilize various modalities for goal conferencing, including live meetings during the school day and after-school tutoring hours, Zoom meetings, and pre-recorded videos between educators and students.

For the Pi Pioneers these cycles of implementation technically never end, although they will likely invest fewer resources and attention in them over time for any given part of the student experience.

You can find some additional guidance and supports around navigating these cycles of implementation using the following QR code:

"From Test Drive to Full Speed": What Just Happened?

- The Pi Pioneers expanded Math Goal Conferencing from the initial group of five students to include all seventh and eighth grade students; doing so required them to change an essential System Element—the schedule to allow for one-hundred-minute Friday math blocks.
- While the implementation process is similar to the test-drive, there is a stronger focus on the quality of materials and preparing educators who were not involved in the initial tests.
- In community-based design, it is crucial to continually update the design vision, even during implementation, to remain responsive to student needs and ensure that practices are effectively achieving the intended outcomes and experiences.

"ZOOM IN AGAIN": DESIGN ADDITIONAL COMPONENTS OF THE STUDENT EXPERIENCE

Key Activities:

1. Craft a detailed vision for another specific aspect of the student experience.

Communities that successfully keep their journeys going and make them deeper work on designing more parts of the student experience over time. If the community has already created a guiding design vision for the whole school or system, like they have in Elm Town, this process can involve going back to that vision and asking similar questions to what led to the first focus on a part of the student experience, such as the following:

- What part of the student experience should we change to reach our goals for graduates and design principles?
- What's one big but possible idea we could try next to keep making progress toward our vision?
- Where does the data show a key area of outcomes or experiences that we should work on?

If the community has not yet created a design vision for the whole school or system—if they skipped that step early on to focus on one part of the student experience—this could be a good time to go back and do that. It can help make sure ongoing efforts work well together and help figure out what new part of the student experience to design next and why. This is suggested but not required; we know of some communities that successfully added several parts of the student experience before going back to look at their overall guiding vision, but that's not the usual way.

It's now January in Elm Town Unified, and the first round of implementation has finished with Math Goal Conferencing. Mr. Wallace and the middle school experience designers, the Pi Pioneers, are ready to "Zoom In Again" on a different part of their learning environment design.

Some communities might add on other parts of the experience—beyond math—as they zoom back in, but Elm Town's Pi Pioneers continue to focus on math, layering in more elements to enhance Customization. They explore online learning experiences to differentiate instruction and meet each student's unique needs, leveraging the abundance of available ed tech tools.

Figure 9.1 illustrates an overview of what that process looks like:

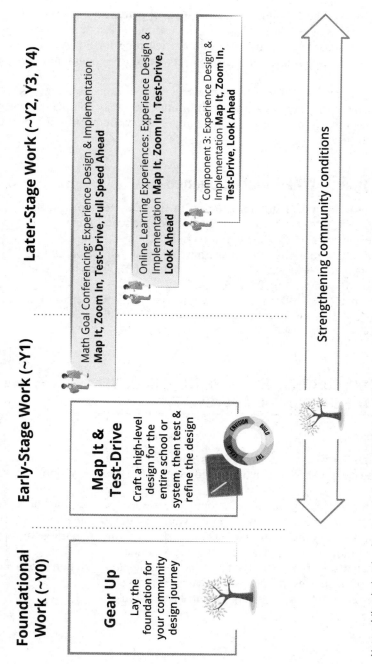

Foundational Work (~Y0)

Gear Up

Lay the foundation for your community design journey

Early-Stage Work (~Y1)

Map It & Test-Drive

Craft a high-level design for the entire school or system, then test & refine the design

Later-Stage Work (~Y2, Y3, Y4)

Math Goal Conferencing: Experience Design & Implementation **Map It, Zoom In, Test-Drive, Full Speed Ahead**

Online Learning Experiences: Experience Design & Implementation **Map It, Zoom In, Test-Drive, Look Ahead**

Component 3: Experience Design & Implementation **Map It, Zoom In, Test-Drive, Look Ahead**

Strengthening community conditions

Note: while whole-school/system design usually begins with a concentrated stretch, communities often return to it over time to update the design vision, build additional elements aligned to it, etc.

FIGURE 9.1

In community-based design, change happens gradually. Communities tackle different aspects of their learning environment design over time, working toward a shared vision of extraordinary learning for all. Attempting to change everything at once is likely to overwhelm the system and the people in it.

As Elm Town proceeds through these cycles with various components over time, moving at the speed that their conditions allow may compel them to pause or slow down the process for one component while prioritizing or accelerating another.

"Zoom In Again": What Just Happened?

- With the first round of implementation in the rear-view mirror, the design teams in Elm Town will now layer on another component of the student experience to take through the Design Cycle.
- At the middle school, the Pi Pioneers have decided to layer on Online Learning experiences, which is another piece of their math multimodal learning environment.
- The Pi Pioneers will follow the same approaches outlined here and in Chapter 7 to learn, envision, build, and test online learning experiences.

"MAP IT AGAIN": CONTINUE TO REFINE THE HIGH-LEVEL VISION FOR THE ENTIRE SCHOOL OR SYSTEM

Key Activities:

1. Make a plan to revisit the guiding design vision.
2. Update the design vision, structures, and execute the updated vision.

Concurrent to layering on more student experiences and taking them through the Design Cycle, Mr. Arthur and Dr. Wallace will unite again to lead the design teams on another important set of work: revisiting, updating, and deepening the guiding design vision for the entire school system. The community will review the vision after the first year of innovation and then revisit it in the third, fifth, and seventh years of the design process.

Figure 9.2 represents their current system-level vision.

MISSION

Elm Town Unified School District is committed to empowering all students to become adaptable, collaborative, and innovative problem-solvers ready to thrive in an ever-changing world.

DESIGN PRINCIPLES

Active Self-Direction	Customization	Relevance	Rigorous Learning

GRADUATE AIMS

Team Players (Growth Mindset & Communication)	Adaptable Futurists (Vocational Knowledge & Skills)	Independent Thinkers (Responsible Decision-Making & Critical Thinking)	Community-Minded (Work Across Lines of Difference & Collaboration)

EXPERIENCES

Blended Learning	Project-Based Learning	Multi-Tiered-Supports	High-Dosage Tutoring	Circle Practice	Community Projects

FIGURE 9.2

Engaging this work is crucial for two reasons:

- Constantly rebuilding Clarity and Conviction among current community members through active engagement with the guiding design vision, embedding it into structures and routines.
- Periodically revisiting and updating the vision to keep pace with the rapidly changing world and evolving community needs, ensuring it remains relevant and effective.

This process strengthens the following:

- *Design*: The design vision and the supports tied to the vision will be updated to better match the community's current context and aspirations.
- *Conditions*: This process involves a re-investing in conviction and clarity in the design vision and in a broad coalition involved and invested in supporting the vision.

"Map It Again" Activity 1: Make a Plan to Revisit the Guiding Design Vision

The process that Elm Town Unified will take to revisit, update, and deepen its guiding system vision is once again anchored in the Design Cycle. This phase of work is valuable for a community as it builds the foundation of Clarity, Coalition, and Conviction in the system's efforts. The design team will use many of the same "look inward and outward" activities and tools described in Chapter 7.

In Elm Town Mr. Arthur will guide the team to ask and answer questions like these: How well is this vision enabling us to meet our mission? To what extent are our students and staff thriving? What is possible or known now that wasn't possible or known when we last crafted or updated this vision?

To generate the plan, the design team leads a monthlong community-wide engagement effort. They are surprised to find that new parents, educators, and students largely reinforced and supported their initial ideas. Elm Town's mission to develop adaptable, collaborative, and innovative problem-solving students seemed more relevant than ever in a time when generative AI was making rapid daily advancements. Educators within the community emphasized the growing importance of teamwork and collaboration, expressing that the district needed to intensify its efforts to provide students with learning experiences and opportunities that foster these skills.

"Map It Again" Activity 2: Update the Design Vision, Structures, and Execute the New Vision

After the design team looks inward and outward, they compare new insights to their current vision and update the design vision to incorporate those insights.

In Elm Town they make a few adjustments to their design vision:

- Adding Connection and Community to design principles emphasizes the importance of relationships and collaboration skills for the future of work.
- Changing "Independent Thinkers" to "Independent and Collaborative Thinkers" acknowledges the value of critical thinking both individually and in dialogue with others.
- Insights from reflection prioritize creating experiences to help students become "Team Players," as young people overemphasized independent thinking.

The updated system design vision is shown in Figure 9.3.

Based on these insights, Mr. Arthur and the design team will revise the materials and resources connected to the guiding vision, such as handbooks, training sessions, plans, and sometimes even the physical space if necessary, perhaps even painting their graduate goals on school walls. Lastly, Mr. Arthur and Dr. Wallace will guide the different teams across the system to put the updated vision into action, making sure their community is working with the most current vision and does not experience a disconnect between what they have agreed on and what actually takes place in classrooms, schools, district offices, and community areas.

With this updated guiding vision, Mr. Arthur and the design teams also have guidance on where to prioritize their efforts. This collaborative exchange among all the stakeholders in a school community is what makes community-based design a productive process. From here, the Elm Town design teams will continue their journey for years to come, building upon the wisdom of the local community and responding to the reality of student experiences and outcomes.

In the next phase of work, you will discover how communities like Elm Town will "Perform Routine Maintenance," attending to the process, people, and leadership over the long haul.

MISSION

Elm Town Unified School District is committed to empowering all students to become adaptable, collaborative, and innovative problem-solvers ready to thrive in an ever-changing world.

DESIGN PRINCIPLES

Active Self-Direction	Customization	Relevance	Rigorous Learning	Connection & Community

GRADUATE AIMS

Team Players (Growth Mindset & Communication)	Adaptable Futurists (Vocational Knowledge & Skills)	Independent & Collaborative Thinkers (Responsibl Decision-Making Critical Thinking)	Community-Minded (Work Across Lines of Difference & Collaboration)

EXPERIENCES

Blended Learning	Project-Based Learning	Multi-Tiered-Supports	High-Dosage Tutoring	Circle Practice	Community Projects

FIGURE 9.3

"Map It Again": What Just Happened?

- Elm Town Unified revisited its system design vision by looking inward and outward.
- By listening to educators, caregivers, and students again, the design team gained new insights about the system design that will impact their future prioritization efforts.

"PERFORM ROUTINE MAINTENANCE": MAINTAIN THE PROCESS AND LEADERSHIP OVER THE LONG HAUL

Key Activities:

1. Manage the process.
2. Actively improve key Community Conditions.
3. Reactively improve key Community Conditions.
4. Create capacity for the Design Partner role.

This chapter began by highlighting some of the forces that can make it challenging to sustain and deepen design journeys. Strengthening conditions is not a one-time event but an ongoing practice of care and attention to keep the environment conducive to the design innovation. This final section examines how these Conditions can be intentionally cultivated, in tandem with the design work, as design journeys mature and evolve over time. There are four main categories of activities that maintain and strengthen the Conditions in parallel with ongoing design efforts.

"Perform Routine Maintenance" Activity 1: Manage the Process

Managing the entire process involves initiating the work each year (or any other designated period of the journey), coordinating planning sessions and reflection meetings for each quarterly "round" (or however you have structured the work within a given stretch), and conducting more comprehensive reviews and planning at the end of each year.

You can find examples of round-level plans and additional tools for stewarding the overall process using the following QR code:

As the design journey moves forward, it's important to keep a strong, dedicated team engaged across the school and the wider system. This team should stay focused and committed to the journey's importance. To do this, you can use different strategies, like regularly sharing the journey's unfolding story, pointing out recent progress, and updating your Community Case for Change when needed to include new insights and developments.

You can find some tools and examples that other communities have used using the following QR code:

Often, there's a journey planning team that drives this work each year, which is usually an evolution of the initial planning team that kicked off the journey. Either way, like with that initial team, this planning team should at least include one or two school or district administrators (ideally including a project manager or "co-pilot" who is not the district superintendent or school principal), as well as any Design Partners supporting the work.

"Perform Routine Maintenance" Activity 2: Actively Improve Key Community Conditions

Second, you'll actively work to improve key Community Conditions for the journey. This is typically included as one or more specific priorities for a given year, such as fundraising, enhancing leadership capacity at the school or system level, or strengthening an aspect of team culture, like fostering inclusion and connection across differences. These priorities are often identified during the annual planning process, discussed at the end of Chapter 7. The guiding question is: "What essential conditions need the most attention to ensure continued progress on our journey?" To answer this, you can draw on your own observations and seek input and feedback from others in your community.

Many communities find it helpful to use a Community Conditions Reflection Guide (use the following QR code) to gather feedback from various members, and teams are sometimes pleasantly surprised by the results. For more information on strengthening leadership capacity, one of the most common proactive priorities, refer to Chapter 10.

"Perform Routine Maintenance" Activity 3: Reactively Improve Key Community Conditions

Third, you'll need to address key Community Conditions as they come up. This might include handling the departure of a key leader, dealing with significant pushback or cultural challenges within the community (from boards and district leaders to school-based leaders, educators, families, and students), or taking advantage of an unexpected opportunity to share a major milestone or secure new funding. A common mistake is when a community "puts their heads down and keeps pushing through" instead of pausing to consider how to address an unexpected issue that impacts the conditions. This can happen because the team underestimates the importance of the issue or, more often, because they have not created the structures or flexibility to reflect and respond. While each specific issue is unexpected, the fact that something unexpected will come up should not be. Anticipate that these types of issues will arise and need to be addressed every year of the journey.

You probably have a lot of experience and strategies for addressing issues that come up with the conditions. Use what you know works well. As you do, also think about the following:

- How can we handle this issue while still keeping our design journey moving forward?
- How can we give this the attention it needs without falling into the trap of leaders spending all their time "putting out fires" instead of leading us toward great learning for everyone?
- How can we use the fact that many other communities like ours are on design journeys and have faced similar issues? What help is available to us in dealing with this issue?

This is another area where being plugged into a network of leaders, communities, and supports can be helpful. You can use the following QR code to find ways to access this network:

"Perform Routine Maintenance" Activity 4: Create Capacity for the Design Partner Role

As with Mr. Arthur in the Elm Town Unified example, Design Partners play a crucial role in supporting communities' design journeys. Typically, communities create capacity for this role. Various people can serve as Design Partners, including district staff or leaders, teachers on special assignment, local nonprofits, or independent consultants. Early in a community's design journey it can be beneficial to have someone outside the school building, such as district staff or an external partner with experience supporting similar journeys, take on this role. As the journey progresses, systems and schools can often handle more of the Design Partner role internally, especially if they intentionally build the capacity of one or more people to fill the role. This is usually done through an apprenticeship-style "I do, we do, you do" approach, working with existing Design Partners to gradually reduce external support and increase local support over time. Communities have various options for building and accessing this essential capacity, which we will discuss in the book's conclusion.

The four communities in Part 2 have been on their design journeys for several years: Van Ness for eight years, Northern Cass for four years, Brooklyn STEAM for seven years, and Intrinsic for nine years. Such continuity in a change effort is rare in the education sector, but it does not have to be. When communities nurture their Conditions both through and alongside their Design Cycles, they give their work the best chance of success and can continue progress toward their vision of extraordinary learning for all students.

In the next part, we focus on several factors that can turbocharge your community's design journey including leadership, the ecosystem you are operating within, and the many sources of support all around you.

How to Turbocharge Your Community Design Journey

In this final part, you will delve into several factors that can turbocharge your design journey, including your own leadership, the ecosystem you're operating within, and the many sources of support all around you.

Chapter 10 helps you examine your own leadership. When we ask ourselves what separates the design journeys that succeed from the ones that stall or fizzle, one thing pops out over and over again: learner-centered leadership. You will walk away understanding what this kind of leadership is all about, how it functions, and what you can do to grow and exert your own learner-centered leadership, whether you are a superintendent, a board member, a teacher, a parent, or even a student.

Chapter 11 explores the number-one challenge that leaders report that makes innovation challenging: policy barriers. This chapter highlights three categories of barriers you'll face: assessment and accountability, seat time and graduation requirements, funding and other resources. For each barrier, you will walk away with strategies for how you can navigate these barriers, including operating within constraints as well as how to push to transform them.

The conclusion outlines the many supports you can draw from and helps you see that you are in good company, even if it feels at times like you might be swimming upstream alone. We emphasize that leading toward designs that enable extraordinary learning for all is not easy. If it were, it would already be happening everywhere. This final chapter will leave you with the good news that you are surrounded by a wide range of supports—including people within your own community, capacity-building experiences you can bring into your community, networks you can join, models you can learn and borrow from, external Design Partners, and more.

CHAPTER 10

Your Leadership Matters

Key Points

- "Learner-centered leadership" is what separates the design journeys that succeed from the ones that stall or fizzle. This special kind of leadership *places learners (of all ages) at the center of all decision-making.*
- This kind of leadership can be exerted by anyone and everyone throughout the system, and this chapter highlights specific actions that people in various roles can take.
- Learner-centered leadership grows from the inside out—through ongoing cycles of action and reflection.

In Chapter 3 you read about Cynthia Robinson-Rivers's relentless thirst for knowledge and personal growth. This learner-centered core drove her desire to both broaden and deepen her experiences and knowledge as an educator: first relocating to Washington DC and teaching in classrooms for three years; then working as an assistant principal, before joining the District of Columbia Public Schools (DCPS) central office working on human capital initiatives related to teacher evaluation, recognition, and retention; continuously visiting many schools in the DC area, observing what distinguished the very best teachers and classrooms; and finally, founding Van Ness Elementary, the remarkable school focused on the whole child that you read about earlier in this book. Throughout this professional evolution, Robinson-Rivers was on a perpetual quest for knowledge, information, and inspiration. She became a fellow at Harvard's Project Zero, exploring learning connected to the arts. There she discovered bold interdisciplinary teaching methods. She studied experts like Howard Gardner and Ron Ritchhart, along with practices like Reggio Emilia, playful learning, teaching for understanding, and visible thinking.

Robinson-Rivers keenly felt her own evolution as an educator and a leader through her professional learning journey, and she wanted the educators working at Van Ness to have the same kinds of experiences to inform their own classroom environments. Moreover, she knew that for the Whole Child Model to be effectively integrated throughout the school, her educators would need a shared learner-centered mindset to support these young people. But this is not something a leader just decides is important and articulates—it necessitates a series of cascading actions to make this commitment to professional learning possible. Robinson-Rivers knew that developing learner-centered educators was critical to Van Ness's success, so she allocated whole staff time for professional learning, dedicated financial resources to fund off-site teacher trainings, and hired a counselor to support mental health of adults on staff. Robinson-Rivers's commitment to her own learning, and developing learners of all ages, is one of the keys to the success and staying-power of the design innovation of the Whole Child Model.

When we ask ourselves what separates the design journeys that succeed from the ones that stall or fizzle, one thing stands out over and over again: leadership.

Running amazing classrooms, schools, and systems has always required strong leadership. But what we have observed is a special kind of leadership—a deep, thoughtful, inquiry-based leadership, grounded in trust and humility, and above all an overarching desire to create an equitable, extraordinary environment with students at the center. This is leadership that can create a culture, as Superintendent Tom Rooney from Lindsay Unified School District (LUSD) (Central Valley, California) put it, "where every learner is loved and feels like they belong and are given what they need, so they come to love learning, love themselves, and advance their own life." Like everything you have read in this book so far, this is not the traditional, industrial-era definition of leadership working in the usual ways within existing systems—this is a version of leadership we call "learner-centered leadership."

Learner-centered leadership places learners (of all ages) at the *center* of systems in order to cultivate the conditions for extraordinary learning for all.

The understanding that successful design journeys depend on engaged and committed leadership stems from nearly a decade of working in the field with hundreds of schools in districts across the country, where system leaders, school administrators, educators, and students have shifted to a mindset of learner-centered leadership. This leadership mindset at all levels, which you will learn about through this chapter, creates conditions for successful community design journeys.

This chapter describes what makes learner-centered leadership so impactful, introduces a framework that shows how it is developed, and reveals how learner-centered leadership empowers learners at all levels to embrace their own sense of agency. To make this tangible, we highlight moments where leaders you have already read about at Van Ness, Brooklyn STEAM, Northern Cass, and Intrinsic advance innovative design journeys through their leadership. Finally, this chapter concludes with action steps for leaders at all levels, from superintendents to students, to support design journeys centered on learners.

A SPECIAL KIND OF LEADERSHIP FOR A SPECIAL KIND OF CHALLENGE

We often fantasize about how much easier this work would be if we were designing schools in a brand-new town, built in a place where no one has ever lived before. There would be no history, no personal politics, no change management to deal with. But most readers of this book, and the leaders spotlighted throughout this chapter, are operating inside of existing systems. All must work within their current structures and cultures to do the very best for learners every day, while simultaneously evolving the design of their learning environments.

Let us be clear: leadership is not the same as occupying a position of authority. We've seen plenty of people in high-ranking positions who are not operating as leaders. In a school, they might be distant or totally inaccessible or completely numbers driven; they may have a title, but they are not creating a nurturing environment for growth in the classroom or in the school culture. Conversely, we have collaborated with many principals, teachers, parents, school board members, and even students who, despite not holding top leadership positions, have demonstrated remarkable leadership. They listen, learn, and take action alongside students and teachers in their schools and in the process build coalitions, foster conviction, and cultivate a culture of innovation.

WHAT DO LEARNER-CENTERED LEADERS DO?

From working with hundreds of leaders across the country and through a national superintendent leadership development program that we run, we have identified six actions that set learner-centered leaders apart from others. As you will read later in the chapter, these actions derive directly from how these leaders conceive of their roles.

Listen to Learners (of All Ages)

Learner-centered leaders are committed to doing what is best for learners, which begins with engaging and listening to them. This seems like an obvious move, but we too often observe decisions impacting young people that are not deeply informed by their voices because many leaders are not asking them questions. Instead, leaders frequently make decisions based on other pressures or assumed needs. Learner-centered leaders deeply listen to learners to make decisions, prioritize tasks, and spend their time on what is most beneficial to learners. The most learner-centered leaders may take this one step further and bring learners to the decision-making table to elevate learners' needs, perspectives, and expertise as part of vision-setting and decision-making. (Side note: this can also create experiences of agency for learners!)

At the most basic, listening begins with asking questions, and to ask questions you need to get people in a room or find a method for soliciting input. Robinson-Rivers at Van Ness increased the listening opportunities by being proactive in building relationships with families. Opportunities to create connection, like monthly coffees and ice cream socials, opened the door for communication. Greeting families at drop-off and learning caretakers' names built trust. More formal speaking engagements were recorded for caregivers who were unable to attend in person.

With this baseline familiarity there was an opportunity to solicit feedback from learners and families, in person or through questionnaires, about what is and is not working in the school. This investment in two-way communication made it possible for parents to share specifics about their children and what they need. Now the classroom, designed where every child has a specific job, is targeted to build the executive function skills of the child that needs them. Principal Robinson-Rivers, listening to parent and student learners, built a culture of trust that made the design itself more effective.

Make Decisions to Serve *All* Learners

Learner-centered leaders make decisions and take action so that the system functions to serve *all* learners in the ways they need and deserve. If the design of the school or the function of the system is not optimally serving learners, a learner-centered leader makes changes. They interrogate all aspects of their system from teaching and learning to human resources to transportation to budgeting and ensure all structures and staff are set up to serve learners.

For example, Principal Robinson-Rivers explored the way breakfast was served at Van Ness. The industrial design of schools assumes that students will eat in a large space with others, typically a cafeteria. But by listening to students who expressed how stressful that environment was for them, the design team redesigned the entire morning to be about what learners needed, not the structural design of the building. Breakfast moved to the classroom as a practice of the larger Strong Start component of the Whole Child Model.

> "All our decisions and actions are in direct response to the unique needs of the students that we serve. We interrogate all our systems, structures, policies, and behaviors, and we are agile to meet the needs of all kids."
> —Learner-Centered Leadership Lab participant

Be the Chief Learner and Model Learning for Others

Learner-centered leaders are first and foremost learners. They model learning by asking questions, seeking diverse inputs and perspectives, approaching challenges with curiosity, and exhibiting a learner mindset. Instead of first giving answers, they pose questions and empower others in the system to find solutions. The humility and curiosity of learner-centered leaders is often part of their core identity. As lifelong learners, these leaders frequently model the work of unlearning and learning that is critical for personal and collective growth.

Dr. Cory Steiner was a chief learner as he led the visioning effort for making the Leaps you read about in Chapter 4. Not only had he learned from surveying the community that they wanted to graduate students that went into college, career, or military, but he also took in what he was learning from additional research, employers, and additional family/student surveys. The insights that Dr. Steiner uncovered during the visioning process helped to inform and validate their graduate profile. A Northern Cass learner would need to be accountable, showing responsibility for all their choices and following through with commitments. At Northern Cass, learners would need a growth mindset—flexible and willing to put in extra effort when things get challenging and always striving to improve.

> One superintendent reflects: "Learner-centered leadership to me means that we are constantly learning from every situation we encounter that challenges our leadership approach. To believe we already have all the answers is to be limited in our approach."
> —LCLL participant

Cultivate a Culture of Learning and Growth

Learner-centered leaders create a culture of learning that encourages the social and emotional development of young people and adults. These leaders build strong, emotionally secure relationships and create spaces with psychological safety. This culture makes it possible for all learners to take the risks necessary for learning and innovation. Further, a culture of openness and empathy creates opportunities for greater alignment of issues and systems. Learner-centered leaders recognize that learning and innovation are not linear processes and make it safe to iterate and grow.

To support learning and professional growth, Principal Robinson-Rivers at Van Ness elementary sent multiple staff members to external trainings with organizations like Conscious Discipline, PBL Works, the Washington International School Summer Institute for Teachers, and even tours of Reggio Emilia classrooms in Italy. This commitment was both a signal that she believed in teacher leadership and growth and that she trusted them to bring back what they learned and share it with the rest of the staff. But it was also a way to clarify the vision for the design of the Whole Child Model, because the trainings encouraged teachers to constantly be in discussion about what they had learned and continually iterate on how to apply it throughout the design itself.

> "Being a learner-centered leader is about making sure there's a safe space for risk-taking to happen. That the focus is on how we learn, which requires both psychological safety and push."
> —Learner-Centered Leadership Lab participant

Empower and Develop Others to Become Learner-Centered Leaders

Learner-centered leaders empower others by building confidence and capacity through leadership opportunities.

This mirrors and encourages a shift to learner agency where learners determine their own path and teachers and administrators elevate student voice. In action this might look like encouraging and supporting structured ways to gather student feedback and then subsequent actions taken as a result of that feedback. It also raises the level of personal accountability for learners of all ages and the confidence that accompanies agency. Equally important is the coaching and development of others that learner-centered leaders provide—these leaders believe every human (young or adult) is capable of growth and worthy of investment to grow their capacity.

In Chapter 6 you read about cofounders Ami Ghandi's and Melissa Zaikos's bold vision for Intrinsic, but like all design journeys there were challenging moments, and the design team led by Ami encountered one in year five when they recorded a drop in academic performance in math. In the long-term visioning, they had planned for a future deep dive into what actually happens in the classroom, and this disappointing academic data expedited the exploration. Ami saw this moment as an opportunity to learn from teachers in the classroom and in so doing strengthen the design.

What this looked like in practice was teachers leading the Design Cycle, running additional pilots to tweak and improve the math features. The process of investigating in detail what was going on in the classrooms built clarity as the teachers aligned the math features with the vision, which in turn built conviction in the model. In this example, you see leadership empowering and developing others to become learner-centered leaders, as well as the way that act positively impacts design evolution and the strengthening of conditions in the process.

> "It's about empowerment; that's the most important thing I do. Thinking about who else can take this on and lead it. Many leaders see the development of others as a part of their role, but learner-centered leaders do this by building trusting relationships and empowering others for the sake of the individual's growth as well as the evolution of the system itself."
> —Learner-Centered Leadership Lab participant

Engage with Other Leaders in the Ecosystem to Create and Support Integrated Experiences for Learners

Learner-centered leaders recognize that education does not end when the school day is over. It does not stop at the walls of school or the borders of the campus. Learning can happen anywhere and everywhere, and factors outside of formal "school" play an enormous role in the school's ability to serve learners. Housing, nutrition, transportation, jobs, health and wellness, safety, and so much more impact learners every day. Rather than focusing only on what happens inside their system, learner-centered leaders are concerned with anything and everything that's relevant for young people's abilities to learn.

Practically, what does this mean for learner-centered leaders? For a closer look at student life, a learner-centered leader can partner with other organizations and agencies (e.g., hospitals, employers, housing, and food service organizations, transportation providers, etc.) and work together to support these learners. These partnerships can also offer experiences that young people find relevant and prepare them to thrive.

Dr. Kayon Pryce of Brooklyn STEAM is a leader engaged with other leaders in the ecosystem to offer experiences where young people can thrive. As a newly immigrated student from Jamaica who was receiving special education services for English as a Second Language (ESL), he was "tracked" by his counselor to a career pathway, not college bound. Disregarding this advice, he earned a doctorate and founded Brooklyn STEAM to create a one-of-a-kind innovative work-based program that offers meaningful and impactful opportunities for students like him. Brooklyn STEAM exists fully integrated within the ecosystem. By engaging other leaders within the ecosystem (New York City Public Schools, Brooklyn Navy Yard, on-site businesses), Dr. Pryce's visionary leadership converged location, community partnerships, and the opportunities to create this exceptional opportunity for young people to prepare for their future. To build a computer in a group setting, install it for a client, run a firewall, and then troubleshooting tech issues builds communication skills, problem-solving skills, and confidence, and it helps a young person understand what they like (and do not like) in a potential job opportunity.

HOW DO LEARNER-CENTERED LEADERS HAVE IMPACT ON CONDITIONS?

Learner-centered leadership grows from the inside out but impacts their systems from the outside in. What do we mean by that? Based on data and insight derived from our work with system leaders across the country, we have created a framework that shows the way learner-centered leadership operates at multiple levels. This leadership both creates conditions for innovation and change and enables design journeys, as shown in the following image:

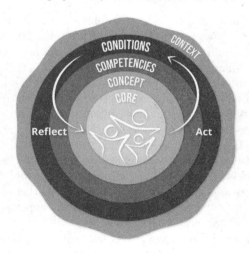

It Starts with Your Core

At the center of your learner-centered leadership is your core—who you are. Think of your core as your values, your identity, and your strongest motivations. Everyone's core is different, but in our work with learner-centered leaders, we see a pattern: leaders who are learner-centered have a strong and abiding belief in the potential of all learners (young and old) and feel called to serve them. For many this belief in the potential of all learners comes from a deeply personal place, perhaps their own limited access to special opportunities or seeing and experiencing the injustice of disparities—racial, economic, gender, or other. Some tap into a faith-based source of motivation to serve others. Whatever it may be, at the core of learner-centered leaders lives an enduring source of strength and direction that they summon and leverage to serve. A strong connection to your core beliefs and values—the ones that drive you to evolve and grow—serves to strengthen your conviction and sustain you.

This core identity is evident in the actions of leaders like Ami Gandhi, the chief learning officer at Intrinsic. It is clear to those around her that she believes in people and their potential, that she thinks of herself as an innovator, and that she is committed to the work of the ever-iterative design journey. Kayon Pryce, principal of STEAM, believes at his core he is an agent for change and considers the STEAM center to be a model for social justice. Lindsay Unified Superintendent Tom Rooney's core includes a deep and abiding love for learners, a sense of personal responsibility for them, and an unwavering will to persevere until they all get what they deserve.

Your Core Is Expressed through Your Concept

A strong core identity as a learner-centered leader alone is not enough to guide your work. Using that core identity to develop a mindset about your role and how you enact it will inform your actions. We call these mindsets about your role, your *concept* of your leadership. For example, do you see yourself as Chief Problem Solver or Chief Empowerer of Others to solve problems? Do you prioritize running an efficient system to satisfy myriad stakeholders, or to serve the unique needs of every learner?

These differences in how you could frame your role in part determine the actions you take. In fact, in many cases a mindset drives learner-centered actions like the ones you read about at the beginning of the chapter. The following table outlines six concept shifts from the industrial-era mindset to a learner-centered leadership mindset:

LEADERSHIP CONCEPTS

Industrial Era	Learner-Centered Era
Represent learner's interests with very little learner input	Listen to learners (of all ages)
Make decisions to serve the system	Make decisions to serve all learners
Be the Chief Director	Be the Chief Learner
Further a culture of performance and compliance	Cultivate a culture of learning and growth
Control a system of roles, rules, and hierarchies	Empower and inspire others to become learner-centered leaders
Manage discrete, fragmented systems	Engage with leaders in the ecosystem to create and support integrated experiences for learners

Your Competencies Translate Your Concept into Action

It is not enough to conceive of your role in a certain way. Competencies, the next ring out of the framework, refer to the specific *abilities* consistent with how you think of your role, and how those abilities lead to impactful action. Some examples of competencies include the following:

- Your skills listening to learners (of all ages) by asking questions, making it safe for them to share honestly, and synthesizing the most important insight you hear
- Your ability to articulate a future vision that inspires all the stakeholders in your system

- Your capabilities at empowering and building capacity in the people around you
- Your skills at engaging diverse stakeholders to invest them in your change effort

Because strong conditions enable school communities to pursue design journeys in every context, the ultimate role of a learner-centered leader is to draw upon competencies and act to foster the community conditions for innovation and change: conviction, clarity, capacity, culture, and coalition.

THE SOURCE OF THIS FRAMEWORK

The perspectives shared in this chapter have been developed collaboratively with learner-centered superintendents over the past five years in a program we call the Learner-Centered Leadership Lab. In 2019, leaders from nine organizations[1] gathered with staff from Transcend and LUSD to conceive of this program. The Lab's core premise is that learner-centered leadership is a critical enabler of system transformation, and much of the framework and insight you have read in this chapter is the result of findings from the lab. Now in its fifth year, the lab serves as a leadership development and insight development engine. The lab has two goals: first, to develop learner-centered leaders who have the support and skills to transform existing school systems into schools where extraordinary experiences and outcomes are possible for all learners; and, second, to produce usable knowledge on learner-centered leadership and system transformation for the education ecosystem to scale beyond the lab.

Most of the participants believed they were learner-centered leaders before joining the lab, but the collaboration introduced more opportunities to ask and listen and deepen their leadership core. Members of each cohort (at the time of this printing there have been six national cohorts, in addition to local spinoffs) realized that to honor the experiences and aspirations of learners, they had to take very seriously all the ways in which systems need to change for those systems to serve every single learner in the way those learners need and deserve. LCLL participants learn ways to lead, which place learners at the center of all of the systems. To learn more about this national program, use the following QR code:

We call it a "lab" and not just a superintendent development program, because the method of the lab is research, data collection, and information sharing. All that leaders share and discuss becomes research fodder to develop new insights about the nature and impact of learner-centered leadership and how that impact might grow over time. Over the course of nine months, participants in LCLL dig into personal and collective development, as well as research questions that build professional knowledge for the nascent field of learner-centered leadership. Participants have used insight from the lab to strengthen conditions within their school districts and subsequently pursued design journeys within their communities.

How Learner-Centered Leaders Grow and Develop

Every day, leaders working to transform conditions in their context encounter major, thorny challenges. Maybe the initiative they set into motion is stalling out. Maybe they are getting resistance from people around them. Maybe the politics around them are dividing the coalition they have worked so hard to build. Whatever it may be, these moments of breakdown are important fuel for breakthroughs in their development as learnercentered leaders. But if—and only if—they use these moments as prompts for reflection.

In our work through the LCLL program, we have found that the best way to support people to develop their learner-centered leadership skills is through deliberate cycles of action and reflection. Using moments of challenge as prompts for reflection means looking at challenges as an invitation to learn and develop oneself. This is a very different orientation than seeing challenges as evidence that someone else is the problem. When leaders do this, they model a learning orientation for everyone around them, which directly contributes to a culture of innovation. Quite intentionally these cycles of action and reflection mirror the design cycle itself, where learning and trying new actions happen in an ongoing, iterative process.

LCLL's Growing Impact

For many LCLL participants, the work goes well beyond the nine months of cohort participation, and they create local versions of the LCLL program that grow capacity within their systems. LUSD Superintendent Tom Rooney and his Assistant Superintendent of Human Resources Brian Griffin have invested thousands of hours in professional development for their district leadership. To create a peer network among these top positions and strengthen the learner-centered mindset across the district, Rooney and Griffin partnered with Transcend to cofound the first local LCLL. Through this experience, LUSD's administrative cabinet and principals worked alongside their peers to explore real-life problems that tested who they are as learner-centered leaders and how their district is moving in its transformation toward learner-centeredness.

In designing the local LCLL, Rooney and Griffin looked to Transcend's national LCLL program, which brings superintendents from across the country together to deepen their commitment to learners by creating conditions that foster a learner-centered environment. By exploring who they are as leaders and bringing in their local context, LUSD participants were able to build deep levels of trust among their cabinet and principal teams and build adaptive approaches to create conditions that would lead to positive outcomes for learners. Because of the extensive benefits of the local LCLL, they asked Transcend to facilitate two more cohorts to further bolster the learner-centered system.

In 2023, all of Rooney and Griffin's principals and directors were in local LCLL cohorts, problem-solving and building their core identities alongside their peers. Rooney's ambitious vision for this local lab is that it serves every person in the LUSD in a leadership role out to the site level to include teacher leaders, counselor leaders, and other people in informal leadership roles but considered leaders among their peers. This comprehensive and inclusive local lab would strengthen the core of individual leaders, define who they are as leaders, and help them articulate their purpose and mission as leaders. With this strength and insight and the support of peers, this collective can create conditions for others to thrive.

"What the local LCLL did for us is deepen our commitment to what it truly means to be learner-centered and strengthen our team. It created the space for vulnerability and space for growth that are not common in many systems," says Rooney. "I know that the team walked out of there with an even deeper commitment to being radically learner-centered." To learn more about this program in Lindsay's district, use the following QR code:

BE A LEARNER-CENTERED LEADER

What does all this mean for you? As we said earlier, you can exert important leadership regardless of the role you play in your school and community. Your leadership actions will strengthen the conditions in your community.

If You Are a Superintendent or Other Administrator

You are in a particularly influential role to start or sustain a design journey in your community. You can do the following:

- Develop your own conviction about what needs to change and why.
- Invite your community to start a "conversations with kids and educators" campaign. Use the following QR code to learn how:

- Diagnose the conditions in your own system. Use the following QR code to learn how:

- Develop your own and your team's learner-centered leadership. Use the following QR code to learn how:

- Apply to join Transcend's programs for superintendents. Use the following QR code to learn how:

If You Are an Educator

How much are you listening to your learners? You can do the following:

- Conduct empathy interviews, survey learners, and even shadow them.
- Invite your learners to co-create new experiences. Ask for their ideas!
- Start—or continue—making the Leaps in your own classroom! For every Leap, there are moves you can make as an educator and things you can do.

- Ask, or advocate, for more opportunities to pilot new and different learning experiences. As you do, collect evidence of impact on your students, not only to help you keep tuning it but also to demonstrate the results of innovation on metrics that your school and district care about. We're not going for different just to be different but different in ways that create better results for kids.

If You Are an Involved Parent or Caregiver

Ask your child about their experiences at school. Here's a list of questions for conversations with kids:

- Get involved in your local parent-teacher-student association (PTSA) and/or advocate for your school and district to explore more innovative learning environments. Read this book together.
- Familiarize yourself with additional resources and options for out-of-school experiences, whether at places like the Boys and Girls Club or the local youth group, or in pods, micro schools, and camps.

If You Are a Student

Recognize that your leadership matters! You have the power to not only influence your own experience and education but also make a difference in your school, your community, and beyond.

- Advocate for your own experience as a student. Familiarize yourself with the Leaps and notice where you fall on each of the dimensions of experience.

- Encourage your teachers and administrators to listen to students through allowing everyone to take the Leaps survey (or something similar) and/or doing a Conversations with Kids or Shadow a Student protocol.

- Join together with other students and develop ideas for how school could work best for you. Share these ideas with your teachers and administrators and ask if you can pilot them.
- Do not stop at the walls of your school or classroom. Look into learning opportunities outside of school—whether online programs, apprenticeships, or projects in your community.
- Take your learning into your own hands!

Robinson-Rivers deliberately developed herself and her team of educators as learner-centered leaders, sending signals about her belief in teacher leadership and their continued growth and her trust in them to bring back their knowledge and share with other staff.

By committing to their professional learning in support of the design vision (remember, the Whole Child Model was underpinned with conscious discipline, Emilio Reggio, and other innovative social-emotional elements), educators are able to deliver integrated student experiences that support academic learning and enable learners to develop critical skills such as empathy, trust, and self-regulation.

That legacy of professional learning continues today as part of the learner-centered culture of the school, even as Van Ness is in its seventh year of success. A teacher-led "Climate Team" supports the emotional well-being and mental health of the team of educators on staff; educators continue to share learnings from trainings they attend with other internal staff; and finally, as part of the Van Ness Elementary sharing journey through DCPS, the educators and administrators can share their learnings with interested observers looking for inspiration for a similar design journey.

Leadership happens at all levels of a design journey and within a broader context, which we call an **ecosystem.** In the next chapter, we look at a few of the key factors that impact learner-centered leaders on these journeys and how they work within the ecosystem to create experiences and outcomes that better serve learners.

CHAPTER 11

The Policy Environment Around You Matters

Key Points

- Design journeys operate within a broader ecosystem, which can either aid or hinder school communities' efforts to innovate. Among the many factors, state and federal policies play a particularly important role.
- School communities who are pursuing design journeys highlight three categories of policy that matter greatly: (a) assessments and accountability, (b) seat-time and graduation requirements, and (c) public funding for innovation.
- Systems and schools have options for navigating these policy realities: optimize within policies and still make important progress on your design journey, or work to shift constraints that are impeding your full vision. This chapter shows you how to do both.

In late 2016 the governor of North Dakota created a task force called the Innovation Education Summit, comprised of several groups: state representatives and other legislators who were strong advocates for education and wanted to fund innovation, the elected Superintendent of Public Instruction and her team, a committee of K–12 educators, and parents and caregivers of students. This group assembled to address growing concerns from system leaders and educators that federal and state policies were limiting their ability to innovate in schools and to define what it meant to be innovative. For example, superintendents, principals, and teachers felt they could better meet student needs if they were not constrained by narrowly defined seat-time requirements for graduation. These education leaders weren't advocating to remove all structures—they were advocating for flexibility so they could design their schools to be more learner-centered and effective. The result of this collaboration was State Senate Bill 2186, which allowed the superintendent of public instruction to selectively waive certain requirements, such as that all students must learn the same content, in the same place, at the same time.

Because Dr. Corey Steiner of Northern Cass had been part of a group of system leaders and educators testifying in front of the legislature in support of the bill, he was poised to submit what he called an "innovation waiver" to the Department of Public Instruction the moment the bill passed. This bill, and House Bill 1478 that shortly followed, made many of the design choices you've read about in Northern Cass's design journey possible.

While all of these aspects of the ecosystem surrounding schools matter greatly, this chapter focuses on policy, since system leaders consistently cite it as one of the biggest constraints to—or enablers of—innovation. The chapter begins with an overview of the policies that most impact communities' ability to pursue innovative school design and suggests alternatives and modifications to those policies that would remove barriers for system leaders to pursue design journeys. Then, in their own words, school and system leaders share their experiences advocating for policy change and working on innovative design journeys within existing federal and state policies. Finally they recommend action steps to advance innovation in any ecosystem.

POLICY IMPACT

Which policies are most impactful in shaping the climate for local innovation? The voices best positioned to answer that question are those in school communities who experience those policies most directly. Access to these communities comes from the Canopy project,[1] a research project and data collection hub that we steward in partnership with the Center for Reinventing Public Education (CRPE). In the most recent Canopy survey,[2] educators and leaders representing thirty-nine states and the District of Columbia cited three policy factors as particularly crucial for their ability to plan and build new models for school:

- Assessment and accountability systems
- Requirements for seat time and graduation
- Funding to support innovation

For each of these policy areas, we provide a brief overview before turning to what matters most for innovation and what changes system leaders can advocate for.

ASSESSMENT AND ACCOUNTABILITY SYSTEMS

Historically, students who had long gone underserved by public education—English learners, students with disabilities, and many students of color or students living in poverty—were invisible, hidden behind averages. Before the creation of assessment and accountability systems that measure student and school performance, identify schools in need of support, and prompt action to raise student achievement, ". . .parents had no way of knowing how well schools were serving their children, equity advocates had no way of knowing whether students were getting the necessary learning opportunities and resources, employers had no way of ensuring graduates they hired would be equipped with the right skills for the job, and states had no real way of identifying schools that needed help to improve and setting them on a course to do so," as the Education Trust has pointed out.[3] Standardized tests aimed to create a comparable, straightforward method to gauge learning outcomes against grade-level standards in a state.

The strategy of setting a common set of desired outcomes (also known as "standards"), measuring student performance against those standards, and then holding schools and districts accountable for results has been at the heart of education policy since the publication of "A Nation at Risk" triggered reforms. Throughout the 1990s and into the 2000s, economists, governors, and business leaders increasingly embraced a "tight-loose" approach to K–12 reform—greater accountability for meeting student expectations in exchange for greater autonomy to meet those expectations. The assessment and accountability systems that grew out of this approach were well-intended efforts to ensure consistency and a universally high standard in public education, on the belief that a combination of incentives and pressure would drive school system improvement. Civil rights groups committed to the students of color who had long been underserved by the education system joined the cause, believing that this kind of accountability system would redirect funding, attention, and qualified teachers to the students and schools facing the most barriers to opportunity. Accountability systems, then, can be a tool for communicating expectations of public education and spurring action, through a combination of pressure and support, to ensure that all learners are served well.

The 2001 No Child Left Behind and 2015 Every Student Succeeds Act (ESSA) reauthorizations of the Elementary and Secondary Education Act introduced different levels of prescription for standards, assessments, and accountability. Requirements for the latter two systems are spelled out in ESSA, which runs 443 pages[4]—even a summary of the law's accountability provisions runs six single-spaced pages.[5] States have implemented their own additional assessments and accountability provisions that aren't required by federal law.

Impact on Innovative Design

We should not be quick to let go of the intended positive purposes that standardized tests and accountability systems were designed to achieve. At the same time, much has been said about how our current generation of standardized assessments, and associated accountability practices, insufficiently measures student aptitude and can hinder learner-centered practices,[6] with criticism that they do the following:

- Narrow curricula toward test competency
- Inhibit innovative teaching methods such as project-based learning, exploratory studies, and interdisciplinary approaches
- Favor a particular type of neuro-typical learner
- Ignore important environmental factors (e.g., a student's physical or mental health the day of the test or the temperature or noise level in the room at the time of testing)
- Have racial/cultural bias inherent in their design

Most principals can describe in excruciating detail the overwhelming array of logistical tasks that testing imposes every spring—from creating new schedules to attending mandatory security training sessions to building materials management plans—all at the expense of time that could be focused on designing extraordinary and equitable learning experiences for young people. For the volume of accountability requirements and testing, this often adds up to systems that "...hold back people's willingness to try new things," according to one principal.[7] Another shared, "We've...seen regulations/accountability get tighter in the past decade which has decreased flexibility...this has led to some loss in creative programming decisions." *Nearly half of the communities we spoke to cited testing and accountability requirements as barriers to their ability to innovate.*

> "Our design focuses on personalization and student interests through internships and project-based learning. With navigating school schedule/seat time/state standards and testing requirements, we are often limited in doing our best work for students and families."
> —Respondent, Canopy (High School)

Accountability systems hinge on assessments to calculate composite school or district ratings, inadvertently suppressing risk tolerance. Depending on the state, consequences of consistently poor performance can include forced conversion, reorganization, or management by a public or private entity. Even schools and districts able to avoid the "accountability clock" may fear public disapproval or loss of enrollment due to poor test results or oversimplified ratings. This focus can create a high-stakes environment that encourages risk aversion rather than fostering experimentation and can dissuade schools from straying from the traditional paths of teaching and learning. Consequently, educators may be reluctant to adopt innovative programs or practices that might not immediately translate into improved test scores. The combined result is less room for activities that promote creativity, character building, and social-emotional development. These are key aspects of a well-rounded education that often fall outside the realm of standardized assessments.

A Promising Path Forward

A significant and growing movement is underway to design assessment systems that inform families, students, educators, policymakers, and the greater public about student progress while also supporting better teaching and deeper, more personalized learning. In particular, we believe that the next generation of assessments must do the following:

- **Encourage more comprehensive learning goals:** Current policy requires assessment of only a narrow slice of the outcomes and experiences that learners need to thrive. Assessment and accountability systems should aspire to measure the full range of outcomes that communities value and employers require. Current policy also focuses disproportionately on measuring outcomes at the expense of measuring the quality of students' experiences, which matter both in their own right and as near-term predictors that can be immediately actionable for educators.
- **Enable personalized advancement rather than mandate a one-size-fits-all approach:** Current policy requires that all students be tested on the same content at the same time, with no flexibility for learners to move at different paces. Instead, students should be able to advance at their own pace, demonstrating proficiency when they're ready and allowing multiple opportunities to demonstrate mastery. With appropriate guardrails for rigor and equity, students should also be allowed to demonstrate mastery in more diverse ways than just written exams completed alone and in silence.

As states navigate assessment requirements that often leave little breathing room for innovation, some have taken advantage of incremental steps to support assessment innovation at the federal level, including through the Competitive Grants for State Assessments and Innovative Assessment Demonstration Authority programs, flexibility within ESSA, and the U.S. Department of Education's authority to waive statutory provisions and regulations. State leaders and school communities are not doing this work in isolation. Organizations like KnowledgeWorks and the Center for Innovation in Education facilitate state communities of practice, create policy frameworks, and convene forward-thinking partners around innovative assessment. In November 2023, U.S. Department of Education (USED) Secretary Miguel Cardona sent a letter to chief state school officers acknowledging that more work is needed to ease state paths to innovation.[8] Most notably, he recognized that our current assessments do not "always meet the mark" and celebrated the emergence of competency-based assessments. "We cannot expect innovation from the field of education while protecting the status quo from Washington, DC," Cardona wrote.

A growing number of states and districts are already working outside of their federally approved accountability systems to create school quality systems that incorporate more locally situated forms of data. State agencies in Colorado, Kentucky, and New Mexico are creating learning partnerships with schools and districts to pioneer new methods that lift up the values of local communities. In Kentucky, the department of education launched an ambitious effort to bring together districts and collectively imagine what community-driven assessment systems could look like. They have convened students, families, educators, policymakers, and other important stakeholders to think through how to balance two essential imperatives: the need for consistent information about student learning across the state to help surface inequities and gaps and the need for communities to have a meaningful say in the kinds of outcomes that their students need to thrive in the world beyond K–12 education. The state was awarded a $3 million Competitive Grant for State Assessments to accelerate this work.

Assessment tool providers are leading encouraging efforts, too. In collaboration with practitioners and policymakers nationwide, the Carnegie Foundation for the Advancement of Teaching and Educational Testing Service (ETS) established a partnership to design and pilot a robust, scalable suite of assessment and analytic tools that captures the full range of behavioral and cognitive skills required for American students to succeed in K–12, postsecondary education and beyond. Their partnership has the potential to transform two of the educational pillars they built: standardized assessment and the Carnegie Unit, covered in the next section.

Dramatically more policy innovation and research and development (R&D) on new assessments is needed to provide states with the capacity to build twenty-first-century systems that understand student learning.

Policymakers have an opportunity to lean into this moment of reinvention to do the following:

- **Federal policymakers** can rethink federal requirements that require the annual assessment of every learner on every grade-level standard in every year and consider alternatives such as assessment in certain milestone years, or assessment by sampling (the approach used by the National Association of Educational Procurement [NAEP]).[9] Either approach would still allow for school-level accountability and meaningful inferences about system-wide learning while reducing the assessment burden experienced by students and teachers. With strong guardrails for rigor and equity, local assessment systems could then be relied upon to provide instructionally useful information to educators and inform families of their individual child's performance. Federal policymakers could also consider offering states flexibility around the designs of the tests themselves, allowing and incenting states to adopt adaptive assessments that incorporate standards from multiple grade levels to better measure growth during the year. Waivers could also give states and local communities the "breathing room" to develop and pilot new generations of assessments that measure the broader range of outcomes and experiences most essential for the twenty-first century, including problem-solving, communication, collaboration, and agency. Schools looking to embrace a student-centered paradigm will need regulatory permission to operate under an alternative accountability structure that maintains the overall objective of college- and career-readiness, allows for more personalized academic pathways, and provides a more precise way of measuring and rewarding learning growth toward proficiency.[10]
- **Federal and state policymakers** could consider expanding accountability systems beyond traditional assessment scores in literacy and numeracy to consider a wider range of indicators reflecting school performance, including student experiences and engagement, social-emotional growth, and post-graduation success. They could also invest in the R&D necessary to invent, test, and validate the new generation of assessments that will be required to assess the broad range of outcomes and experiences that young people need to thrive beyond school. This could come in the form of National Science Foundation (NSF) grants to researchers and tool creators, Education Innovation & Research (EIR) grants to districts that are piloting these tools, increased funding for CGSA, or other mechanisms.
- **State policymakers** can develop and pilot competency-based assessment and accountability systems. Done well, competency-based assessment and accountability can align the instructional incentives embedded within statewide assessment and accountability systems to a student-centered

paradigm. They can also provide parents, students, and teachers with more precise and transparent information on the progress each student makes toward proficiency than current state assessments afford.[11] Under the requirements of federal law, states would likely need to operate a competency-based assessment system as a supplement to current, state-summative assessments. However, as federal policy evolves, states may one day be able to give schools a choice about whether to implement a grade-level-based or competency-based assessment and accountability system.

SEAT TIME AND GRADUATION REQUIREMENTS

Seat time and graduation requirements, defined by states or school districts, are a second set of interconnected policy factors cited by innovative schools as crucial for reinvention. Starting in the early twentieth century, students earned credit for a particular course after spending a specific amount of time in a classroom—typically 120 hours. The "Carnegie Unit" became the stand-ard measure for graduation from high school and admission to college and often dictated that all students learn the same content, in the same place, at the same time, and pass a uniform assessment to demonstrate mastery. Since the 1980s, states and districts have increased their graduation requirements to include coursework consistent with academic content standards adopted by states.[12] As of 2023, forty-six states and the District of Columbia identify minimum credit requirements to earn a standard diploma. Typically, students must complete a certain number of courses in core subjects in addition to sub-jects such as computer science, financial literacy, or physical education.[13] Not surprisingly, these one-size-fits-all, industrial-era holdovers are a significant barrier for communities seeking to create more personalized and customized student experiences.

Impact on Innovative Design

The original intent behind the Carnegie unit—to ensure that students are exposed to an extended course of content and put a meaningful floor beneath student learning—still makes sense. But seat-time policies inherently chal-lenge innovation by prioritizing time spent in a classroom over the skills and knowledge that students attain. In the modern age, competency-based learning, online courses, and project-based learning have emerged as power-ful strategies. These formats tailor education to the unique strengths, needs, modalities, preferences, and pace of each student but are harder to do inside current requirements. Seat-time requirements have until recently also limited opportunities outside of school, such as internships, apprenticeships, and other career-connected learning opportunities, since that time hasn't counted as student time "in their seat."[14]

> "State policy on seat time and other flexibilities are in the way of providing personalized learning overall. These are important factors to get changed in policy."
>
> —Respondent, Canopy (High School)

Likewise, while having a set of expectations that need to be met by graduating students is essential for maintaining a baseline of educational quality, many states' rigid requirements often fail to reflect or support the diversity of students' talents, interests, and career paths. Furthermore, this formulaic approach leaves little room for students to delve deeply into areas they are passionate about or that are relevant to their future careers. It can discourage schools from experimenting with interdisciplinary or project-based learning programs, which might offer students a more holistic understanding of real-world issues. These innovative approaches often blur the lines between traditional subject boundaries, making it challenging to fit them neatly into the conventional boxes of graduation requirements.

A Promising Path Forward

States are able to create some flexibility for schools and districts to allow for the demonstration of knowledge and the awarding of credit based on a student's mastery of standards or competencies rather than a traditional Carnegie unit. They may also permit students to satisfy some graduation requirements through personalized models, such as performance assessments, portfolios, or projects.

In fact, as some states have shifted away from seat time and toward mastery-based demonstrations of student learning; they have also begun using graduation requirement policy as a lever to increase flexibility and support personalized opportunities for students. In its most recent (2023) fifty-state comparison of high school graduation requirements, the Education Commission of the States found that forty-four states and DC permit students to substitute specific courses, assessments, or other experiences for those existing credit requirements, and twenty-one states have multiple diploma options or pathways to graduation.[15] How many schools and districts within these states have actually seized the opportunity to replace traditional graduation requirements with deeper forms of learning is less well-known.

In a 2022 brief on state policies to support student-centered learning, the Education Commission of the States and KnowledgeWorks captured

Colorado's example.[16] There, the state board of education develops graduation guidelines to support the development of local graduation requirements. Within these guidelines, districts can offer students a variety of options to demonstrate competencies required for graduation, including a work- or project-based capstone project, portfolio of work, or performance assessment. To support districts in implementing these personalized options, the Colorado Department of Education (CDE) convened a work group of educators, administrators, and representatives from postsecondary institutions and community organizations that developed guidance on capstone projects and portfolio graduation requirements.[17] CDE elevated promising district examples, including districts using digital portfolios to track student progress and districts with capstone requirements. The state further created the Innovative Learning Opportunities Program, which allows schools to apply for flexibility from attendance and seat-time requirements to create these learning opportunities. As of the 2023 school year, 161 of the state's 178 school districts have adopted a "performance-based" graduation requirement.[18]

Though school systems have been slow to free students from seat-time requirements and institutions of higher education have been slow to recognize or value mastery-based demonstrations of learning, all states, in fact, now allow for students to receive mastery-based credit in some way.[19] There are encouraging signs of progress. In its enabling legislation for competency-based pilot grants, Utah included a requirement that institutions of higher education shall recognize and accept a diploma earned in a competency-based program. The New England Secondary Schools Consortium, a collaboration of five states that encourages mastery-based graduation and personalized learning pathways, has secured a statement of support from 85 public and private institutions of higher education which "states—unequivocally—that students with proficiency-based grades and transcripts will not be disadvantaged in any way" in the admissions process.[20]

State policymakers can continue to examine their regulatory landscape and create space for school communities looking to transition to a student-centered paradigm by *reforming seat-time and graduation requirements so that students can earn credit—and schools can receive funding—for a diverse array of meaningful activities*, not just time spent physically in school buildings. Flexibility allows school districts to support personalized opportunities for students or prioritize certain knowledge and skills needed for success in college, career, and civic life.

FUNDING FOR INNOVATION

A third policy factor that innovative communities have highlighted as especially relevant for their ability to go on design journeys is funding. One school leader shared that "we can and will do our innovative work within a variety of parameters. . .but public schools must receive adequate funding to support innovative work that often involves increased staff capacity." Many innovators also raised the need to devote precious time to fundraising for design work and pilots, such as one school leader, who told us "Funding is an issue for innovation. We are consistently writing grants to get the things that we need in our innovative site. . .we spend a lot of time trying to find funding."

Schools and systems largely do not have line items in their budgets for innovation—whether for their own people's time on it, for support from external design partners, or for models they adopt. Pulling from existing funds or devoting limited time to fundraising aren't sustainable or scalable ways for school and system leaders to start and sustain design journeys, yet they are necessary in federal and state funding environments where education R&D is not financially supported. Compared to other sectors that serve the public good, a strikingly low amount is spent on education R&D, an important vehicle for innovation. In FY2022, the U.S. Department of Education's budget authority for R&D was $405 million—less than 0.1% of the elementary and secondary education budget. Meanwhile, the Department of Defense invested $65 billion in R&D, and the Department of Health and Human Services, $42 billion. The Department of Agriculture spent more than $3 billion on research related to food and agriculture.[21]

Impact on Innovative Design

If young people were having extraordinary learning experiences, it would be possible for schools to repurpose funds they currently spend on remediation, discipline, and attendance toward more fruitful aims. Getting from "here" to "there" requires innovation, which means communities need to undertake design journeys. But without funding to support design journeys—including innovative models they can borrow from—most communities find it difficult to innovate. They gravitate to smaller point solutions that can be more readily implemented but that do not enable them to fundamentally transform the design of schooling. When pockets of funds appear, they are able to pilot new ideas, but many of those pilots stall or evaporate when resources dry up.

A Promising Path Forward

The idea for a national K–12 center focused on R&D has circulated since President Obama's 2012 budget proposal invoked the example of Defense Advanced Research Projects Agency (DARPA), the advanced defense research agency that is credited with bringing about technological innovations such as weather satellites, the Global Position System (GPS), and the internet. Since then, coalitions like the Alliance for Learning Innovation have generated momentum for **federal policymakers** to take action on several ideas:

- Two important legislative initiatives would employ research, development, and statistical collection to improve the way that children learn: the Advancing Research in Education Act (AREA)[22] and the New Essential Education Discoveries (NEED) Act.[23] The latter would establish a national center to promote high-impact education research to enable experimentation and rigorous evaluation that in turn helps to develop and disseminate innovative, data-based practices and tools that create breakthroughs.
- Efforts to support the supply of innovative learning models must be complemented with those to overcome the barriers to their adoption.[24] One way to support supply-side and demand-side incentives would be to allow states to apply for federal funding to offset the cost of model implementation at early adopter schools. State entities that receive federal funding could then host a subgrant competition in which schools access funding to support adoption-related costs of innovative learning models over a fixed period of time. Funding could also be used by state agencies to fund the administrative costs associated with overseeing, supporting, promoting, and evaluating the impact of innovative learning models.

It's not just the federal policymakers who could be doing more to support education R&D. In recent years, many states have focused on the task of making their school funding formulas more adequate and equitable to meet the learning needs of young people. This is admirable, but there is a disconnect when those investments are confined to the industrial model of schooling. In tandem, **state policymakers and agencies** could do the following:

- Invest in high-quality collaborative education R&D efforts (such as research-practice partnerships, youth participatory action research, or networked improvement communities) and develop and sustain local capacity for design journeys. Innovation grants could go directly to schools and systems and take many forms, including funding for those participating on community design teams, model adoption, external design partners, or design support roles within districts.
- Invest in the development of innovative learning models aligned to state standards and in the organizational capacity of model providers. In Montana and North Dakota, federal pandemic recovery dollars were used to create Math Innovation Zones, incentivizing elementary and middle school partnerships with innovative learning models, tools, and technical assistance providers so every student has a personalized pathway to proficiency.[25] In Tennessee, state legislators made a historic $500 million investment "to bring Innovative School Models to every

public high school and middle school in the state."[26] Virginia has made $100 million available for planning and starter grants for approved "laboratory schools,"[27] designed to "stimulate innovative programs, provide opportunities for innovation in instruction and assessment, provide teachers with an avenue for delivering innovative instruction and school scheduling, management and structure, and. . .develop model programs." These kinds of state-level investments in innovation can help harness the educational, technological, and creative capacities within states so the innovative learning models it oversees are more closely aligned to state standards.

NAVIGATING YOUR POLICY ENVIRONMENT

In the face of these challenges and opportunities for transformation, what's a learner-centered leader to do?

In the sections that follow, through the insights and actions of system leaders and administrators, we share concrete steps that school and district leaders can take to navigate within policy constraints and shift limiting policy factors in the medium-term. We highlight system leaders who have done both to lead successful design journeys.

Optimize Within Existing Policies

A number of years ago, we had the fortune to work with a district in a special waiver program, which exempted them from having to follow an overwhelming set of state regulations. They ran with this special set of permissions and created powerful innovations for personalizing learning, partnering with local employers, incorporating far more projects, and much more. We asked the district leaders which freedoms from state regulations were proving to be most important to them. They thought for a moment and said, "You know, we actually could have done any of these things under the existing regulations. We just never thought we could until we had the permission to do so."

Optimize Within Current Regulations

While not yet the norm, several states, including Colorado, Idaho, Indiana, Michigan, South Carolina, and Utah, have tried to assist schools' efforts by creating "flexibility guides"[28] detailing the ways that state laws and regulations create room for more student-centered learning environments. Indiana's flexibility guide, for example, provides step-by-step instructions for the three primary flexibility tools available to schools and districts: "flexibility through request," "flexibility through innovation program participation," and "flexibility through state delegation of authority—home rule."

Cynthia Robinson-Rivers, the principal you read about in Chapter 3 at Van Ness Elementary School in Washington DC, had no policy exemptions or waivers when she led the envisioning work for Van Ness's Whole Child Model. The model was designed to function within district and boundary policies, which meant it adhered to all of the traditional requirements laid out in this chapter for things like standardized assessments and instructional hours and days.

Principal Robinson-Rivers got creative. Working within the parameters set by the district, the design team followed the math block time requirement but shifted the curriculum to be more learner-centered and inquiry-based, improving students' emotional relationship with math. Next, because they knew their students needed time to move their bodies to prepare their brains to learn, they tweaked minutes to borrow time from other blocks of the day to add some time to recess. Finally, to support students who were behind grade-level in academics, Principal Robinson-Rivers allocated her federal recovery money toward extra teacher pay to add a month to the school year for the learners who needed support catching up.

Tweak the Systems that Aren't Working

In many school districts, report cards have an academic section and a behavioral section. Typically the behavioral section is designed to be compliance-based, focused on "following directions" and being nondisruptive. But based on the Van Ness design team's insights from the Learn phase of R&D for the Whole Child Model, they knew that language and perspective made a big impact on how equitable a classroom experience might be. As a result, the Van Ness design team advocated for a change of language. Instead of a compliance-based "follow directions" standard, they worked to change the language to "share and take turns balancing the needs and rights of themselves and others." This may not seem like much, but it shifts the tone of teaching to be about facilitating cooperation and respect between students in the classroom. And it shifts the student perspective to focus on empathy and self-advocacy, yielding a more equitable environment for young learners. By evaluating systems and identifying elements that are not working for an overall vision for equitable learning, you can start small to make a big impact.

Allocate Existing Funding to Support Innovative Design

According to former Superintendent Lynn Moody in North Carolina, most schools use federally allocated Title I funds to lower class size or hire tutors for students facing the most barriers to opportunity. She instead encouraged her educators to think creatively about how those funds could be used to bring their design vision to life—for student learning experiences that were "passion and interest-driven, personalized and customized"—whether inside or outside of the classroom.

The kindergarten teachers took students on a fishing trip, with corresponding prelaunch, launch, and postlaunch units to support the learning. There was a writing assignment around the experience, a chart about the trash observed and collected that formed a math unit, and a library research unit where students could explore categories of individual interest associated with the trip. This integrated approach, which included a unique experience for these young learners, indelibly shaped their first year of all-day school. All it required was thinking creatively about the use of existing funds.

Sustainable funding streams like Title I (the largest federal aid package to schools and local education agencies, targeted to meet the educational needs of low-income students in our nation's highest poverty schools) and Title IV (intended to provide all students with access to a well-rounded education, improve school conditions for student learning, and improve the use of technology) can be used to spark and sustain redesign efforts.

Advocate for Policy Change

"Iowa passed a competency-based law[29] that removed seat-time requirements if you were Comp-based. Without this law we couldn't have started [our program]" —Respondent, Canopy (High School)

"We are able to provide flexibility with scheduling for students and families because of the ability to modify how we meet the requirements of the school calendar. With the seat-time status, students are able to attend courses from outside the school; this allows for more flexibility with scheduling."

—Respondent, Canopy (High School)

Learner-centered leaders, by definition, see it as part of their job to push on the broader systems around them when those systems aren't serving learners. These leaders can look at the entire ecosystem and think of every person as a learner, every connection as an opportunity for growth. That mindset informs a sense of collaboration with policymakers, board members, union leaders, and other community members that can lead to change in many layers of the ecosystem.

This front-end advocacy is evident in the Central Valley of California, where Superintendent Tom Rooney regularly travels to Sacramento to speak up for policy changes that will deliver what he believes learners deserve. Most pressing in Rooney's district is a push to use more comprehensive and varied evidence of learning to determine the success of learning environments and student performance; he believes less emphasis should be placed on a state test for many of the reasons discussed earlier in this chapter. He advocates to include robust local and nonacademic measures, such as attendance, life skills, engagement, behavior, career aspirations, and meaningful activities outside the classroom to generate a more robust picture of a child's learning competence.

System leaders who successfully advocate for state policy shifts are prepared with data and facts that support their recommendations. They build community support and momentum for their initiatives and leverage their professional relationships to build their own skills and support network.

"When approaching policymakers, it's crucial to use hard data and facts to support your arguments. Data can offer objective evidence of the effectiveness of innovative practices in your schools. Be proactive in collecting this data. Consider tracking student progress, gathering feedback from teachers, parents, and students, and documenting the impact of innovation on student engagement and outcomes. Use this data to show policymakers the tangible benefits of these innovative practices and their potential for scalability."
—Canopy Participant

- **Come Prepared with Evidence.** Data supporting the Van Ness Whole Child Model came from a survey administered to teachers, who highly rated the asynchronous professional development units that Robinson-Rivers and her Transcend partner put together from a piece of the "Strong Start" practice. The momentum generated from this positive feedback was a catalyst for expanding Van Ness's model sharing, which in turn led to more schools in the DC area adopting the design itself.

"As a superintendent, you have a unique platform for advocacy. Use it. Engage in public forums, write op-eds, speak at community events, or leverage social media. Each of these avenues offers opportunities to voice your perspectives, share success stories from your district, and engage a broader audience. Policymakers are more likely to take notice if there is public support for your initiatives."
—LCLL Participant

- **Activate Community.** Leveraging the success of her previous design innovation, superintendent Lynn Moody advocated for and received waivers from the North Carolina legislature to develop a pilot school program, SparkNC. Superintendent Moody describes the SparkNC design as a high-tech accelerator; the outcome is career and technical education, achieved through a deep dive that incorporates ethics, durable skills, and real-life experiences with businesses and industry. This innovative design is possible only because the degree is not tied to accountability models; for example, seat time isn't a feasible standard to meet when the on-site industry experience is part of the curriculum. Moody is collecting stories from learners, educators, and community participants in the pilot program and working with other advocates who will help her deliver those stories to the North Carolina General Assembly. Ultimately, she hopes to replicate and iterate the model in other places.

> "Remember, you are not alone in your endeavors. There are other superintendents, education leaders, and organizations that share your vision. Connect with these professional networks. They can provide support, share insights, and collaborate on joint advocacy efforts. Collective action can often amplify your voice and influence."
>
> —LCLL Participant

- **Leverage Your Networks.** In Chapter 10 you read about the Learner-Centered Leadership Lab. Unlike standard state conferences, the format and program for the lab make idea-sharing, problem-solving and collaboration possible. This community of superintendents is unique in that it creates a network of peer-resource support to leverage for perspectives and solutions. This professional network, and the inspiration to create a similar program for assistant superintendents and principals within those districts, can generate momentum for change.

CONCLUSION

This chapter began with important legislative developments in North Dakota. The state's progressive policy direction certainly played a role in sparking the design journey for Northern Cass, but it wasn't the whole story. A learner-centered leader—committed to bringing community stakeholders into the conversation, including the teacher's union, elected officials, and educators—also made innovation possible. Today, Dr. Steiner is focused on sustaining the design innovation his district has implemented over the past several years. The annual report he submits to the Department of Public Instruction, which granted his waiver under 2186, includes data tracking, outcomes, and community feedback as part of a variety of metrics that show how Northern Cass continues to evolve and improve on the goals outlined in the waiver.

As Dr. Steiner and his design team continue to evolve and expand the model within Northern Cass, he continues to seek support for innovation to sustain and scale the design. In fact, Dr. Steiner sees his role in North Dakota extending beyond his own district. More than a year before each upcoming legislative session, he meets with elected officials to talk about funding talent requirements, information systems, and other support necessary to implement and sustain innovative education. He regularly meets with the union and other community stakeholders to advocate for policies that he recommends rise to the Legislature, and during legislative years regularly hosts forums (as well as annually in non-legislative years) that bring legislators to the table to share ideas.

Challenge: How might you support design journeys within your ecosystem? If you are a system leader, think about what you wish you could do, and ask yourself how you might be able to make it work while still complying with regulations. And, how might you advocate to shift policy?

Conclusion: You Are Not Alone

If there is one key takeaway from this book, we hope it's the inspiration to embark on your own community-based design journey, ready with the knowledge, tools, and support needed to redesign your school for the success of all learners. We understand that while this work is worthwhile and possible, it's not easy. If redesigning our systems were simple, it would have already been accomplished by the incredible innovators, educators, and leaders who preceded us. However, we believe that our generation of system leaders and educators possess the collective wisdom and humility gained from past efforts and the new tools at our disposal to create learning environments that truly serve all children.

To support every community with opportunities to engage in a design journey, we have identified four key enablers that assist in meaningful and lasting transformation:

- Availability and access to codified, Leaps-aligned learning models, so school communities do not have to start their journeys from square one.
- The presence of Design Partners who can help in the facilitation and implementation of design journeys.
- Access to ongoing learning and professional development opportunities that build the local capacity to start and sustain the work.
- A network of like-minded innovators who are also on design journeys.

EXPLORE NEW MODELS THAT MAKE THE LEAPS

Throughout this book, we have demonstrated that our current educational model is persistently and consistently rooted in early 20th-century ideas about learning, the optimal organization of children and adults, and society's workforce and leadership needs. These beliefs collectively contribute to the creation of the industrial model that reflects this vision.

We define innovative models as integrated programs that fundamentally reshape the educational experience. In our experience, nearly all communities benefit from incorporating proven innovations into their learning environment designs. Communities looking to reshape parts or all of their

247

learning environment design can adapt and adopt learning models, tools, resources, and other support from schools or organizations that have tackled and overcome similar challenges. We also find that visiting innovative learning models in action through "inspiration visits" can be transformational for schools. These visits to peer schools, like the ones Mr. Arthur conducted for the educators of Elm Town Unified in Chapter 7, uncover what is possible and celebrate potential for change.

We believe that the educational system we seek to change is so deeply entrenched and intertwined with American life that it will require an immense amount of effort, commitment, and momentum to move beyond the industrial model. The gravitational pull and the inertia of the existing system continues to be incredibly strong, which is why models that are making the kinds of Leaps we define in Chapter 1 are essential. These models serve two critical purposes. First, they provide a foundation to build upon, preventing communities from having to start their design journeys from scratch. Second, they present a coherent direction to move toward, with clear standards of excellence that a community can strive for.

To support schools in discovering, introducing, and implementing new educational models, Transcend has developed the Innovative Models Exchange. This free, searchable database provides educators with inspiration and practical resources to transform the learning experience in their communities.

Use the following QR code to find further information:

FIND A DESIGN PARTNER

Over the years, we have learned that having a Design Partner, like Mr. Arthur from Chapters 7 and 8, is one of the keys to a successful design journey. Design Partners collaborate closely with communities to align on a vision for the entire school system. They support a community to progress toward that vision and iterate on it over multiple years.

School administrators and educators are already stretched beyond their limits as they attend to the obligations and responsibilities of their current roles. Managing the status quo alone is challenging enough, let alone envisioning and executing bold change. A Design Partner will support you in this journey and provide insight based on past experiences that help reduce the stress of taking on something new.

Here are some specific things that Design Partners do to support communities on design journeys:

- Assist a community to understand the components of a successful design journey
- Support a community in identifying its assets (e.g., people, organizations, networks) that can contribute to progress in its journey
- Design and facilitate learning experiences that enable a community to utilize its assets effectively in pursuing its vision
- Identify opportunities for communities to learn how to access and use supports more independently as they continue their journey beyond the first year
- Hold and steward the overall vision for the school/system design, bringing specialized skills and other experts to the community-based process

In the four case study examples featured in Part II, you witnessed the results of a Design Partner's collaboration. In the case of Van Ness Elementary, their Design Partner played a crucial role in codifying the Whole Child Model into a cohesive set of practices, adult professional development, and supporting tools. Without this support, the cohesive and coherent design of the Whole Child Model might have been lost or attributed to one innovative principle at one point in time. At Northern Cass, their Design Partner introduced them to the Design Cycle methodology, helping to structure and guide the innovative drive within their community.

In the cases of Brooklyn STEAM and Intrinsic, the Design Partner helped the respective communities learn from and adapt innovative approaches developed elsewhere. For STEAM, career technical education is not a novel concept, but the specificity, alignment to the local marketplace, and access to real-world industrial professionals represent a significant Leap for these types of programs. Similarly, "Choice Day" at Intrinsic is not an entirely new idea, but the educators in this community have tailored the concept to fit their specific needs, balancing academic and other experiences to help students navigate how to make the choices they need to succeed.

We have all experienced systems where there is an abundance of energy and willing educators, but without clarity, methods for assessing progress, and disciplined efforts, initiatives can fizzle out and disappear due to turnover and fatigue. In all of these examples, the design partner facilitated reflection, brainstorming, and meaning-making as a team. The Design Partner provides essential additional capacity so that school teams can undertake the challenging work of making Leaps toward extraordinary learning for all while still executing the normal school day. Design Partners are instrumental to maintain the flame of possibility and vision within school communities.

WHERE DO I FIND DESIGN PARTNERS?

Unfortunately, Design Partners do not yet exist at scale within the education sector, but there are many organizations around the country that serve as Design Partners.

Transcend is one such organization filled with Design Partners—a diverse team of educators, innovators and changemakers with experience as school and system leaders—who support communities across the country. We work hand-in-hand with communities to align on a whole-school vision that they can progress (and continue to iterate) toward over multiple years. We support you to implement, learn, and scale changes that improve your community's learning experience. You read about four design journeys in Part II of this book, and at the time of this printing we have reached 2,350 schools representing 1.2 million students nationwide.

Transcend is not the only organization working in partnership to support design innovation. There are other organizations, such as Springpoint, Throughline Learning, Learner-Centered Collaborative, Redesign, and LEAP Innovations, that support design journeys with different resources and methods. There are also organizations that do this in the context of specific models, including Big Picture Learning, New Tech Network, and others.

There may also be people in your own community who are ready to be design partners, or could be ready with the right training. These partners might be individual consultants, local organizations that support schools, or even people who are employed by your system or your schools—people like directors of innovation, heads of educational technology, or even highly motivated principals or assistant principals. We offer training through Transcend Institute, which can give people the knowledge, skills, tools, and support network to become a Design Partner—use the following QR code to learn more:

Integrating Design Partners into Education

We envision a future where every school community has a Design Partner to support ongoing journeys, allowing schools to continually evolve as the world and communities change. Imagine a world where design supporters are part of the infrastructure of school systems, just like literacy coaches, social-emotional learning (SEL) heads, and deans of culture. If this were the case, what Leaps would be possible for young people? When this becomes a reality, it will pay for itself, not only in terms of better experiences and outcomes but also because proactively designing more engaging, motivating, and science-based learning environments can reduce issues related to discipline, remediation, or other learning distractions.

BUILD YOUR OWN CAPACITY

Your role in a community-based design process is important, regardless of your specific position. We have seen in our experience that community members need access to sustained learning and development that deepens their skills and expertise, puts them in contact with like-minded others, and continually strengthens their belief in the design process.

We developed the Transcend Institute with these goals at heart. The Institute's purpose is to build the capacity of education innovators through human-centered and relevant adult learning—high-quality course offerings, apprenticeships, and cohort-based experiences—that supports and enables community-based design journeys. The Institute offers different levels of support depending on where a community may find itself, whether they are years into their journey and need support in running effective design cycles or they are completely new to the idea of community-based design.

The Learner-Centered Leadership Lab, introduced in Chapter 10, is a Transcend initiative specifically designed for the most forward-thinking and visionary systems leaders who are committed to putting learners first. Throughout their progression, these leaders work collaboratively and support each other to create conditions that will enable learners to thrive in a world that is constantly evolving. As part of this program, these innovative leaders have access to a national network of like-minded individuals who are just as passionate about transforming education as they are. Throughout their experience in the Lab, participants continue to reflect on this central question: "How do I evolve my leadership to address the challenges I face to transform my system so all learners have extraordinary and equitable outcomes and experiences?"

To learn more, use the following QR code:

JOIN A GROWING NETWORK

There is a growing number of schools and systems nationwide exploring rede-sign efforts. You may not have identified them as such because they are on a small scale, but they are happening all around you. You read about four larger-scale examples in the beginning of the book: Northern Cass, Van Ness, Intrinsic, and Brooklyn STEAM—all four of those design teams observed many models for inspiration, and all four of them today share their design in some way. But these are just four of many.

In the Transcend community, we convene thousands of innovative education leaders pursuing this work through online summits and training, in-person conferences, and access to an enormous body of supporting con-tent. Through this free, vibrant network, innovative leaders in education con-nect to, seek help from, get energized by, and learn with like-minded others. We know networks are a powerful lever for social change, and we hope you will join the thousands of people who have joined together to reimagine what school looks like by using the following QR code:

EXTRAORDINARY LEARNING FOR ALL

For a long time we have tried to improve our schools by asking more of eve-ryone in the system: higher and harder expectations for students to achieve, longer hours for teachers to plan and work, more accountability regimes for administrators, and longer days in school for everyone. We have learned a lot from these efforts, and some of them have been successful in various places. Even one child with access to more opportunity and able to make agency-driven choices in their lives is important. But as a sector, we impact so many more futures, hopes, and dreams. The growing consensus in our country is that we are missing out on tremendous talent and possibility by not evolving and dramatically improving our education system. The system has improved by increments, but we need Leaps and bounds improvements to help children to thrive and transform the world.

Remember Ali from "Two Schools, Two Districts, Two Possible Futures" in the book's introduction? Ali is motivated to be at school. His learning environment is designed in such a way that he gets to practice new skills, learning from his triumphs and failures. Ali has some sense of control over his learning, able to pick how fast or slow he progresses through content. Ali has agency in his own learning, a sense of belonging in his school community, and the confidence to try new things. Every day, he is provided with opportunities to increase his self-understanding, and he feels that he belongs to this extraordinary community.

Imagine a world where every child has a learning experience like Ali's. Now, let us design it.

Endnotes

INTRODUCTION

1. Larry Cuban and David Tyack coined the term "grammar of schooling" in their 1995 book, *Tinkering toward Utopia: A Century of Public School Reform*.
2. In the 2019 article "Implications for Educational Practice of the Science of Learning and Development" in *Applied Developmental Science*, authors Darling-Hammond, Flook, Cook-Harvey, Barron, and Osher demonstrate how science of learning and development insights have been used to develop teaching practices that promote children's learning and well-being.
3. In the article "Precision Education: How K–12 Schools are Embracing AI" published by *Forbes* in 2023, Sahota asserts that AI is revolutionizing learning by enhancing personalized learning experiences, aiding in curriculum development, and providing innovative teaching methods.
4. Myriad research and news articles show how polarization has been on the rise in our country. Some examples include:
   a. Pew Research from September 2023 titled "Americans' Feelings about Politics, Polarization and the Tone of Political Discourse" found that many Americans show negative sentiments toward politics.
   b. "What Happens When Democracies Become Perniciously Polarized?" by Jennifer McCoy and Benjamin Press of the Carnegie Endowment (2022) describes increasing polarization in Washington and in the day-to-day life of Americans, referencing examples such as the phenomenon that Americans are less likely to marry across political divides and increasingly partisan media.
   c. A Brown University study titled "Cross-Country Trends in Affective Polarization" (2020) by Levi Boxell, Matthew Gentzkow, and Jesse M. Shapiro posits that polarization has "grown rapidly in the last 40 years—more than in Canada, the United Kingdom, Australia, or Germany."
   d. Education is also seeing increased polarization, as evidenced by school board elections and debates around Critical Race Theory. School board elections have "been a flash point for the culture wars," says Julie Marsh, codirector of University of Southern California's Center on Education Policy, Equity, and Governance, in an interview on *PBS NewsHour*.

5. The landscape of nonprofits focusing on experience design is expanding, with notable examples such as the following:
   a. IDEO's evolution of design thinking now encompasses experience design beyond physical products, highlighting its significance in creating meaningful experiences.
   b. The National Equity Project employs Liberatory Design, which targets equity issues and catalyzes change within intricate systems by crafting transformative experiences.
6. The Center of Education Policy at the George Washington University Graduate School of Education and Human Development published a 2020 briefing titled "History and Evolution of Public Education in the U.S.," which argued that advocates of common schools emphasized the civic, economic, and social advantages of accessible public education, especially for children from low- and middle-income families, by equipping them with the skills needed for improved employment prospects. This focus on widespread education was aimed at fostering unity among social groups, mitigating poverty and criminal activity, and enhancing the overall welfare of American society.
7. Research and experts show that despite public education in the United States being touted as the great equalizer, young people from different social backgrounds get vastly different learning experiences and educational outcomes, ultimately perpetuating social inequalities:
   a. The 2017 study "Education Inequalities at the School Starting Gate" conducted by the Economic Policy Institute highlights how public schools in the United States perpetuate social inequality by allowing performance gaps based on social class to emerge early in children's lives, which typically fail to narrow as they progress through the education system. This means that children who begin their education at a disadvantage tend to remain behind, struggling to catch up and rarely bridging the initial gap.
   b. Policies on school funding, resource allocation, and tracking result in disparities for minority students, such as limited access to quality books, curriculum materials, and technology, as well as larger class sizes, less experienced teachers, and lower-quality curriculum, as outlined in Linda Darling-Hammond's chapter titled "Inequality in Teaching and Schooling: How Opportunity Is Rationed to Students of Color in America."
   c. In 1998, the *Brookings Review* published "Unequal Opportunity: Race and Education" by Linda Darling-Hammond, which argued that minority children often face unequal access to important educational resources such as good teachers and quality curriculum, which impacts their learning outcomes more than their race itself.
8. Our work builds on research and thought leadership from organizations like Education Reimagines, New Classrooms, Gradient Learning, KnowledgeWorks, Deeper Learning, Digital Promise, and others that have studied the American school system, what we can learn from its history, and how we can think about the future.

9. Previous reform efforts have resulted in limited educational opportunities for students of color compared to their peers. Research by Linda Darling-Hammond in "Inequality in Teaching and Schooling: How Opportunity Is Rationed to Students of Color in America" shows that students of color often attend underfunded schools in urban or rural areas, lacking qualified teachers and quality curriculum and instruction, unlike predominantly white schools.

10. See, for example, Next Generation Learning Challenges' synthesis of research in 2020 highlighting two key factors: a) stereotype threat, which is the fear of realizing a negative stereotype results in marginalized students' poorer performance; and b) bias in the questions standardized tests ask that assume background understanding that may not be the norm across young people from different neighborhoods, backgrounds, family financial standing, or exposure.

11. See Lary Cuban's book, *Confessions of a School Reformer*.

12. See, for example, Jal Mehta's book, *Reimagining American Education: Possible Futures: Toward a new grammar of schooling*.

CHAPTER 1

1. Examples of organizational frameworks for a broader set of student outcomes include:
   a. Hewlett Foundation's Deeper Learning Skills Framework
   b. Roots of Action's The Compass Advantage Framework
   c. UNICEF's Conceptual Framework for Measuring Outcomes of Adolescent Participation
   d. National Council for the Social Studies' College, Career, & Civic Life (C3) Framework
   e. Battelle for Kids' P21 Framework for 21st Century Skills.

2. The Christensen Institute synthesizes research demonstrating a growing mental health crisis in their 2022 report, "No, The Kids Aren't Okay. Here Are Four Social Supports that Can Make a Difference."

3. The study "Do Teachers' Beliefs About Children's Math and Reading Abilities Predict Children's Self-confidence in These Subjects?" published in *Education Psychology* in 2015 tracked three cohorts (N = 849 students) in elementary school over four years to understand how teachers' views on their students' abilities affected the students' self-confidence in math and reading. The study found that when teachers had high expectations of their students' abilities, the students felt more confident and capable in both math and reading.

4. Research demonstrates that holding young people to high expectations positively impact their learning, such as the following sources:
   a. "Teacher Expectation Effects on Need-Supportive Teaching, Student Motivation, and Engagement: A Self-Determination Perspective" by Lisette Hornstra in *Educational Research and Evaluation* (2018) revealed that when teachers believe in their students and support their needs, it leads to higher student motivation in class, both from within and in how they behave.

     b. The study "Do Teachers' Perceptions of Children's Math and Reading Related Ability and Effort Predict Children's Self-Concept of Ability in Math and Reading?" by Katja Upadyaya and Jacquelynne Eccles in *Educational Psychology* (2015) found that when teachers believe in students' abilities and effort, it positively impacts students' self-confidence, emphasizing the role of high expectation and learning opportunities in helping young people succeed.

     c. "Linking Black Middle School Students' Perceptions of Teachers' Expectations to Academic Engagement and Efficacy" by Kenneth Tyler and Christina Boelter in *Negro Educational Review* (2008) demonstrated that students' perceptions of teachers' expectations directly impact their academic engagement and efficacy.

5. Information about Da Vinci Rise is available at davincischools.org and on the Innovative Models Exchange, a free, searchable database powered by Transcend that offers educators inspiration and practical resources to reshape the learning experience, accessible at http://exchange.transcendeducation.org.

6. Abrams' report "Kids' Mental Health in Crisis" (2023), published by the American Psychological Association, reveals an emerging youth mental health crisis exacerbated by the COVID-19 pandemic. The report notes a concerning rise of about 40% in persistent feelings of hopelessness and sadness, as well as suicidal thoughts and behaviors among young people over the decade leading up to the pandemic.

7. According to a survey conducted in the study "Are They Really Ready to Work? Employers' Perspectives on the Basic Knowledge and Applied Skills of New Entrants to the 21st Century U.S. Workforce" by the Conference Board, Corporate Voices for Working Families, the Partnership for 21st Century Skills, and the Society for Human Resource Management (2006), which involved approximately 400 employers nationwide, employers highly value applied skills such as collaboration and self-direction.

8. The report "Social, Emotional, and Academic Development through an Equity Lens" published by the Education Trust (2020) asserts that education systems need to focus on the whole child to foster learning environments that provide students with the full support they need to succeed in school. Additionally, Shi and Cheung's meta-analysis published in the *Journal of Youth and Adolescence* (2024) emphasizes that high-quality Social Emotional Learning programs significantly enhance K–12 students' social-emotional skills, academic performance, attitudes, and prosocial behaviors, highlighting the crucial role of SEL in fostering holistic development within educational contexts.

9. Information about Van Ness Elementary is available at vannesselementary.org and on the Innovative Models Exchange, a free, searchable database powered by Transcend that offers educators inspiration and practical resources to reshape the learning experience, accessible at http://exchange.transcendeducation.org.

10. Research supports that rigorous learning significantly impacts young people's learning experiences, such as:

     a. In "Inequities in Advanced Coursework," a report published by the Education Trust's Kayla Patrick, Allison Rose Socol, and Ivy Morgan (2020), report that without rigorous learning, students are forgoing crucial opportunities that could prepare them for success in both college and careers.

b. Zeiser et al.'s study "Evidence of Deeper Learning Outcomes: Findings from the Study of Deeper Learning" (2014) published by the American Institutes of Research reveals that students in deeper learning schools reported increased levels of collaboration skills, academic engagement, motivation to learn, and self-efficacy.

11. In the article "These are the top 10 job skills of tomorrow—and how long it takes to learn them" published by the World Economic Forum (2020), Kate Whiting asserts that problem-solving and critical thinking are top skills employers believe are growing in prominence. Additionally, the report "It Takes More Than a Major: Employers' Priorities for College Learning and Student Success" published by Hart Research Associate (2013) summarizes findings from an online survey of 318 employers with at least 25 employees, highlighting that the majority of employers emphasize the importance of field-specific knowledge and a broad range of skills for recent college graduates' long-term career success.

12. Information about Long-View is available at long-view.com.

13. Research supports that increasing relevance positively impacts learning; some examples include:

a. In her article "Relevant Curriculum is Equitable Curriculum" (2021), published by the Association for Supervision and Curriculum Development, Chaunté Garrett emphasizes the pivotal role of relevant curriculum in supporting the success of students from marginalized communities by dismantling barriers to their achievement.

b. "Promoting School Valuing Through Career Relevant Instruction" by Roderick Rose and Patrick Akos (2014) published in the *Journal of the Society for Social Work and Research* illustrates that career-relevant instruction in math, science, and social studies increases the extent to which students value school.

c. A study that examines teachers' communication and student experiences, "Classroom Goal Structures and Communication Style: The Role of Teacher Immediacy and Relevance-Making in Students' Perceptions of the Classroom" (2021) by Ryan Iaconelli and Eric M. Anderman in *Social Psychology of Education: An International Journal*, found that when teachers effectively communicate the relevance of the content, students also perceive a higher mastery goal structure.

14. Information about Gibson Ek is available at http://gibsonek.isd411.org.

15. For more about Big Picture Learning, see www.bigpicturelearning.org.

16. A body of research supports that affirming learners' identities supports their success. Some examples include:

a. "How all students can belong and achieve: Effects of the cultural diversity climate amongst students of immigrant and nonimmigrant background in Germany" (Schachner, M. K., Schwarzenthal, M., van de Vijver, F. J. R., & Noack; 2018) indicates that both (perceived) equality and inclusion and cultural pluralism were associated with a higher sense of school belonging, and higher school belonging in turn was associated with better outcomes (i.e., higher achievement, academic self-concept, and life satisfaction).

b. The study "Two Brief Interventions to Mitigate a 'Chilly Climate' Transform Women's Experience, Relationships, and Achievement in Engineering" by Walton, Logel, Peach, Spencer, and Zanna (2020) demonstrates that interventions designed to affirm the identity of underrepresented groups in STEM fields can significantly improve their sense of belonging and academic achievement.

c. Research conducted by Yeager, Walton, Brady, Akcinar, Paunesku, Keane, and Dweck titled "Teaching a Lay Theory Before College Narrows Achievement Gaps at Scale" (2016) shows that interventions aimed at promoting a growth mindset and affirming students' abilities can lead to improved academic outcomes, particularly among marginalized groups.

d. The study "The Impacts of a Middle School Self-Affirmation Intervention on African American and Latino Students" by Geoffrey Borman (2021) found that a self-affirmation program, tested in eleven middle schools, reduced the achievement gap by 50% annually from seventh to twelfth grade and raised on-time graduation rates for students of color by ten percentage points, compared to students not in the program.

17. Information about nXu's model is available at nxueducation.org and on the Innovative Models Exchange, a free, searchable database powered by Transcend that offers educators inspiration and practical resources to reshape the learning experience, accessible at http://exchange.transcendeducation.org.

18. Information about RevX is available at revxedu.org.

19. Research underscores the importance of relationships and social connections on learning and positive development; examples include:

a. Jean Lave and Etienne Wenger's seminal work *Situated Learning: Legitimate Peripheral Participation* (1991) published by Cambridge University Press illuminates that learning extends beyond internal cognitive processes; it encompasses active social interaction and contextualized knowledge. This perspective emphasizes that learning is fundamentally a social process rather than solely a cognitive activity.

b. The Student Experience Research Network's research brief "Structures for Belonging: A Synthesis of Research on Belonging-Supportive Learning Environments" (2021) reinforces the assertion that fostering strong relationships with educators and peers can positively influence students' experiences and improve their sense of belonging.

20. Information about St Benedict's Prep is available at sbp.org and on the Innovative Models Exchange, a free, searchable database powered by Transcend that offers educators inspiration and practical resources to reshape the learning experience, accessible at http://exchange.transcendeducation.org.

21. Research and scholars support that tailoring learning experiences for young people can enhance their experiences; some examples include:

a. The article "Diversity, Equity, and Inclusion in Personalized Learning" by Noah Dougherty demonstrates that tailoring learning experiences to accommodate the diverse needs and identities of young people can enhance their sense of self, motivation, and overall learning outcomes.

b. Zheng et al.'s meta-analysis "The Effectiveness of Technology-Facilitated Personalized Learning on Learning Achievements and Learning Perceptions"

(2022) shows that technology-facilitated personalized learning, tailored to learners' needs, pace, path, and materials, had a positive impact on students' learning perceptions, including interests, enthusiasm, attitudes, motivations, and satisfaction levels.

c. McCarthy et al.'s study (2020) in the *Journal of Research on Technology in Education*, "Appraising Research on Personalized Learning: Definitions, Theoretical Alignment, Advancements, and Future Directions," highlights that high school students who were able to select their reading materials based on their reading level and interests experienced an enhanced sense of learning, with notable improvements in reading skills, particularly among less-skilled readers.

22. Information about the Met is available at themethighschool.org.

23. The impact of student-directed learning on motivation and outcomes is evident in research. Examples include:

a. A key takeaway from "Active Learning Improves Academic Achievement and Learning Retention in K–12 Settings: A Meta-Analysis" by Özgür Tutal and Taha Yaza is that active learning pedagogies, when compared to traditional lecture-based instruction, notably enhance both academic achievement and learning retention for K–12 students.

b. Additionally, "Countering Deficit Thinking: Agency, Capabilities and the Early Learning Experiences of Children of Latina/o Immigrants" discusses how agency and capabilities play a role in shaping the early learning experiences of children from Latinx immigrant families, challenging deficit-oriented perspectives.

24. Research supports that Anytime, Anywhere learning can cater to the specific needs of learners, such as:

a. "States and School Systems Can Act Now to Dismantle Silos Between High School, College, and Career" by Georgia Heyward, Sarah McCann, and Betheny Gross (2021) highlights the persistent silos between K–12 education and industry and advocates that integrated learning systems present opportunities to innovate and enhance learning by engaging with the community.

b. Cavanaugh et al.'s meta-analysis "The Effects of Distance Education on K–12 Student Outcomes" (2004) published by Learning Point Associates indicates that there is no significant difference in performance between students enrolled in online programs versus those in traditional K–12 classrooms suggesting that the benefits of distance learning are substantial and not overshadowed by perceived concerns about its effectiveness.

c. Chung Kwan Lo & Khe Foon Hew's article, "A Critical Review of Flipped Classroom Challenges in K–12 Education: Possible Solutions and Recommendations for Future Research" (2017) reveals that using a flipped-learning approach significantly improved student performance compared to traditional teaching methods, highlighting the potential benefits of learning outside of the classroom.

25. Information about Teton Science Schools and their place-based model is available at tetonscience.org and on the Innovative Models Exchange, a free, searchable database powered by Transcend that offers educators inspiration and practical resources to reshape the learning experience, accessible at http://exchange .transcendeducation.org.

CHAPTER 3

1. The focus on shifting young people from the "survival state" to the "learning state" is inspired by Conscious Discipline, which equips educators to support young people's transition from emotional or "survival states" to an executive or "learning state" focused on problem-solving. Understanding the brain state model underscores the critical role of safety, connection, and problem-solving in shaping effective learning environments.
2. This statement draws on Dr. Bruce Perry's research and his concept of the three Rs—Regulate, Relate, and Reason—which are integral to facilitating students' access to the learning brain.
3. This language construction that follows the guiding structure: "I don't like it when you . . . Next time . . ." incorporated in the Whole Child Model stems from the Conscious Discipline approach outlined in the book *Conscious Discipline: Building Resilient Classrooms* by Dr. Becky A. Bailey.
4. Advances in the science of learning and development demonstrate that many aspects of learning transcend a narrow focus on reading, writing, and arithmetic. Example of supporting research include:
   a. Research demonstrating that social, emotional, and well-being factors influence learning:
      i. A study led by Christina Cipriano, PhD, from Yale University's Child Study Center, "The State of Evidence for Social and Emotional Learning: A Contemporary Meta-Analysis of Universal School-Based SEL Interventions," found that students who participated in SEL programs demonstrated increased academic achievement, improved social and emotional skills, and better overall well-being.
      ii. "The Influence of Affective Teacher-Student Relationships on Students' School Engagement and Achievement: A Meta-Analytic Approach" by Roorda et al. (2011) shows that teacher-student relationships (both positive and negative) have a medium to large (.25–.40) correlation with student engagement and a small to medium (.10–.25) correlation with student achievement.
      iii. "The Impact of Enhancing Students' Social and Emotional Learning: A Meta-Analysis of School-Based Universal Interventions" by Durlak et al. published in 2011 found that social-emotional learning programs significantly improve academic performance (as measured by both test scores and grades) from kindergarten through high school.
   b. Developments in brain science expand our understanding of learning:
      i. Research like "Executive Function: Implications for Education" (2017) published by the Institute of Education Sciences highlights that skills like attention regulation, goal maintenance, and inhibition, which are part of executive functioning, are essential for staying focused, avoiding distractions, and making thoughtful decisions—all of which are crucial for academic success in school.
      ii. The article "Science Shows Making Lessons Relevant Really Matters" in Edutopia summarizes research, demonstrating that "the brain stores information in the form of neural pathways, or networks. If a student acquires new information that's unrelated to anything already stored in his brain, it's tough for the new information to get into those networks because it has no scaffolding to cling to."

    iii. A study titled "Effects of Prior-Knowledge on Brain Activation and Connectivity During Associative Memory Encoding" by Liu, Grady, and Moscovitch found that building on prior-knowledge increases memory encoding.

5. Dr. Bruce Perry's Neurosequential Model is a developmentally informed, biologically respectful approach to working with at-risk children. More information can be found at neurosequential.com.

6. Dr. Brooke Stafford-Bizard's Building Blocks for Learning is a framework that represents the skills and mindsets that students use to access, acquire, and apply the academic content prioritized in classrooms. The framework includes five kinds of building blocks: healthy development, school readiness, mindsets for self and school, perseverance, and independence and sustainability. More information can be found in Turn Around for Children's report "The Building Blocks for Learning: A Framework for Comprehensive Student Development."

7. The "Strong Start" materials from Whole Child Model can be accessed on their website. For more details, refer to https://www.wholechildmodel.org/strong-start.

8. The Edutopia article "Building a Culture of Unconditional Positive Regard" suggests that when students connect with adults who are not in strictly authoritative roles, it reassures them of the adults' trustworthiness and reliability. This fosters the ideal environment for developing unconditional positive regard.

9. Research shows that connectedness at school influences social, emotional, and academic outcomes for young people:

    a. "Examining School Connectedness as a Mediator of School Climate Effects" by Alexandra Loukas, Rie Suzuki, and Karissa Horton in the *Journal of Research on Adolescence* (2006) found that school connectedness was predictive of higher school satisfaction and positive behavior at school.

    b. The Relationship of School Connectedness to Adolescents' Engagement in "Co-Occurring Health Risks: A Meta-Analytic Review" by Rose et al. (2022) found that school connectedness has a significant protective association with mental health, substance use, violence, sexual health, as well as their co-occurrence. For students of color, school connectedness had the strongest protective effect on mental health risks.

    c. "How Informal Mentoring by Teachers, Counselors, and Coaches Supports Students' Long-Run Academic Success" by Matthew Kraft, Alexander Bolves, and Noelle Hurd shared by the *National Bureau of Economic Research* (2023) demonstrates that having a school-based mentor increases academic performance and academic attainment for all adolescent students and has a larger effect for students of lower socioeconomic status.

10. Flamboyan Foundation empowers leaders, teachers, and communities in Washington DC and Puerto Rico through strategic support, family engagement initiatives, innovative partnerships, and impactful philanthropy to improve educational outcomes for children. The foundation works to strengthen family engagement in schools through school partnerships and leadership development programs, aiming to create authentic relationships between families and educators for improved student outcomes.

CHAPTER 4

1. The White House's analysis on chronic absenteeism (2023) shows a significant increase in students missing school, nearly doubling from 15 percent in 2018–2019 to 30 percent in 2021–2022 after the pandemic. This widespread increase in absenteeism across all states with available data highlights the profound disconnect experienced by students regarding the relevance of traditional schooling experiences.
2. Stephanie Sowl, Rachel Smith, and Michael Brown's study "Rural College Graduates: Who Comes Home?" (2021) in *Rural Sociology* underscores the reality of talent drain in rural communities, as graduates of four-year colleges frequently move from small-town rural areas to larger cities for economic opportunities.
3. Building 12 is an organization that has developed a competency-based school model that adapts to meet learners where they are and helps them to pursue their interests and passions on a pathway to college and career success. They have lab schools as well as a network of affiliated schools. Information can be found at Building21.org.

CHAPTER 5

1. Relevant learning experiences are shown to increase motivation, according to research:
    a. "'What's in it for me?': Increasing Content Relevance to Enhance Students' Motivation" by Ann Bainbridge Frymier and Gary Shulman in *Communication Education* (1995) demonstrates that relevance influences student motivation, finding a positive correlation between motivation and teachers' efforts to make content connected to students' lives.
    b. "Promoting School Valuing Through Career Relevant Instruction" by Roderick Rose and Patrick Akos in the *Journal of the Society for Social Work and Research* (2014) found that career-relevant instruction in math, science, and social studies increased student valuing of school (emotional engagement) for all students.
    c. Brain science shows that relevant, meaningful activities are connected to emotional engagement, memory encoding, and motivation, according to Sara Bernard's synthesis "Science Shows Making Lessons Relevant Really Matters" in Edutopia (2010).
2. On March 26, 2014, the Civil Rights Project at University of California, Los Angeles published the report "New York State's Extreme School Segregation: Inequality, Inaction and a Damaged Future" that examined enrollment and school segregation patterns from 1989 to 2010 at the state and regional levels and found severe segregation.
3. The National Bureau of Economic Research Working Paper, "The Race Between Education and Technology: The Evolution of U.S. Educational Wage Differentials," 1890 to 2005 by Claudia Goldin and Lawrence F. Katz claims the college wage premium (the average difference in wages for college graduates versus those with a college diploma) saw a rapid increase after 1980. The article "Changes in College Skills

and the Rise in the College Wage Premium" by Jeff Grogger and Eric Eide (1995) further describes the rise of the college wage premium during the 1980s, especially for recent labor market entrants.

4. MHA Labs designed a common set of easy-to-understand 21st century skill targets called The Building Blocks, which comprise 35 core social, emotional, and cognitive skills deemed critical for college, career, and life success. Information can be found on their website, mhalabs.org.

5. In March 2021, Edutopia interviewed Dr. Linda Darling-Hammond, president and CEO of the Learning Policy Institute, about Project-Based Learning (PBL) and its alignment with the science of learning and development. According to Dr. Darling-Hammond, PBL students perform equally on standardized tests but excel in real assessments, demonstrating stronger problem-solving and critical thinking skills essential for long-term success in academics and real-life situations.

CHAPTER 6

1. Research shows that students are more likely to learn when they feel physically and psychologically safe.
   a. In 2020, America's Promise Alliance published a report based on a survey of high school students. The findings revealed that positive relationships, a sense of belonging, and feelings of empowerment significantly improved young people's engagement and meaningful learning experiences.
   b. Navigate 360's article "Why Is School Safety Important?" introduces the idea of "Maslow before Bloom." This concept emphasizes that students need to have their basic needs, such as physical, social, and emotional safety, met before they can fully participate in academic learning.
   c. The National Center on Safe Supportive Learning Environments states that school safety is tied to better student and school outcomes. They emphasize that emotional and physical safety in schools directly impact academic performance.

2. Long-View is a micro school in Austin, Texas, that serves roughly eighty students from grades two to eight. Their innovative approach to math is where math blocks are typically two hours and within that time they engage young mathematicians in two Thought Exercises, a Concept Study (our version of a lesson), and Studio (work time that typically involves partners collaborating at whiteboards but also sometimes involves individuals working on paper). You can find out more at long-view.com.

3. Summit Learning is a comprehensive program that helps students gain mastery of core subjects that is utilized by more than 300 schools across the United States. They developed the Summit Learning Platform, a free online tool that allows every student to have a personalized learning experience because it is geared to each individual student's goals, aspirations, and dreams. On the platform, students set individual goals, create roadmaps to achieve them, learn content at their own pace, and dive into meaningful projects that connect to the real world. You can find more information at summitlearning.org.

4. According to the article "Reframing After-School Programs as Developing Youth Interest, Identity, and Social Capital" (2020), affluent families use after-school enrichment to enhance education and readiness for college and careers, leading to a gap in engagement between those with and without the financial means to access such programs.
5. Low-income students have fewer chances for academic enrichment compared to their wealthier peers according to the article "Developing Talents Among High-Potential Students from Low-Income Families in Out-of-School Enrichment Program" (2010) published in the *Journal of Advanced Academics*.

CHAPTER 10

1. One of the participants, Devin Vodicka, wrote a book we recommend, *Learner-Centered Leadership: A Blueprint for Transformational Change in Learning Communities*.

CHAPTER 11

1. The Canopy Project is a collaborative effort stewarded by Transcend and the Center for Reinventing Public Education (CRPE) to surface a diverse set of innovative learning environments and document the designs they are implementing. Schools are nominated for notable work to design school-wide equitable, student-centered learning environments. You can find more information at canopyschools.org.
2. In February 2024, 189 innovative schools completed a 20-minute school design survey with questions about policy's role in their ability to redesign school. The insights represented come from that survey data.
3. The EdTrust article "New School Accountability Systems in the States: Both Opportunities and Perils" provides an overview of accountability systems in recent history and explains how before accountability was codified in law, marginalized students and their families did not have adequate access to information about how they were performing in school.
4. The Every Student Succeeds Act (ESSA) was signed into law in 2015, reauthorizing the 50-year-old Elementary and Secondary Education Act (ESEA), the national education law and commitment to equal opportunity for all students. The law's text can be accessed at https://ed.gov/essa.
5. The U.S. Department of Education's summary of final ESSA regulations related to just the bill's accountability, state plans, and data reporting provisions runs six single-spaced pages.
6. According to research and leaders in the field, current approaches to standardized assessments have been shown to inadequately measure student learning and present barriers for learner-centered orientations:
   a. *The Testing Charade: Pretending to Make Schools Better* by Daniel Koretz asserts that high-stakes standardized testing is problematic, diverts instructional time to test-prep over meaningful experiences, and has led to widespread cheating, corner-cutting, and inflated scores.

    b. Jack Shneider and Ethan Hutt's book *Off the Mark: How Grades, Ratings, and Rankings Undermine Learning (but Don't Have To)* argues that grading, rating, and ranking, the primary technologies that make up our current approach to assessment, do not paint a holistic picture of how a student is performing in school; rather, they hinder learning and exacerbate inequities.

    c. *The Death and Life of the Great American School System: How Testing and Choice Are Undermining Education* by Diane Ravitch critiques how standardized testing pressures teachers to "teach to the test" at the expense of broader academic and life skills, narrows the curriculum, does not sufficiently account for critical or creative thinking, and puts extra burdens on schools in disadvantaged communities who may face additional barriers meeting benchmarks and thus face funding cuts or closures.

7. In February 2024, 189 innovative schools completed a 20-minute school design survey with questions about policy's role in their ability to redesign school. Quotes from principals in this chapter about their sentiments toward policy come from that survey data.

8. On November 20, 2023, Secretary of Education Miguel Cardona wrote a letter to chief state school officers clarifying several key provisions of the Innovative Assessment Demonstration Authority (IADA) and identifying ways USED is working to improve implementation and encourage state participation.

9. Each assessment cycle, a sample of students in designated grades within both public and private schools throughout the United States is selected for the National Assessment of Educational Progress (NAEP), with a selection process that utilizes a probability sample design in whichever school and student has a chance to be selected. The samples of public schools and their students in each state are large enough to support state-level estimates.

10. This sentence is quoted from Transcend and New Classroom's collaborative report, "Out of the Box: How Innovative Learning Models Can Transform K–12 Education" on page 46.

11. Information about how competency-based assessment and accountability can align to a student-centered paradigm is adapted from pages 48–49 of Transcend and New Classroom's collaborative report, "Out of the Box: How Innovative Learning Models Can Transform K–12 Education."

12. The National Center on Educational Outcomes (NCEO) focuses on the inclusion of students with disabilities, English learners, and English learners with disabilities in instruction and assessment. Their summary of how state graduation requirements have changed over time can be accessed at https://nceo.info.

13. The Education Commission of the States published a 50-state comparison of 2023 high school graduation requirements for a standard diploma, which can be found at https://ecs.org.

14. Leading organizations in the field emphasize that seat time limits learning opportunities outside of the school building. Some examples include the following:

    a. In the book *Learner-Centered Leadership: A Blueprint for Transformational Change in Learning Communities*, Devon Vodicka describes how seat-time requirements are antiquated and prioritizes time spent on a task over authentic learning.

   b. "Moving from Seat-Time to Competency-Based Credits in State Policy: Ensuring All Students Develop Mastery" by Dale Frost at the Aurora Institute states that "School leaders find once they begin to optimize their instructional models using anytime, anywhere learning, state policies that reinforce seat time become a barrier to innovative approaches delivering highly-personalized learning experiences for all students."
   c. The Education Next article titled "A Post-Pandemic Opportunity to Think Differently About Instructional Time" states that "The seat-time system constrains the ability of educators to meet their students where they are academically and to provide the necessary personalized supports to help students either accelerate to mastery or go deeper in the content."
15. The Education Commission of the States published a fifty-state comparison of 2023 high school graduation requirements for a standard diploma, which can be found at https://ecs.org.
16. This example is adapted from Education Commission and KnowledgeWorks' 2022 brief "State Policies to Support Student-Centered Learning" by Ben Erwin and Gerardo Silva-Padrón.
17. Beginning in fall 2013, CDE convened seven work groups to inform the implementation of graduation requirements, including a Capstone Projects work group. Recommendations and resources can be accessed at https://www.cde.state.co.us/postsecondary/gg_workgroups.
18. This comes from Dr. Amy Spicer's 2022 dissertation research, "Colorado's Graduation Guidelines: An Implementation Study," which analyzed graduation requirements in all of Colorado's 178 school districts.
19. In May 2023, *Education Week* published the article "Every State Now Lets Schools Measure Students' Success Based on Mastery, Not Seat Time" reporting that all states now provide some degree of flexibility for students to be assessed on their subject mastery rather than hours spent in a classroom.
20. On its website, newenglandssc.org, the New England Secondary Schools Consortium (NESSC) shares a resource on the relationship between mastery-based systems and the college admissions process titled "85 New England Institutions of Higher Education State that Proficiency-Based Diplomas Do Not Disadvantage Applicants."
21. Facts and figures we share about the Department of Education's R&D spending and comparisons to the Departments of Defense, Health and Human Services, and Agriculture come from the Congressional Research Service's 2022 report "Federal Research and Development (R&D) Funding: FY2023."
22. In December 2023, the Senate HELP Committee voted to advance to the full Senate the Advancing Research in Education (AREA) Act, a bipartisan bill focused on improving education research and evidence use in the classroom and modernizing how states track student data and outcomes from preschool to postsecondary. As a reauthorization of the Education Sciences Reform Act (ESRA) passed 20 years ago, it also reauthorizes the Institute of Education Sciences (IES), the Statewide Longitudinal Data Systems, and the National Assessment of Educational Progress (NAEP).

23. In December 2023, U.S. House members introduced bipartisan legislation to establish a national center to promote high-reward education research, the NEED Act. The National Center for Advanced Development in Education (NCADE) would develop and disseminate innovative, data-based practices and tools.

24. More information about building the supply of innovative learning models can be found in the report "Out of the Box: How Innovative Learning Models Can Transform K–12 Education" by NewClassrooms and Transcend.

25. Montana's Office of Public Instruction launched the state's Math Innovation Zone (MIZ) Program "to help prepare schools to transition to personalized learning models in math." The Greater Math in North Dakota Program is that state's grant opportunity, made available through ESSER funds, to promote the use of blended learning instructional approaches in third- through eighth-grade math classrooms.

26. Information about Tennessee's investment in innovative school models can be found on the Tennessee Department of Education website, https://tn.gov/education.

27. Information about Virginia's grants available for laboratory schools can be found on the Virginia Department of Education website at http://doe.virginia.gov.

28. Several states, including Colorado, Idaho, Indiana, Minnesota, South Carolina, and Utah, have published "flexibility guides" to promote the state-level waivers and flexibilities available to schools and districts.

29. The Iowa Department of Education provided guidance in 2019 to "help educators create multiple pathways for students to earn credit in addition to traditional seat time" as stated in the resource "Competency-Based Education (CBE) Program Standards Guidance."

Index

271